Balanced Wonder

Balanced Wonder

Experiential Sources of Imagination, Virtue, and Human Flourishing

Jan B. W. Pedersen

LEXINGTON BOOKS
Lanham • Boulder • New York • London

Published by Lexington Books
An imprint of The Rowman & Littlefield Publishing Group, Inc.
4501 Forbes Boulevard, Suite 200, Lanham, Maryland 20706
www.rowman.com

6 Tinworth Street, London SE11 5AL

Copyright © 2019 by The Rowman & Littlefield Publishing Group, Inc.

All rights reserved. No part of this book may be reproduced in any form or by any electronic or mechanical means, including information storage and retrieval systems, without written permission from the publisher, except by a reviewer who may quote passages in a review.

British Library Cataloguing in Publication Information Available

Library of Congress Cataloging-in-Publication

Names: Pedersen, Jan B. W., author.
Title: Balanced wonder : experiential sources of imagination, virtue, and human flourishing / [Jan B. W. Pedersen].
Description: Lanham, Maryland : Lexington Books, 2019. | Includes bibliographical references. | Summary: "In Balanced Wonder: Experiential Sources of Imagination, Virtue, and Human Flourishing, Jan B. W. Pedersen digs deep into the alluring topic of wonder and argues in a scholarly yet accessible way that the experience of wonder when balanced serves as a strong contributor to human flourishing. Along the way Pedersen describes seven properties of wonder and shows how wonder is distinct from other altered states, including awe, horror, the sublime, curiosity, amazement, admiration, and astonishment. Examining the contribution of both emotion and imagination in the experience of wonder--filtered through the Neo-Aristotelian work of philosophers Douglas Rasmussen, Alasdair MacIntyre, and Martha Nussbaum--Pedersen also makes it clear that wonder may contribute to human flourishing in various ways, such as widening of perception, extension of moral scope or sensitivity, a wondrous afterglow, openness, humility, an imaginative attitude, reverence, and gratitude. Importantly, for wonder to act as a strong contributor to human flourishing one needs to wonder at the right thing, in the right amount, in the right time, in the right way, and for the right purpose"-- Provided by publisher.
Identifiers: LCCN 2019039862 (print) | LCCN 2019039863 (ebook) | ISBN 9781498587778 (cloth) | ISBN 9781498587785 (epub) | ISBN 9781498587792 (pbk)
Subjects: LCSH: Wonder (Philosophy)
Classification: LCC B105.W65 P43 2019 (print) | LCC B105.W65 (ebook) | DDC 158.1--dc23
LC record available at https://lccn.loc.gov/2019039862
LC ebook record available at https://lccn.loc.gov/2019039863

For Ayako and Mai

Contents

Acknowledgments		ix
Introduction		1
1	The Lure of Wonder	11
2	Wonder and Emotion	67
3	Wonder and Imagination	95
4	Implications of the Role of Imagination in Wonder	131
5	Wonder, Human Flourishing, and Virtue	151
Conclusion: Wondering about Wonder		203
Bibliography		215
Index		225
About the Author		231

Acknowledgments

To wonder about wonder is an unsettling affair and during the course of researching and writing this book I have ever so often found myself trapped in what seemed an inescapable mire. In such situations, unless one like Rudolf Erich Raspe's adventurous character Baron Munchhausen has the ability to pull oneself out of trouble by ones own hair, deliverance depends on the good will of others. I am no Munchhausen and thus I would like to take this opportunity to thank some of the excellent people whose wisdom, knowledge, and skills have enabled me to complete the work.

First and foremost I must express my debt to Professor Martyn Evans and Dr. Angela Woods of Durham University who offered helpful guidance, careful critique, and corrective comments at numerous stages in the writing process.

I also wish to thank Professor Robin Attfield of Cardiff University, Dr. Simon Forrest of Newcastle University, Dr. Ian Kidd of the University of Nottingham, Professor Jane Macnaughton of Durham University, Professor Stephen Pattison of the University of Birmingham, Dr. Lutz Sauerteig of Newcastle University and Dr. William Viney of Goldsmiths, University of London for their many courtesies and academic advice.

Thanks also to Dr. Anders Schinkel and Professor Doret de Ruyter at Vrije University, Amsterdam for propelling my wonder studies forward and inviting me to participate in *The Wonderful Education Project*.

My friends Geoff Beyers, Jakob Mølbjerg, the late Matthew Neale, and Lone Petersen deserve special thanks for their many thoughtful suggestions and critical comments. Likewise, I have benefitted from many conversations with Allan Beattie, Fabio Cicarelli, David Clinnick, Thomas Hirst, Frank Kauff, Fredric Maron, Catherine Racine, Astrid Polato, Claus Simonsen, Sam Walkwell, and Colin Wild.

Furthermore, I am grateful to my mentors, Dr. Hans Fink and Professor Steen Wackerhausen of Aarhus University for inspirational lectures that still live on in me and for their encouragement to advance my philosophical studies.

My gratitude also goes to Peter Martin Fogh-sensei, Seido Ryu for extending "Os (オス)!" at a critical time and Ethan Monnot Weisgard-sensei, head of Copenhagen Aiki Shuren Dojo, for teaching me the mental application of "Tai no henko (体の変更)," which I have frequently put to use during my years of writing.

I am also grateful to my editors, Trevor F. Crowell and Jana Hodges-Kluck, and to an anonymous reviewer for Lexington Books for their kind encouragement and professionalism.

This book could not have been completed without the support and inspiration of my family. I extend my thanks to Kiyo Wakatsuki, Tetsuyuki Wakatsuki, Keiko Wakatsuki, Kirsten Pedersen, Flemming Pedersen, Lars Bjerggaard Pedersen, Kim Pedersen, Pernille Dohn, and my nephew, Villads Bjerggaard Dohn.

My greatest indebtedness is to my wife Ayako and my daughter Mai. Mai is responsible for an important example of wonder used in this book and Ayako has more than often pulled me out of "the mire." I cannot express how grateful I am for her fortitude, kindness, patience, and unshakeable support, not forgetting her careful critique and suggestions, which have saved me from a variety of errors. Ayako and Mai, you are endless sources of wonder to me—O brave new world that has such creatures in't!

Elements of chapter 1 can be found in two of my earlier publications including "On Lovecraft's Lifelong Relationship with Wonder" appearing in *Lovecraft Annual* No. 11, edited by S. T. Joshi (Hippocampus Press, 2017) and "Howard Phillips Lovecraft: Romantic on the Nightside" in *Lovecraft Annual* No. 12, edited by S. T. Joshi (Hippocampus Press, 2018). The elements in question are used by kind permission of Derrick Hussey, Hippocampus Press, www.hippocampuspress.com.

Jan B. W. Pedersen
Frederiksberg, Denmark
June 2019

Introduction

In *De Inventione* Cicero writes: "In the difficult case, if the auditors are not completely hostile, it will be permissible to seek to win their good-will by an introduction."[1] This book argues that cultivating a balanced sense of wonder is a strong contributor to living a flourishing human life. For the argument to be convincing, a somewhat in-depth understanding of what is meant by "balance," "wonder," and "a flourishing life" is key, but it is the notion of wonder that will receive the most sustained attention.

This book is philosophical in nature and seeks not only to clarify what wonder is, understood as a psychological state, but also brings the resources of philosophy to bear on how wonder makes living well possible. It does so by generating philosophical understanding of the role of imagination in human life, by providing philosophical perspectives on how wonder elicits imagination, and by generating philosophical criteria to evaluate the virtues arising from experiences of wonder—criteria that is not only personal but also ethical and political.

In this respect what you are about to read can be considered an antidote to the confusion of modern life as it stakes out a distinct and important perceptive on the topic of wonder and charts a philosophical path to flourishing, involving three prominent and contemporary neo-Aristotelian philosophers: Douglas Rasmussen, Alasdair MacIntyre, and Martha Nussbaum.

Since wonder is the centerpiece of the book, presenting a preliminary identification of wonder is in order. Wonder is a sudden experience that intensifies the cognitive focus and awareness of ignorance about a given object. It is typically an unsettling yet delightful experience that makes one aware that there might be more to the perceived object than meets the eye. That wonder is delightful is supported by various philosophical sources and one might begin by pointing out that in the *Poetics* Aristotle writes that "wonder is pleasant."[2] The *Poetics* is interesting because there are discrepancies between some of the translations of this particular work, which is relevant to the study of wonder. Joe Sachs's 2006 translation, which is cited here, clearly states that wonder is pleasant but Stephen Halliwell's 1995 Loeb Classical Library translation states that "awe is pleasurable."[3] This is confusing and draws attention to the curious fact that in the literature wonder and awe are in some cases used interchangeably. To complicate matters, literary scholar Dennis Quinn informs us that admiration and wonder are also sometimes used interchangeably[4] and that when we read, for example, Aristotle's *The Art of Rhetoric*, where he writes "that which excites admiration is pleasant,"[5] it is important to keep in mind that it is possible to read this particular citation as "that which excites wonder is pleasant." This paints a somewhat muddled picture of wonder but also adds to the allure of the subject as it invites us to begin to think about "a taxonomy of altered states" specifying possible distinctions between wonder, awe, and admiration. Mounting further support for the idea that wonder is pleasant one might, besides Aristotle, also point to philosopher Conelis Verhoeven who indirectly supports the notion as he argues that one can only wonder if one is in a safe place or wonder would turn into loathing and panic.[6] Contemporary philosophers Philip Fisher and Derek Matravers likewise support the idea that wonder is joyful. Fisher writes that "wonder is a sudden experience of an extraordinary object that produces delight"[7] and Matravers mentions in his work that wonder has a hedonic tone.[8]

Moving away from the notion that wonder is delightful, one might also point out that there is a suddenness to wonder. The experience hits you unannounced like lightning and it seems evident that it may arise from various sources. Seeing a rainbow in the sky or falling in love or witnessing someone pass away may prompt an experience of wonder. Particular books and works of art are wonder inducing as they invite us to see things from a different and even particular perspective. Verhoeven suggests that like pathos, wonder is granted or inflicted[9] and in this respect wonder is not something we can will ourselves to experience; however, it is something we might have a talent for.[10] Philosopher Paul Martin Opdal is of a similar opinion as he speaks of children having a capacity for wonder that might be turned into philosophical reflection.[11] Further still, it seems plausible that one can develop a balanced sense of wonder[12] that transcends childhood wonderments and brings forth an informed and mature kind of wonderment. What I refer to here is a sense of wonder that by no means is of the extreme. It is to be in a place between extremes that neither accommodates the immediate wonderments of a fool or a child nor displays the outright hostility to wonder attributed for the sake of argument to the vulgar, crude, and reductive adult. To harbor a balanced sense of wonder involves being able, at least to some degree, to harness or control wonder. It is a product of refinement where one's wonderment turns out to be just right.

This particular line of thinking might, to some, evoke Aristotelian ideas of virtue, and rightly so. For Aristotle virtue is connected to the notion of the mean, which is located between excess and deficiency. Experiencing a sense of wonder while pondering that bachelors are not married is wondering in excess.[13] It is to wonder foolishly or immaturely that such wonder would rest uneasily with any sensible person. To believe that so-called experts or authorities would have the answer to all questions and that one can escape wonderment by consulting such would be to harbor a deficient sense of wonder which equally would sit ill with any tempered person. To wonder in a balanced way is by no measure an easy task, as we humans, unlike the pendulum, do not automatically reach the place of equilibrium. It is something we actively have to work for. Now investigations into a balanced sense of wonder represent a rather unexplored area and more work is to be done if a richer account is to see the light of day. It would be interesting to see what possible consequences could entail too little or too much wonderment and if either of these had any bearing upon the flourishing of the person doing the wondering. I shall say more about this in a later chapter but for now let me briefly address the other supporting constituent, the flourishing life.

The idea of a flourishing human life is an idea that has gained increased popularity since philosopher Elizabeth Anscombe published her now famous article "Modern Moral Philosophy."[14] In the article she presented human flourishing as a new translation of the old Greek word "*eudaimonia*," which Aristotle thought to be the highest good or the very goal of human life. Until Anscombe's publication, *eudaimonia* had been translated as "well-being" (taken to be almost synonymous with "happiness"), which gave the concept a distinctly subjective feel. The new translation worked in the opposite direction and suggested that although the idea of human flourishing in a modern sense does not encompass presenting a complete objective account of what characterizes a good human life, it nevertheless suggests that there may be more to the good life than individual subjective accounts might reveal. Furthermore, it suggests that a flourishing life has to be measured over the course of a whole human life. Aristotle writes: "One swallow does not make a spring, nor does one fine day, and similarly one day or a brief period of happiness does not make a man supremely blessed and happy."[15] The main message here is that in order to live a good human life or a flourishing human life—it is not enough to feel happy the split second before you take leave of it. Nor is it good enough to have experienced, for example, two years of absolute bliss in a lifetime while the remaining time was, for want of a better word, dreadful.

There are at least two reasons why an inquiry into the linkage between a balanced sense of wonder and human flourishing is important. First of all there is a gap in the literature on the subject matter. References can be found in works that deal with wonder and ethical development but none that addresses the subject matter directly. This makes it important and worthwhile pursuing. Secondly, it would be of interest to examine the possibility that a life encompassing a balanced sense of wonder might flourish to a larger degree than a life embracing wonderment in excess or no wonderment whatsoever. A balanced sense of wonder could harness the positive sides of wonderment, which in turn can be used as inspiration for how to live a flourishing life. Such wonder might facilitate a critical openness toward the world, which in turn would help keep the notion of human flourishing free from negative constraints. In addition, a balanced sense of wonder may prompt the discovery of new sources of flourishing and in effect prove the antidote to complacency. Most people will, over time, become set in their ways and develop a scope of vision that may reach far but is still limited by habits that one might be unaware of. A balanced sense of wonder could prompt openness to the positive sides of everything from religious, political, scientific, or philosophical thoughts to particular cultural outlooks, ways of life, or praxis.

So far very little has been said about wonder but it is a captivating subject that has received increased attention in recent times from a variety of different scholars.[16] It is captivating for several reasons, one being that as a subject wonder is elusive and hard to fully grasp. Unlike the optical meteorological phenomenon of the rainbow, wonder does not present itself as an external object that can be readily studied and explained by objective science. Wonderment seems to be an entirely human phenomenon[17] and it can spring from various situations. Witnessing something spectacular like a rainbow, the aurora borealis, the birth of a child, or the success of a free solo climber[18] may very well produce a sense of wonder. To reflect upon something is another wonder-inducer as it ever so often takes us to the edge of our knowledge and makes us wonder about the implications of the questions we ask. Big questions like: What is the meaning of life? Where did the universe come from? Is the universe finite or does it extend into eternity? Why it is there at all and how does one devise a wise answer to the question of how one should live? are wonder-inducing questions. The reason for this is that they are huge and difficult questions that have a tendency to lift us up above the immediate practicalities of life and make us think about our place in the universe and what we are doing with the time given to us. Another reason why wonder is fascinating arises from the curious fact that no discipline within academia has claimed it as its own. Despite having been addressed by a variety of different scholars hailing from different disciplines, wonder remains itinerant and unsettled. To illustrate just how widespread and diverse the academic interest in wonder is, one could start by drawing attention to the discipline of philosophy. Philosophy has a long-standing relationship with wonder, which goes back to Plato and Aristotle. Their writings support the idea that philosophy begins in wonder.[19] Similarly, in the area of theology, wonder comes across as the starting point for theistic experience.[20] Professor of religious studies, Robert C. Fuller, seems to support that notion, as he believes the experience of wonder can lure us into extended engagement with what lies beyond the limits of rational engagement and that this is key in terms of understanding spirituality.[21] Furthermore, Fuller observes that experiences of wonder "are principal sources of what historians variously call nature religion or aesthetic spirituality."[22] This is to say a sensibility to the sacredness of nature; the mystical or a particular pantheistic feeling toward the universe may emerge from wonderment.[23] In addition, theologian and philosopher David B. Burrell points out that wonderment in the Abrahamic faiths is connected to questions about creation, the contingency of being, and examination of this contingency together with our lived experiences "that is both expressed in such accounts and is in turn cultivated by them."[24] Wonder is also relevant to the field of aesthetics where objects such as the Elgin Marbles[25] have inspired wonder and indeed helped generate new wonders like John Keats's poem "On Seeing the Elgin Marbles" from 1817 which dwells on the pangs of mortality and wonders of Grecian grandeur.[26] Wonder can also be associated with modern science because as philosopher Howard L. Parsons writes: "A scientist can find a molecule or protozoan or child or galaxy wonderful because he can be excited by the known and imagined meanings that his scientific community has surrounded him with."[27] Popular writer Richard Dawkins also thinks that wonder and science walk hand in hand and he argues that scientific investigation can be inspired by wonder and, like art, science is capable of generating new wonders. Dawkins writes:

> Newton's dissection of the rainbow into light of different wavelengths led on to Maxwell's theory of electromagnetism and thence to Einstein's theory of special relativity. If you think the rainbow has poetic mystery, you should try relativity.[28]

Scientific discoveries and developments like these can produce what Dawkins calls a feeling of "awed wonder," which he deems one of the uppermost experiences a human being can experience.[29] Now leaving aside the question of whether there is such a thing as a hierarchy of experiences that can support Dawkins's view, and what such a hierarchy actually looks like, it is safe to say that not everyone would readily subscribe to Dawkins's view. In support of this claim stands philosopher Ian Kidd who distinguishes between shallow and deep wonder and argues that wonder merely presents itself in a shallow way for the scientist and there is a deeper kind of wonder fused with the ethical dimension that the scientist simply misses out on.[30] Now Dawkins's conjunction of awe and wonder reminds us that wonder is a complicated subject, because as much as one might agree with Dawkins and think his conjunction fitting for the experience he is describing, one would be inclined to think it peculiar because as much as it is possible to merge awe and wonder, it is also possible to view awe and wonder as two completely different states of mind, prompting us to find out in what sense they differ from one another.

But why does wonder travel? Why is it not at home with one discipline, specialty, or branch of learning? Quinn points out that it might simply be because wonder does not fit any specialty and it may prove difficult for one branch of the academic tree to give an exhaustive account of wonder. There is, as Quinn puts it, "something as inherently absurd in the idea of a wonder expert as in the idea of an expert on life."[31] In other words, if one wishes to learn more about wonder it might be prudent not to get too fixated on disciplinary lenses, but look to wonder as something that digs beyond the disciplinary barriers of academia. Perhaps wonder in this regard is initially best understood by evoking the image of the primordial soup advocated by evolutionary scientists. It is a place of origin. It is a state of mind, which potentially can give rise to a desire for inquiry and for the academically inclined subsequent works, be they either scientific or artistic in outline or composition.

Nevertheless, the present inquiry is a philosophical one, and although philosophy is hard to define one might say that a part of philosophy, at least since the time of Socrates, has been concept analysis and the critical scrutiny of ideas. Since the success of the present inquiry relies partly on a clear, rigorous presentation of particular key concepts, notions, and ideas evoking philosophical inquiry as "method" is apt. To strengthen this notion one might point out that since philosophy has a long history of addressing wonder, balance (understood as virtue), and human flourishing, it seems a good choice to turn to philosophy. In addition, it must be said that the philosophy or philosophical lens through which wonder is explored qualifies as neo-Aristotelian, meaning that it draws on the work of Aristotle and a selection of contemporary philosophers to whom Aristotle is a substantial source of inspiration. Other approaches to flourishing do exist but the present book does not consider such alternatives, nor does it in any way represent a thorough apology for neo-Aristotelianism. The neo-Aristotelian angle on flourishing is a tool chosen purely because it enables us to paint a rich picture of wonder.

The inquiry is divided into seven parts, including an introduction and a conclusion. Chapter 1, "The Lure of Wonder," aims at providing the reader a preliminary understanding of wonder. The chapter opens with the presentation and brief examination of seven examples of wonder, which gives the reader a basic insight into the phenomenon of wonder. Next, the etymological roots of wonder and how wonder can be seen as a noun, a verb, an adjective, and an adverb, which can be seen as an additional guide to wonder is examined. Thirdly, a brief history of wonder is presented with the purpose of making the reader appreciate that wonder changes over time. The fourth movement will examine a selection of altered states by addressing wonder's relationship with awe, horror, the sublime, curiosity, amazement, admiration, and astonishment with a view to further clarifying what wonder is. This is followed by an examination of the "enemies of wonder" in order to make clear why we sometimes avoid wonderment. Finally in the interest of presenting a preliminary understanding of wonder that transcends naïve sentiments and crude rationalizations, attention will be drawn to some contemporary writers on wonder and their views on the subject. Furthermore, additional research questions, including if wonder can be exclusively seen as an emotion; what the role of imagination in wonder is, and in what sense wonder contributes to human flourishing shall be highlighted with the purpose of paving the way for the subsequent chapters. Thus, the first chapter by no means provides the final word on wonder, but is merely a stepping-stone to further investigations into the subject matter.

Chapter 2, "Wonder and Emotion," investigates in what respect we may label wonder as an emotion and if it is possible to label it exclusively so. The first movement involves an elaboration of the rationale for addressing wonder as an emotion followed by an inquiry into the nature of emotions. By committing to the cognitive approach to emotions represented by contemporary philosopher Aaron Ben-Ze'ev, the chapter later explores an idea put forward by the likewise contemporary philosopher Adam Morton, depicting wonder as an epistemic emotion. This is followed by an application of Ben-Ze'ev's cognitive approach and Adam Morton's notion of wonder, as an epistemic emotion to some of the examples depicting wonder as an emotion provided in the first section in order to show in what respect the examples reflect wonder as an emotion. Finally, the chapter explores what we may call other faces of wonder and argues that as much as it can be said that wonder qualifies as an emotion, and indeed an epistemic one, wonder does not qualify exclusively as such because wonder may indeed also be looked upon as a mood, a value, and an attitude.

Chapter 3, "Wonder and Imagination," begins by recapturing and expanding the rationale for investigating imagination in connection with wonder. This is followed by an introduction to imagination that aims to clarify the vastness of the subject matter. Subsequently, the work on imagination done by philosophers Mary Warnock, Ronald Hepburn, and Roger Scruton will be presented in order to put forth a modern account of imagination. The choice of philosophers rests on the fact that they are all contemporary thinkers who, through their individual work, have expressed a singular and bold view of imagination that, when synthesized, will help us establish in what capacity a modern conception of imagination is involved in the wondering or wonder-filled experience. Furthermore, these philosophers elucidate how imagination leads us from intense personal experience to subsequent modes of living

Chapter 4, "Implications of the Role of Imagination in Wonder," examines an array of new examples from art, space-travel, and philosophy that are particularly wonder provoking with the purpose, not only to further solidify how the imagination is active in wonderment, but also to show how an experience of wonder may: (1) influence our perception; (2) increase our moral scope and sensitivity; and (3) facilitate a wondrous afterglow and deep wonder.

Chapter 5, "Wonder, Human Flourishing, and Virtue," engages with three contemporary neo-Aristotelian philosophical approaches to flourishing, and the first involves the work of Douglas Rasmussen who, in his approach to flourishing, focuses heavily on the individual. Secondly, I shall engage with Alasdair MacIntyre, whose notion of flourishing alerts us to the social side of flourishing, and is grounded in the idea that we are dependent rational animals with the ability to become independent practical reasoners. Finally, attention will be drawn to politically engaged Martha Nussbaum, whose account of flourishing includes the notion of the "thick, vague conception of the good," by which she offers a basic list of human functional capabilities indicating what is essential to every human life. The three approaches complement one another in the sense that as we progress from Rasmussen to MacIntyre and finally to Nussbaum, we will see a continuing exploration of human nature that will bring about a refined notion of what human beings have in common rather than where they differ. The picture of human flourishing that emerges from engaging with these contemporary thinkers will be utilized as a reference point in the second half of this chapter, which examines how wonder can be a source of flourishing. The second half starts with a survey of what it means for something to be a source of flourishing and the following candidates: literacy, friendship, humor, and physical exercise will be explored. Following this brief engagement I shall argue that wonder also qualifies as a source of flourishing by looking at how wonder may evoke reverence and gratitude, help foster an imaginative attitude, and give birth to openness and humility. Finally, wonder as a virtue will be addressed and I shall argue that a balanced sense of wonder is a strong contributor to human flourishing.

The conclusion, "Wondering about Wonder," recaptures the important findings from the previous chapters and concludes that cultivating a balanced sense of wonder strongly contributes to human flourishing.

By this introduction I hope the good will of the reader has been won and that it is clear that wonder is a most alluring subject matter that deserves attention.

NOTES

1. Cicero, *De Inventione*, trans. H. M. Hubbell, LCL (Cambridge: Harvard University Press, 1989), 1, 21–23.
2. Aristotle, *Poetics*, trans. J. Sachs (Bemidji, MN: Focus Publishing, 2006), 1460a16.
3. Aristotle, *Poetics*, trans. S. Halliwell, LCL (Cambridge: Harvard University Press, 1995), XXIV.
4. Dennis Quinn, *Iris Exiled—A Synoptic History of Wonder* (Lanham, MD: University Press of America, 2002), 4.
5. Aristotle, *The Art of Rhetoric*, trans. J. H. Freese, LCL (Cambridge: Harvard University Press, 1926), III. i. 9–ii. 3.

6. Conelis Verhoeven, *The Philosophy of Wonder* (New York: The Macmillan Company, 1972), 43.

7. Philip Fisher, *Wonder, the Rainbow and the Aesthetics of Rare Experiences*, (Cambridge and London: Harvard University Press, 2003), 55.

8. Derek Matravers, "Wonder and Cognition" in *Practices of Wonder: Cross-Disciplinary Perspectives*, S. Vasalou (Eugene, OR: Pickwick Publications, 2012), 166.

9. Verhoeven, *Philosophy of Wonder*, 13.

10. Ibid., 27.

11. Paul Martin Opdal, "Curiosity, Wonder, and Education seen as Perspective Development" in *Studies in Philosophy and Education*, 20, 2001, 332.

12. According to psychologists William Compton and Edward Hoffman, the phrase "sense of wonder" was coined in the 1920's by Hugo Gernsback, writer and editor of American pulp magazines: *Wonder Stories* and *Amazing Stories*. See William C. Compton and Edward Hoffman, *Positive Psychology: The Secret of Happiness and Flourishing* (Boston: Wadsworth Cengage Learning, 2013), 243. However this might be disputed because the phrase can also be found in English writer W. H. Hodgson's tale *The Searcher of the End House*, published in *The Idler Magazine* between 1910 and 1912. See William Hope Hodgson, "The Searcher of the End House" in *The Casebook of Carnacki the Ghost Finder* (Knoxville: Wordsworth, 2006), 8, 89. The phrase also figures in the title of American biologist and conservationist Rachel Carson's famous 1965 book *The Sense of Wonder*. See Rachel Carson, *The Sense of Wonder* (New York: HarperCollins, 1984). Unless stated I shall make no distinction between the word "wonder" and the phrase "sense of wonder" as they can be seen as different expressions of the same thing.

13. I owe this point to Ronald W. Hepburn. See Ronald W. Hepburn, "The Inaugural Address: Wonder" in *Proceedings of the Aristotelian Society*, Supplementary Volume, 54, 1980, 6.

14. See G. E. M. Anscombe, "Modern Moral Philosophy" in *Philosophy*, 33, 1958, 1–19.

15. Aristotle, *Nicomachean Ethics*, trans. H. Rackham, LCL (Cambridge: Harvard University Press, 2003), I, vii, 16.

16. See, for example, Robin Attfield, *Wonder, Value, and God*, (London: Routledge, 2017); Martyn Evans, "Medical Humanities and the Place of Wonder" in *The Edinburgh Companion to the Critical Medical Humanities*, ed. A. Whitehead and A. Woods (Edinburgh: Edinburgh University Press, 2016); Robert C. Fuller, *Wonder: From Emotion to Spirituality* (Chapel Hill: The University of North Carolina Press, 2006); Caspar Henderson, *A New Map of Wonders: A Journey in Search of Modern Marvels* (London: Granta, 2017); Genevieve Lloyd, *Reclaiming Wonder after the Sublime* (Edinburgh: Edinburgh University Press, 2018); Jan B. W. Pedersen, "On Lovecraft's Lifelong Relationship with Wonder" in *Lovecraft Annual No. 11*, ed. S. T. Joshi (New York: Hippocampus Press, 2017); Anders Schinkel, "The Educational Importance of Deep Wonder," *Journal of Philosophy of Education*, 2017; Sophia Vasalou, *Wonder: A Grammar*, (New York: SUNY Press, 2015).

17. It is possible that nonhuman animals can experience wonder because the brain structures, for example, of mammals, like dolphins and chimpanzees, are similar to that of human beings.

18. Free solo climbing also known as soloing implies that the climber does not rely on any safety equipment and foregoes the use of ropes, harnesses, etc., and relies entirely on her skills for the climb to be successful.

19. See Plato, *Theaetetus*, trans. H. N. Fowler, LCL (Cambridge: Harvard University Press, 1989), 155c-d and Aristotle, *The Metaphysics*, trans. H. Tredennick, LCL (Cambridge: Harvard University Press, 1989), I.

20. See Hepburn, "The Inaugural Address," 1; Sam Keen, *Apology for Wonder* (New York: Harper & Row, 1969).

21. Robert C. Fuller, *Wonder*, 14.

22. Robert Fuller "From Biology to Spirituality: The Emotional Dynamics of Wonder" in *Practices of Wonder: Cross: Disciplinary Perspectives,* ed. S. Vasalou (Eugene, OR: Pickwick Publications, 2012), 85.

23. Ibid., 85.

24. David B. Burrell, "Wonderment Today in the Abrahamic Traditions" in *Practices of Wonder: Cross-Disciplinary Perspectives,* ed. S. Vasalou (Eugene, OR: Pickwick Publications, 2012), 235.

25. The "Elgin Marbles" is a popular term referring to the collection of stone objects—sculptures, inscriptions, and architectural features—acquired by Lord Elgin during his time as ambassador to the Ottoman court of the sultan in Istanbul. At the present time they can be viewed at the British Museum.

26. John Keats, *The Poems of John Keats* (Cambridge: Harvard University Press, 1978).

27. Howard L. Parsons, "A Philosophy of Wonder" in *Philosophy and Phenomenological Research* 30(1), 1969, 89.

28. Richard Dawkins, *Unweaving the Rainbow: Science, Delusion and the Appetite for Wonder* (New York: Penguin, 2006), 42.

29. Ibid., xii.

30. Ian Kidd presented this idea in a paper entitled "Deep and Shallow Wonder" given at the Centre for Medical Humanities (CMH), St Mary's College, Durham, UK, on March 19th, 2014.

31. Quinn, *Iris Exiled,* xi.

ONE
The Lure of Wonder

According to the Roman Stoic philosopher Seneca it is "by the labors of others we are led to the sight of things most beautiful that have been wrested from darkness and brought into light."[1] To bring wonder into the light; to begin to see and understand what wonder is, it is useful to look in detail at specific scenarios in which wonder emerges. In what follows, seven such situations will be presented and interpreted, which together ground the concept of wonder as it will be investigated in the book as a whole.

To begin, let us focus on a scenario that most of us would probably recognize as wonder-filled: namely, the rare, unexpected, and extraordinary encounter with grandiose natural phenomena. Over the course of three consecutive nights from November 12 through November 13, 1833, one of the most spectacular meteor showers in recorded history took place. Elder Samuel Rogers witnessed the spectacle and in his autobiography he writes:

> I heard one of the children cry out, in a voice expressive of alarm: "Come to the door, father, the world is surely coming to an end." Another exclaimed: "See! The whole heavens are on fire! All the stars are falling!" These cries brought us all into the open yard, to gaze upon the grandest and most beautiful scene my eyes have ever beheld. It did appear as if every star had left its moorings, and was drifting rapidly in a westerly direction, leaving behind a track of light, which remained visible for several seconds. Some of those wandering stars seemed as large as the full moon, or nearly so, and in some cases they appeared to dash at a rapid rate across the general course of the main body of meteors, leaving in their track a bluish light, which gathered into a thin cloud not unlike a puff of smoke from a tobacco-pipe. Some of the meteors were so bright that they were visible for some time after day had fairly dawned. Imagine large snowflakes drifting over your head,

so near you that you can distinguish them, one from the other, and yet so thick in the air as to almost obscure the sky; then imagine each snowflake to be a meteor, leaving behind it a tail like a little comet; these meteors of all sizes, from that of a drop of water to that of a great star, having the size of the full moon in appearance: and you may then have some faint idea of this wonderful scene.[2]

Rogers was an educated man and knew about meteor showers; yet the extraordinary intensity, the grandeur and beauty of what he saw filled him with wonder, and thus his world was in a way enlarged or renewed as he became aware that it could indeed hold such qualities. Indeed, he acknowledges that his description may leave us with only a "faint idea" of what was going on, which could indicate that what is truly wonder-filled is beyond words to describe and that in order to obtain a richer understanding of wonder one must experience it personally. However, the subjective nature of this experience does not make it solipsistic: Rogers's account speaks clearly of the potential communality of wonder and the notion that experiences of wonder at least to some degree can be shared (figure 1.1).

Moving away from wonder-provoking natural phenomena but keeping the focus on the rare, unexpected, and extraordinary, the second example concerns philosopher Juan de Pasquale's account of a life-altering event, which took place in his youth. Following the funeral of his seventeen-year-old cousin Richie, de Pasquale found himself in a charged emotional state back in his mother's apartment. De Pasquale writes:

> We were drinking coffee when all of a sudden I regained the sense of my body's presence but simultaneously felt I was going to faint. I went into the bathroom and began to furiously splash water on my face, not so much to wash away the tears as to vainly try to wash away my overwhelming sense of death. When I looked up into the mirror I not only saw Richie's face staring back at me, but my face, my mothers face, my father's face, my sister's face—Everyman's face. There and then, suffering the most unbearable of sorrows that a person can feel, I knew I had uncovered something big, the biggest thing there is.[3]

"The biggest thing there is," is for de Pasquale the realization that we human beings are mortal creatures. Realizing one's mortality for the first time can induce wonder because it is a defining moment where one is presented with an imposing reality beyond one's own and seemingly anyone's control. Confronted with death, we realize that all that a person is, all that she knows and cares about will at some point disappear. Realizing one's mortality leads to a series of imposing existential questions: What should one do with the time one has been given? How should one live? Is there something one must do before the end? Is there a goal or purpose to human existence and who or what would, and indeed could, operate as guarantor for any answer to such questions? As no quick

Figure 1.1. The Leonid Storm of 1833. *Courtesy of the Seventh-Day Adventist Church.* This nineteenth-century woodcut shows an impression of the extraordinary meteor shower that took place on November 13, 1833.

answer capable of withstanding critical scrutiny is easily obtainable facing such existential queries may well provoke wonderment, although this will, to an extent, depend on how our individual mindsets and circumstances influence our experiences and perception. In this, as in all the examples discussed here, the aim is not to claim essential or universal qualities of the experience of wonder, but rather to develop an insight into its possible constituents. De Pasquale's example reveals the intensely subjective quality of wonder—he is, after all, the only one seeing the different faces in the mirror. Furthermore, this is a sudden and extraordinary experience because the different faces should not be there and yet spring upon him from nowhere.

A state of wonder may also spring from experiencing something that contradicts all that one knows or takes for granted. To illustrate this, the third example looks to the beginning of Shakespeare's tragedy *Hamlet*, where we find Horatio, the learned friend of Prince Hamlet, joining the night watchmen Marcellus and Bernardo on their late and bitter cold watch at Elsinore Castle. On the previous night the watchmen sighted what appeared to be the ghost of the late king of Denmark, yet in order to give further weight to their observations they have called upon Horatio to validate their perceptions and speak to the ghost should it reappear. Being an educated man Horatio is at first skeptical of the whole business but as the apparition comes the following scene takes place:

MARCELLUS   Peace, break thee off. Look where it comes again.
BERNARDO   In the same figure like the king that's dead.
MARCELLUS   Looks 'a not like the king? Mark it, Horatio.
HORATIO   Most like: it harrows me with fear and wonder.
MARCELLUS   It would be spoke to.
BERNARDO   Speak to it, Horatio.
HORATIO   What art thou that usurp'st this time of night,
            Together with that fair and warlike form
            In which the majesty of buried Denmark
            Did sometimes march? By heaven I charge thee, speak[4]

Horatio declares that his response embraces both fear and wonder, due to the unexpected and extraordinary encounter, which in this particular case involves the paranormal. The ghost is an anomaly. It is thing that should not be there and its very presence displaces Horatio because the world he inhabits has suddenly become a stranger to him. We might even say that seeing the ghost diminishes his self because not only does it challenge what he thought to be real or otherwise a reasonable picture of how the world works; it also gives rise to an identity crisis involving questions about what and who he is. What he thought to be real or otherwise a reasonable picture of how the world works now stands challenged, and so does indeed his identity. Furthermore, the scene indicates that experiencing wonder, at least to some degree, can be an arresting or astonishing affair that may last only temporarily. The example informs us that wonder is an experience, which starts with an intense moment of surprise and dislocation, but swiftly leads to a strong desire to know more and indeed to act.

Literature offers vivid examples of wonder arising from unexpected encounters, and the fourth example is concerned with German author Thomas Mann's novel *The Magic Mountain*. In a sanatorium in Davos, high up in the Swiss Alps, we find the young protagonist Hans Castorp attending an X-ray examination of his tubercular cousin Joachim Ziemssen who is in the care of the chief medical doctor Hofrat Behrens:

> "Clear picture," said the Hofrat, "quite a decent leanness—that's the military youth. I've had paunches here—you couldn't see through them, hardly recognize a thing. The rays are yet to be discovered that will go through such layers of fat. This is nice clean work. Do you see the diaphragm?" he asked, and indicated with his finger the dark arch in the window, that rose and fell. "Do you see the bulges here on the left side, the little protuberances? That was the inflammation of the pleura he had when he was fifteen years old. Breathe deep," he commanded. "Deeper! Deep, I tell you!" And Joachim's diaphragm rose quivering, as high as it could; the upper parts of the lungs could be seen to clear up, but the Hofrat was not satisfied. "Not good enough," he said. "Can you see the hilus glands? Can you see the adhesions? Look at the cavities here, that is where the toxins come from that fuddle him." But Hans Castorp's attention was taken up by something like a bag, a strange, animal shape, darkly visible behind the middle column, or more on the right side of it—the spectator's right. It expanded and contracted regularly, a little after the fashion of a swimming jelly-fish. "Look at the heart," and the Hofrat lifted his huge hand again from his thigh and pointed with his forefinger at the pulsating shadow. Good God, it was the heart, it was Joachim's honour-loving heart, that Hans Castorp saw! "I am looking at your heart." He said in a suppressed voice. "Go ahead." Answered Joachim again; probably he smiled politely up there in the darkness. But the Hofrat told him to be quiet and not betray any sensibility. Behrens studied the spots and the lines, the black festoon in the intercostal space; while Hans Castorp gazed without wearying at Joachim's graveyard shape and bony tenement, this memento mori, this scaffolding for mortal flesh to hang on. "Yes, yes! I see!" he said, several times over. "My God, I see!"[5]

The scene is wonder-filled for a number of reasons. First of all the protagonist is experiencing wonder when he, via the X-ray apparatus, beholds the insides of his living cousin, including the pulsating heart and parts of his skeleton. The X-ray machine is a technological wonder that gives Castorp a kind of augmented sight allowing him momentarily to see something that normally lies beyond our senses. Second, Castorp's new found "ability" sharpens his cognitive focus and gives rise to thoughts about life and death. Thus the example is complementary to de Pasquale's as it brings into view big questions about the nature of existence, which if we were to extrapolate, is to say that although we may feel very much alive and well, our existence is transient and one day things inevitably will come to an end without us fully knowing why and why it was we have been alive in the first place. In support of this stands Mann's use of the Latin phrase "memento mori," which translates into "remember that you have to die"[6] and the exclamation "My God, I see!" which is emotionally charged and brings to our attention that Castorp (and perhaps the reader as well) just "saw" or realized something of the utmost importance. Third, it gives rise to awareness of ignorance or lack of knowledge because suddenly, courtesy of augmented sight, to perceive parts of the world that hitherto have remained hidden is also to become aware that our knowledge of the world, or what it encompasses, is incomplete. Fourth, it invites us to wonder about what technologies are yet to be discovered that can aid us in beholding aspects of reality that have so far escaped us.

As a fifth example let us turn to the seventeenth-century natural philosopher Robert Boyle, who in relation to one of his observations has interesting things to say about wonder. Boyle writes:

> Yesterday, when I was about to go to bed, an amanuensis of mine, accustomed to make observations, informed me, that one of the servants of the house, going upon some occasion to the larder, was frighted by something luminous that she saw (not withstanding the darkness of the place) where the meat had been hung up before. Where upon, suspending for a while my going to rest, I presently sent for the meat into my chamber, and caused it to be placed in a corner of a room capable of being made considerably dark, and then I plainly saw, both with wonder and delight, that the joint of meat did, in divers places shine like rotten wood or stinking fish; which was so uncommon a sight, that I had presently thoughts of inviting you to be a sharer in the pleasure of it.[7]

What is interesting from Boyle's description is that his first reaction on seeing the luminous meat is wonder accompanied with delight. This is, in other words, an emotional upheaval, but unlike in the example focusing on Horatio from Shakespeare's *Hamlet*, it is not connected to fear because Boyle (but not his servant) is not frightened by what he witnesses but takes pleasure in the mysterious glow and quickly sets out to investigate the reason for its existence. Historians Daston and Park explain that to Boyle, wonders such as the glowing meat were considered "prime objects of investigation," and that Boyle was so pleased by the uncommon sight of it that it kept him awake into the early hours of the morning, despite the fact that he was nursing a cold he had caught while testing a new telescope.[8] This detail is important because it not only highlights the temporality of wonder, indicating that experiences of wonder can be momentary as well as enduring, but also that the emotion or feeling of pleasure arising in conjunction with wonder perhaps fuels the experience.

The sixth example of wonder draws on another philosopher's reflections on events from his youth, namely Sam Keen, who writes of an ordinary day in the city of Maryville, Tennessee:

> When I was six years old I was walking by a courthouse in a small town in Tennessee. A man came out, followed by a large crowd. As he walked past me, he pulled a knife from his belt and said, "I present you with this knife." Before I could see his face or overcome my shock and thank him, he turned and disappeared. The knife was a strange and mysterious gift. The handle was made out of the foot of a deer, and on the blade there was something written in a foreign language which no one in town could translate. For weeks after this event I lived with a pervasive sense of gratitude to the stranger and with a wondering expectancy created by the realization that such a strange and wonderful happening could occur in the ordinary world of Maryville. If nameless strangers gave such gifts, what surprises might be expected in the world?[9]

While it, too, emphasizes the sudden and unexpected, Keen's experience of wonder springs from something as ordinary as gift-giving and is characterized by a long-lasting "wondrous afterglow" that involves a sense of gratitude and wondering expectancy. Keen's experience of wonder contrasts with those of Rogers's and de Pasquale's in that it emerges in a much less dramatic or emotionally charged environment. Keen's example shows that wonder can emerge from a small abnormality in the ordinariness of the everyday, and suggests that in wonder our capacity for imagination is put to use as we try to understand the implications of our experience and answer the "what if" questions it gives rise to.

That experiences of wonder can be contained within the everyday is also the theme of the seventh and final example. On an ordinary afternoon in the autumn of 2014 it occurred to me to show "the duck-rabbit" to my then four-year-old daughter Mai. The duck-rabbit is an ambiguous figure made famous in philosopher Ludwig Wittgenstein's *Philosophical Investigations*[10] and consists of an image in which both a duck and a rabbit can be identified. Upon showing the duck-rabbit to my daughter she readily recognized the duck, which prompted me to ask her in a teasing manner "are you sure"? Puzzled by my question and mischievous look she once again turned her attention to the image and after a few seconds I observed her eyes widening and her mouth opened slightly before she gently uttered, "it's a rabbit." My daughter's experience, the intensification of her cognitive focus, and the particular expression on her face[11] during her moment of aesthetic appreciation, reveal this experience as one of wonder. The encounter with the duck-rabbit produced a small rift in the ordinary, understood as what she takes for granted, including the idea that she has a one-to-one relation with the external world and that this world is reliable and consistently predictable. Through her experience of wonder she suddenly "saw" new patterns, which introduced her to a world where things are not always as they first appear to be and may depend in part on the beholder. This suggests to us that perception is an inherent dynamism in the experience of wonder (figure 1.2).

These examples give us a preliminary idea of what can give rise to, and is involved in, the experience of wonder. Rogers's report covering the 1833 Leonid meteor shower shows that wonder can be accompanied by a sense of grandeur and beauty and prompts us to see the world anew. De Pasquale's case brought to our attention that wonder might arise from a sudden, extraordinary and personal experience that reveals our mortality to us for the first time. From the paranormal goings on in Shakespeare's *Hamlet* we found that wonder can be accompanied by fear and that it temporarily displaces or diminishes the self and inspires a desire for knowledge. The example from Mann's *The Magic Mountain* brought us in connection with "augmented sight" and seeing a part of the world that under normal circumstances is hidden to us. We also became familiar with the idea that awareness of ignorance or lack of knowledge is a part of wonderment in the sense that through wonder we become aware that our knowledge is incomplete. Boyle's experience brought to our attention that wonder is connected with emotional upheaval such as delight, and that one might take pleasure in the experience of wonder to such a degree that it may fuel a sustained inquiry into the object of wonder. Keen's narrative told us that wonder might arise from an ordinary event, that it intensifies the use of the imagination, and can be accompanied by a sense of gratitude and expectancy. My daughter's wonder at the ambiguity of the duck-rabbit alerted us to the notion that in wonder the cognitive focus is intensified and that wonder opens us up to a world where things are not always as they seem.

Examining real life situations and imaginary ones is clearly of great value when it comes to building a preliminary notion of wonder, as they provide insight into the constituents of wonder and invites further inquiry as they carry with them important questions, including is wonder an emotion or feeling? What is the role of imagination and perception in

Figure 1.2. *Kaninchen und Ente* (Rabbit and Duck). The depiction first appeared in the October 23, 1892, issue of the German humor magazine *Fliegende Blätter*.

wonder and in what capacity is it beneficial or good for us to wonder? Questions like these and more will be addressed throughout the book but for now, and in order to continue to build a preliminary account of wonder, let us focus on the name and root of wonder.

THE NAME AND ROOT OF WONDER

Plato's dialogue *Cratylus* emphasizes that the correctness of names is a big part of gaining knowledge and understanding.[12] It also stipulates that obtaining the right understanding of a particular word is a tricky matter and that etymology as a teaching is compromised by the crippling conflict between, on the one hand, Hermogenes (conventionalist), and, on the other, Cratylus (naturalist). The conventionalist would argue that there is no correct usage of a particular name besides what is supported by local convention. For instance the aurora borealis is called "aurora borealis" only because learned people situated in a particular culture have settled upon that label. For the naturalist, things are different and here we find the argument that names are not chosen arbitrarily and that a particular name belongs naturally to a particular object. According to Cratylus, it is important to realize that if one attempts to speak of something by calling it any name other than its natural name, one is completely failing to address it at all. Given this unsettled conflict the use of etymology in the exploration of wonder is connected with an element of uncertainty. Etymology is not an exact science and cannot be used alone to pinpoint the meaning of a word. It can also be argued that it has no purpose in a philosophical inquiry, as it does not provide any security in terms of the meaning of the word. Nevertheless, etymology is not completely useless to our current endeavor. Etymology can be used to indicate the root of wonder, its possible variation in meaning over different languages, and reveal whether its meaning changes depending on how one uses the word. On that note let us have a closer look at what etymology can tell us about the thing called "wonder."

According to Chambers Dictionary of Etymology the word "wonder" derives from the Old English word "wundor" meaning marvelous thing. The word has links to the Old High German "wunter," which in modern German has become "wunder." It can also be ventured that wonder has connections to the Old English "wundian" and the German "wunde," meaning wound or cut, suggesting that to be wonderstruck is to be wounded in a sense, and that it is an experience that no doubt puts a person into sharp focus as no wound is likely to be inflicted without causing some suffering and pain.[13] On a less dramatic note, lexicographer Eric Partridge points out that the Old English "wunder" may be connected to the German "wonne," meaning joy or delight.[14] This particular idea of wonder finds academic support. Literary scholar Philip Fisher, for example, connects wonder with delight and admiration and points out that the Latin root of admiration is "mira" which also is the Latin name for wonder, and furthermore, the root of the word miracle.[15] Historians Daston and Park also support this notion and add that admiration and objects of admiration called "mirabilia," "miracula," or "ammiranda" as terms seem to have root in the Indo-European word for "smile."[16] Literary scholars Robert M. Theobald and Dennis Quinn also favor this connection and claim that writers in English such as playwright William Shakespeare often use the Latinate "admire" as a synonym for wonder.[17] Furthermore, Quinn suggests that "admire" is a word of the senses, of passions, and of the intellect, and relates to both seeing and knowing. This he relates to the Greek word "thau," which may connect to wonder or to look at something in wonder. Wonder in Greek is "thauma," derived from "thea."[18] This root is incorporated in the English word "theatre" which refers to a place where one can encounter spectacular sights and sounds. Finally Quinn informs us that "thea" relates to the word "theory," which to the ancient Greeks was the word for philosophical contemplation.[19] Daston and Park are supportive of this as they point out that the roots of the Greek word "thauma" is found in the verb "to see."[20] However, what this means is unclear, because on one hand it might suggest that wonder appeals to the visual sense, which is a notion strongly supported by Fisher who writes: "Wonder binds the mind to a visual experience that has called attention to itself by its beauty, its strangeness, and its order."[21] On the other, it might entail that wonder has to do with perhaps visualization or the imaginings of the mind's eye, which points to understanding or knowledge. I can offer no verdicts as to which one of these stands is correct but for our purposes, suffice it to say, that they are two faces of the same marvelous coin.

Wonder also bears resemblance to the Old Icelandic word "undr," which in Denmark is known as "under." For something to be an "under," it is (attributed to) an extraordinary object, event, or person of admirable composition or character. For example, it can be well said that the Great Pyramid of Giza is a wonder or extraordinary object because of its uniqueness. The same can be said about Mahatma Gandhi's Salt March to Dandi in 1930 that alerted the world to the burgeoning Indian independence movement.

In the Danish language one also finds the similar but more inquisitive word "undre." This is equivalent to the English "wonder," understood in the context of "I wonder what, I wonder why, I wonder if and I wonder how" and it allows us to say that "wonder" can be used both as a noun and a verb. One way of illustrating this is to return to the paranormal goings on at Elsinore Castle. Seeing the ghost of the late king is to the learned Horatio a wonder (noun) but seeing the king also made him wonder (inquisitive verb) about the nature and purpose of the ghost. In addition "wonder" also presents itself as an adjective and an adverb. If "wonder" is used as an adjective it is used to describe a property of something, meaning that if we, for example, say that Horatio is a wondering (adjective) man we are giving voice to one of the parts that make up the person called Horatio. Wonder can also be used as an adverb in the sense that we can do something wonderingly (adverb) indicating that the focus is no longer on the wonder-filled thing in itself (noun) or that we actively wonder about something (verb) or that we are describing a property of someone or something (adjective) but on wonder as in "we are doing something in a particular way." We might say that after Horatio learned about the existence of the ghost he approached it wonderingly or in a wondering fashion (adverb).

As mentioned, etymology is not an exact science and cannot dictate how we should think about wonder. Because of this, understanding based entirely on etymology can be dangerous as we may end up being misled as much as guided. Nevertheless, for our purposes here, the etymological examination heightens our understanding of wonder as it points out some of the various different meanings and connotations "wonder," as a word, may have. Wonder can be seen as a wound but also something that produces smiles, joy, and delight. It may be that it is synonymous with marvel and admiration and that it is a sensation connected to the senses. Furthermore, it is interesting that wonder can be used both as a noun, a verb, an adjective, and an adverb, indicating that wonder is not just a phenomenon that one can study but also an action of sorts—something that one does, and perhaps in a particular way. With this in mind let us look to wonder from a historical perspective.

A HISTORY OF WONDER

The following historical account of wonder leans heavily on Dennis Quinn's book *Iris Exiled—A Synoptic History of Wonder*, which stands as one of the more comprehensive histories of wonder in the literature. Despite being synoptic, this book stands alone as a wide-ranging and lengthy historical account of wonder. To support Quinn's work, references to a number of accounts targeting selected periods or themes in the history of wonder, such as philosopher Sylvana Chrysakopoulou's essay "Wonder and the Beginning of Philosophy in Plato,"[22] which focuses on philosophy's beginning in wonder and John Onians's essay "'I wonder . . .': A short history of amazement,"[23] highlighting how wonder reveals itself through art and engagement with natural history will also be made. Likewise the historical account builds upon Daston and Park's *Wonders and the Order of Nature*,[24] which focuses on wonder from the medieval period through to the enlightenment and historian Frank Nadis's *Wonder Shows: Performing Science, Magic and Religion in America*, which begins where Daston and Park end their study, namely, with the "vulgarization of wonder."[25] Now it is important for the reader to realize that the framework of this book does not allow a full history of wonder; hence the headline "A History of Wonder" and not "The History of Wonder." This may be disappointing but given that we are merely seeking a preliminary understanding of wonder, an incomplete historical account of wonder depicting where the conception of wonder takes a significant turn will be excused. Bearing this in mind let us begin by addressing what may be called early cultivators of wonder, the ancient Greeks.

The ancient Greeks encompassed a civilization that dominated Greece from the eighth to sixth centuries BC to 600 AD, which signaled the beginning of the early Middle Ages and the continuing rise of Byzantium. This period offers the early musings on wonder and saw the birth of what we now label "classic" poetry and philosophy. The first speculations on wonder can be traced back to the poet Hesiod, who in the *Theogony*[26] informs us that the sea god Thaumas (wonder) married Electra and had three daughters, including Iris (rainbow) and the beautiful-haired harpies Aello and Ocypete.[27] Iris is particularly significant for our purpose here because she functions as messenger of the gods[28] and as Onians has pointed out she represents "the supreme wonder, a miracle linking heaven and earth."[29] In a way she ties the land of humans together with the realms of the gods just like the rainbow does in Norse mythology,[30] yet, despite being a messenger of the gods, it is possible to view her primarily as a representative of her father. As a divine courier, her beauty, shape, array of colors, and to the ancient Greeks inexplicable appearance in the sky, would make hearts leap just as poet William Wordsworth's did many centuries later.[31]

Although one nowadays may dismiss the poetry of Hesiod as mere mythology it is evident that Iris plays an important role in Greek classical philosophy. The reason for this is that Plato, through Socrates, mentions her in the dialogue *Theaetetus*, which centers on epistemology. The dialogue's youthful namesake exclaims upon the realization that he does not know what knowledge is itself, "By the gods, Socrates, I am lost in wonder when I think of all these things, and sometimes when I regard them it really makes my head swim."[32] Socrates replies:

> Theodorus seems to be a pretty good guesser about your nature. For this feeling of wonder shows that you are a philosopher, since wonder is only the beginning of philosophy, and he who said that Iris was the child of Thaumas made a good genealogy.[33]

By reading the *Theaetetus*, we learn that for Plato philosophy begins in wonder and has close ties to ignorance or lack of knowledge.[34] We also learn that, metaphorically speaking, beholding Iris or being in a state of wonder can be an uncomfortable and destabilizing experience inclined to make one's head swim.[35] As daunting as this may sound it is nevertheless the pathos and trademark of a philosopher as Socrates clearly states. This attitude to wonderment encapsulates the very childhood of wonder in Western philosophical thought. To reach what Quinn calls mature wonder we have to go further ahead in time and address the church fathers of the Middle Ages, but not before setting aside a little attention for Roman philosophy.

Roman philosophy is based on Greek philosophy and emerged in 155 BC via the efforts made by an Athenian embassy, together later with Cicero and Varro, who sought to make Greek philosophy accessible to the average Roman. However, the Romans were practical people and dedicated little time to philosophy. What normally is referred to as Roman philosophy are the deliberations of moralists, including Cicero, Seneca, Marcus Aurelius, and Plutarch, but to moralize does not necessarily evoke wonderment nor does it necessarily mean that it is philosophy. Moralizing demands rather the application of ethical principles to the act of correct living.[36] Nevertheless, the Romans treasured Epicureanism[37] and Stoicism[38] and thus philosophically inclined. However, both philosophies originate in Greece and come with a particular bitterness that leaves little room for wonderment. The hedonistic element in Epicurean ethics that flags pleasure and encourages the individual to satisfy her wishes and desires to gain well-being ultimately entails a singular bitterness as the avoidance of pain easily becomes identical with pleasure itself. Potentially this prevents the Epicureans from enjoying such human goods as love, physical exercise, family life, and indeed the activity of philosophy, as all of these present themselves as a combination of pain and pleasure. For the Stoic Romans the chances of encountering wonderment were equally low because, as represented by Seneca, Epictetus, and Marcus Aurelius, the concern for moral and psychological questions was given precedence over metaphysical, logical, and cosmological ones. Seneca hints at this in a letter to Lucilius named "On the Philosophers Seclusion," where he states "nothing except the soul is worthy of wonder; for to the soul, if it be great, naught is great."[39] The advice given to Lucilius draws on the Stoic precept of "nil admirandum" or "nil admirari," which I shall return to later when addressing wonder in connection with the Enlightenment and Romanticism.

Because of their idealism and youthful wonderment the Greeks could be cheerful like Socrates in the *Theaetetus*, but due to their realism the Romans were soberly mature and very much in lack of wonderment.[40] One might argue that poet and philosopher Lucretius stands out as a potential "thaumaturgist" in Roman times because his *De Renum Natura* (On the Nature of Things) is in part concerned with the formation of the world and the emergence of civilization. However, as exciting as it can be to read Lucretius and think him a sort of proto-scientist and his work a forerunner to Darwinian evolutionary theory, his habit of explaining away things sets him apart from the youthful Greek wonder and closer to the mature Roman "anti-wonderers" mentioned earlier.

With the Roman emperor Constantine the Great's embrace of Christianity, the lack of wonderment among the Romans was about to change. However, the reintroduction of wonder in Roman life never restored wonder to its original youthful and distinctly Greek form. It remained sober and mature yet gained a crucial new element, namely, fear or rather the fear of God. For the Christian thinker the ultimate good was God and to gain knowledge about God was alongside the love of God, considered the ultimate goal.[41] To be without these elements or to think otherwise was to stand outside Christianity. For the Christian, this would mean a constant striving toward God motivated by the fear of standing outside the light of God. Alternatively one can point out that the fear of an eternity in the infernal regions of creation, which Christianity also promised if one did not embrace Christianity, would no doubt prompt motivation.[42]

As the various territories of the Roman Empire during the fifth century began to fall to hostile armies, it marked the decline of the Roman Empire and the coming of the early Middle Ages. This was a troublesome period for the Roman Christians and culminated with the sacking of Rome by the Visigoths in 410 AD[43] and the demise of Romulus Augustus, the last emperor of the Roman Empire in 476 AD. Some people saw the fall of the Empire as punishment for abandoning the old Roman gods. In response to this the philosophically interested church father Augustine offered his grand work *The City of God*,[44] aimed at aiding the doubtful by strengthening their belief in Christianity.[45] However, before attending to Augustine's magnum opus let us take a look at his earlier autobiographical work, the *Confessions*. Augustine's confessional autobiography is relevant because in book X we find his reflections on memory, which has interesting things to say about wonder. Augustine writes:

> Great is this force of memory, excessive great, O my God; a large and an infinite [roominess:] who can plummet the bottom of it? Yet is this a faculty of mine, and belongs unto my nature: nor can I myself comprehend all that I am. Therefore is the mind too strait to contain itself? So where could that be which cannot contain itself? Is it without itself and not within? How then doth it not contain itself? A wonderful admiration surprises me, and an astonishment seizes me upon this. And men go abroad to wonder at the height of mountains, the lofty billows of the sea, the long courses of rivers, the vast compass of the ocean, and the circular motions of the stars, and yet pass themselves by, nor wonder that while I spake of all these things I did not see them with mine eyes; yet could I not have spoken of them, unless those mountains, and billows, and rivers, and stars which I have seen, and that ocean I believe to be, I saw inwardly in my memory, yea, with such vast spaces between, as if I verily saw them abroad. Yet did I not swallow them into me by seeing, whenas with mine eyes I beheld them. Nor are the things themselves now within me, but the images of them only. And I distinctly know by what sense of the body each of these took impression in me.[46]

From reading Augustine it is clear that even though the height of mountains and the billows of the sea may indeed foster a sense of wonder, one needs not travel far or rely solely on natural wonders in order to experience wonder. Reflection upon the mystery of how we remember or recall past experiences can prove quite a sufficient source of wonder, and if not, it may flow easily from realizing that we human beings are unable exhaustively to comprehend ourselves. In a way Augustine is urging the reader to get to know herself just like Socrates did, and so with Augustine we see a minor resurrection of the Greek wonder. By dedicating time for introspection, Augustine claims we will discover that human beings are truly wonderful as we are beings that cannot fully grasp or understand ourselves.

Moving on to Augustine's later work *The City of God*, we find that it encapsulates the idea that human history so far has consisted of a battle between the City of God and the City of Earth. The City of God refers to people of the Christian faith seeking the eternal truths of God. By contrast, the City of Earth refers to pagan people who made the finite earthly life their business and pleasure. In time and if human kind embraces Christianity, the idea is that the City of God will stand triumphant. For our purposes book XXI of *The City of God* is particularly interesting because here Augustine discusses a multitude of natural wonders and wonder inducing mekhanemata[47] from Roman naturalist Gaius Plinius Secundus's, also known as Pliny the Elder's encyclopedic *Natural History*. Among these wonders we find the legendary fire salamander[48] that was thought to live in fire; the seemingly ever-active yet ever-lasting volcano Mt. Etna,[49] and an iron picture suspended between two magnetic stones in a nameless temple giving the spectator the impression that it floated in mid air.[50] Augustine used the first two examples in his argument for the idea that not everything that is on fire will be consumed. This played an important part in his outlook on divine punishment and the idea that sinners in the afterlife had to undergo purification by eternal fire in order to gain entrance to Heaven.[51] The third example helped illustrate the existence of wonders developed from human ingenuity and possibly with demonic aid, which could lead people away from the Christian path.[52] Additionally, Augustine points out that the created universe is a wonder designed for human pleasure and delight and that it in itself surpasses the wonder of the things it contains.[53] By this notion Augustine points out that even though the world contains many objects of wonder the greatest of wonders lies in the mystery and omnipotence of God who created it all. Additionally, as pointed out by Daston and Park, it is Augustine's view that there is "no inherent way to distinguish between apparently commonplace and apparently marvelous phenomena since all depended on divine will."[54] Thus, everything in God's creation is wonderful.

Despite the efforts of Augustine it was not until the late Middle Ages, around the twelfth century, that Christianity recovered from the collapse of the Western Roman Empire. By then the first universities had emerged and Christendom saw the reappearance of ancient Greek texts coming from the Arab countries. Among these texts, translated into Latin from both Greek originals and Arabic translations, we find the nearly complete philosophical corpus of Aristotle. The reemergence of Aristotle posed a new "threat" to Christianity as it offered a seemingly well thought-through pagan alternative to Christianity, claiming that the world was eternal and no such thing as an immortal human soul existed.[55] As a response to this danger Thomas Aquinas, in his writing, sought to reconcile Aristotelian thought and the Catholic faith.[56] In doing so he, like Augustine, also managed to recover a bit of the youthful Greek wonder that had been lost during the previous centuries. In his *Summa contra Gentiles* he writes:

> Man has a natural desire to know the causes of whatever he sees, and so through wondering at what they saw, and not knowing its cause, men first began to philosophise, and when they had discovered the cause they were at rest. Nor do they cease inquiring until they come to the first cause . . . Therefore man naturally desires, as his last end, to know the first cause. But God is the first cause of all things. But God is the first cause of all things. Therefore man's last end is to know God.[57]

The Thomistic idea of wonder being a desire for knowledge draws on Aristotle, which becomes clear when reading the opening sentence of Aristotle's *Metaphysics*: "All men naturally desire knowledge."[58] This is shortly followed by the confirmation that philosophy begins in wonder:

> It is through wonder that men begin and originally began to philosophize; wondering in the first place at obvious perplexities, and then by gradual progression raising questions about the greater matter too, e.g. about the changes of the moon and of the sun, about the stars and about the origin of the universe. Now he who wonders and is perplexed is thought ignorant (thus the myth-lover is in a sense a philosopher, since myths are composed of wonder); therefore if it was to escape ignorance that men studied philosophy, it is obvious that they pursued science for the sake of knowledge, and not for any practical utility.[59]

Whereas the highest form of knowledge for Aristotle was *scientia*,[60] for Thomas this comprised of knowledge that precedes faith. Thomas introduced another kind of knowledge that acknowledges the mysterious dimension of faith, referring to the kind of knowledge that will not be revealed by reason, but in principle can only be known with the aid of divine revelation.[61] This allows us to say that although Thomas evokes the notion that philosophy begins in wonder, and that we all seek knowledge and absence of ignorance, he also teaches us that the knowledge of God is the highest form of knowledge and therein lies the greatest of wonder.

Thomas completed his *Summa Theologiae* between 1265–1274 AD and one can argue that with its publication the Middle Ages or scholasticism reached a thriving high point. However, over the next couple of centuries a series of major calamities spun the European High Middle Age culture into an inevitable decline. The Great Famine (1315–1317) is one of these calamities as it ended the lives of millions of Europeans. The Black Death (1348–1350) also qualifies, as it ravaged and robbed Europe of 40–60 percent of its population.[62] Furthermore, the fall of Constantinople to the Ottoman Empire in 1453 was a considerable disaster for Christendom and can be seen as the final blow to the High Middle Ages.

The early Modern Era is a historical term that describes the period starting from approximately the year 1500 AD and ends with the beginning of the Enlightenment in the eighteenth century. The era covers a number of cultural movements, such as the Renaissance, the Age of Discovery, and the Reformation, which all generated an atmosphere of change and departure from the scholastic orientated Middle Ages. During the beginning of the early Modern Era, neo-Platonism[63] presented a strong intellectual current and influenced the philosopher Nicholas of Cusa. Nicholas's main inspiration was Plotinus and in his *De Docta Ignorantia* (On Learned Ignorance) he stated that since the infinite God stands in contradiction to all that is finite, we human beings, understood as finite beings, can have no knowledge of God.[64] To a degree this also extends to the natural world, which for Nicolas was scarcely knowable due to its close connection with God.[65] When it comes to wonderment the new idea is that wonder ultimately prompts us to embrace our ignorance and after that simply rest in faith. We cannot know God and so we are left to wonder.[66]

Often portrayed as the first humanist, Giovanni Pico della Mirandola, in his 1485 oration, *The Dignity of Man*, gave utterance to the notion that man is the most wonderful of earthly beings.[67] This may at first glance seem unexciting and to a certain extent this is the whole point. Quinn suggests that the way Pico is using the word "wonderful" is synonymous with "estimable" or "exalted" and that the oration marks a crucial turning point in the history of wonder. The reason for this is that here we find literary evidence for an early hyperbolization of wonder.[68] Another reason why Pico is important to a study of wonder is because of the radical idea he proposes regarding human nature and the human condition. Pico reveals in the oration that man is great because he has, in fact, no nature and can be anything he chooses to be. Human beings lack conditioning, as philosophers Elisabeth and Paul Richard Blum express.[69] In this light human beings have infinite potential and have the freedom to, on one hand, act at the level of beasts and, on the other, elevate themselves to become something more.[70] Regardless, it is important to realize that no matter what one chooses to be, one fact remains, and that is that one is human. The thing that makes us human has nothing to do with what kind of life we chose to live or what actions we perform. It rests solely with the peculiar and most wonderful fact that human beings have the capability for rational thought.[71]

The early Modern Era also laid the foundation for what was to be known as the new philosophy or science dedicated to the study of nature removed from all things spiritual. One of the pioneers was the empirically minded Francis Bacon, and to the student of wonder he signals the next step in the history of wonder. According to Bacon's *The Advancement of Learning* from 1605 AD the new philosophy does not "presume by the contemplation of nature to attain to the mysteries of God."[72] The examination of nature does indeed produce knowledge but "having regard to God no perfect knowledge, but wonder, which is broken knowledge."[73] Bacon offers no elaborations on what he means by wonder as broken knowledge, but might refer to the idea that studying nature provides no knowledge about the nature of God and that the student will remain ignorant in that department regardless of what he might discover in relation to nature. To Bacon, wonder is the "seed of knowledge";[74] however when one uses the contemplation of nature as a lever to obtain knowledge about God, wonder no longer answers to that description and comes to a full stop. From this moment on, gaining knowledge becomes impossible and we are once again left to wonder.[75]

Wonder as a passion is also important to another prominent figure of the early Modern Age: Rene Descartes. Descartes was a reformer and his work *Discourse on Method* aimed at arriving at clear and distinct ideas without, for example, appealing to authority, which was widely practiced in scholasticism. In his treatise on the rainbow that accompanied the *Discourse on Method* Descartes's explanation of the enigmas of the rainbow completely put an end to the supremacy of the Aristotelian account, which is to be found in Aristotle's *Meteorology*.[76] Descartes's work was so successful that today it remains a major source of knowledge with regards to explaining the features of the rainbow.[77] Although scientific work on the rainbow is interesting as it offers an alternative to the myth of Iris it is, nevertheless, Descartes's work *The Passions of the Soul* that is most appealing to the student of wonder. From here we learn that:

> When the first encounter with some object surprises us, and we judge it to be new or very different from what we formerly knew, or from what we supposed that it ought to be, that causes us to wonder and be surprised; and because that may happen before we in any way know whether this object is agreeable to us or is not so, it appears to me that wonder is the first of all the passions.[78]

It is clear that to Descartes wonder is the first of all the passions.[79] This rests upon the notion that when we find ourselves in a state of wonder as a result of encountering something new we are not in a position to judge whether "the new" is beneficial to us. We do not know whether the object of wonder will aid us or cause us harm. We are oblivious to whether the object is to be loved, hated, desired, or shunned, as each of the responses would depend on knowing whether it is useful or harmful, good for us or bad for us. For Descartes, wonderment is situated between deficiency and excess. Never to wonder equals stupidity as it spells out a mind that never observes or takes notice of anything. Wonder in the excess is the reverse of stupidity and encompasses being astonished[80] by literally everything one experiences. In Cartesian optics, not being able to marvel at the aurora borealis the first time one encounters it is just as bad as when one is constantly astonished by cheap parlor tricks. Cartesian wonderment acknowledges ignorance when something new is encountered but prompts investigation of the object of wonder. Furthermore, once an investigation has identified the object of wonder or woven it into the fabric of the familiar, perhaps as a variation of a particular phenomenon or object, wonderment comes to an end.[81] In this light it can be said that Cartesian wonderment is effectively dismissed by science.

Descartes also informs us that wonder fades as we become more accustomed to the experience of wonder. He writes:

> And although this passion seems to diminish with use, because the more we meet with rare things which we wonder at, the more we accustom ourselves to cease to wonder at them, and to think that all those which may afterwards present themselves are common, still, when it is excessive, and causes us to arrest our attention solely on the first image of the objects which are presented, without acquiring any other knowledge of them, it leaves behind it a custom which disposes the soul in the same way to pause over all the other objects which present themselves, provided that they appear to it to be ever so little new. And this is what causes the continuance of the malady of those who suffer from blind curiosity—that is, who seek out things that are rare solely to wonder at them, and not for the purpose of really knowing them: for little by little they become so given over to wonder, that things of no importance are no less capable of arresting their attention than those whose investigations is more useful.[82]

From this passage we learn that not only must the object of wonder be new to us but also the whole experience of wonder must be new in order for us to experience wonder. The consequences of such an outlook are devastating to wonder because once we familiarize ourselves with the experience of wonder our ability to entertain a sense of wonder is declining. Said in another way the more experiences of wonder we sample the less likely we are to experience wonder again. Cartesian wonder is bound to become a less frequent experience as we grow older simply because the experience of wonder becomes a cliché.

The work of Descartes contributed to the end of the early Modern Era and the beginning of what is known as the Age of Reason, The Age of Enlightenment, or merely the Enlightenment. The Enlightenment was a period that began roughly from the mid-seventeenth century and lasted throughout the eighteenth century. It was a period characterized by the application of reason and empirical science in the interest of advancing knowledge. It was an intellectual revolution and as with all revolutions there were casualties. For the student of wonder the scientific revolution further diminished the importance of wonderment as wonders became quantifiable through the empirical lens. The singular quality of, for example, Theaetetus's wonderment became marginalized or of minor importance to contemporary intelligentsia.

One of the interesting intellectuals who engaged with wonder directly during this period is economist and philosopher Adam Smith. At the outset of his *History of Astronomy* he cautiously makes a distinction between wonder, surprise, and admiration. Smith writes:

> What is new and singular, excites that sentiment which in strict propriety is called wonder; what is unexpected, Surprise; and what is great or beautiful Admiration.[83]

From Smith's distinction we learn that wonder arises from the new and novel but that it is distinct from what is unexpected, which brings surprise, and from the great or beautiful, which calls for our admiration. Quinn notes that Smith's distinctions became popular during the Enlightenment but that the identification of wonder with novelty would eventually denigrate wonder and admiration would gradually lose its momentum due to it being separated from wonder.[84] What Smith means by sentiment is unclear but it can be argued that he uses the word "sentiment" as synonymous with "passion." The idea that wonder is a passion comes under attack when we look to the work of German philosopher Immanuel Kant. In his *Critique of Judgment* he reveals that *Vervunderung*, which translates into "astonishment" or "wonder" is "the affection produced by the representation of novelty exceeding our expectations."[85] For Kant, wonder is not a passion but an affection contrasting *Bewunderung*, which translates into "admiration" or "esteem." This distinction is important because, according to Kant, we do not put an end to our "admiration" or "esteem" of someone or something just because the novelty has worn off. To Kant, admiration or esteem is more enduring than wonder and the reason for this is that admiration or esteem is free from any contaminating feelings.[86]

Let us now pay attention to the Enlightenment poet Alexander Pope. Pope is interesting because of his dedication to scientific thought and neoclassicism, which forced a sturdy discontent with wonder. In *Essays on Criticism* he states: "For Fools admire, but men of sense approve"[87] and in the sixth epistle of the first book of Horace addressed to Mr. Murray he goes to even greater lengths to express his aversion. Here he writes: "Not to admire is all the art I know, To make men happy, and to keep them so."[88] The expression "not to admire" is not coined by Pope himself but originates in the expression "Nil Admirari" used in the epistles written by the Roman poet Horace. In here Horace links the notion of Nil Admirari to human happiness by writing: "Marvel at nothing—that is perhaps the one and only thing, Numicus, that can make a man happy and keep him so."[89]

It can be argued that Cicero also embraced this viewpoint. Written around 45 BC Cicero's *Tusculan Disputations* offers contemplations on what possible wisdom can facilitate the alleviation of distress; Cicero arrives at the following notion on what wisdom is:

> The thorough study and comprehension of human vicissitudes, in being astonished at nothing when it happens, and thinking, before the event is come that there is nothing which may not come to pass.[90]

According to Cicero one must, in order to be wise and to prevent stressful situations, anticipate every possible outcome of a given situation and not be astonished by anything that might actually happen.[91]

Horace, Cicero, and Pope might refer to different states of mind due to their respective use of "admiration," "marvel," and "astonishment." However, it is possible that Pope's "not to admire," Horace's "marvel at nothing," and Cicero's "being astonished at nothing" all are synonymous with the notion "wonder at nothing." The reason for this is that Pope uses the same Latin phrase as Horace and when we consider Pope's support of science and belief that wonder is for fools it appears likely that "Nil Admirari" may refer to wonder at nothing. Upon considering why Horace should have less regard for wonderment one possible reason is that Horace finished his formal education at the Academy in Athens. At the time, Stoic and Epicurean philosophy dominated the Academy and it is likely that Horace's aversion to wonder springs from a deep involvement with those particular philosophies.[92] On a different note, one could point out that Cicero does not use the Latin phrase "Nil Admirari" but "Nihil Admirari"[93] and therefore he is referring to something entirely different from Horace and Pope. However since "nil" and "nihil" refer to "nothing" in Latin it would seem futile to counter argue on this basis.

Despite negative exponents of wonder, like Pope, and the fact that wonder by the early eighteenth century was connected with the vulgar, that is, "the barbarous, the ignorant and the unruly" people who celebrated "enthusiasm, superstition, and imagination,"[94] wonder was soon to enjoy a Renaissance. As the eigteenth century matured a countermovement to the Enlightenment known as Romanticism arose questioning the Age of Reason and its disregard for the passions. Romanticism also referred to as "The Romantic Era" took place approximately between 1760 and 1850. It is a movement that is notoriously hard to frame and define but it is commonly accepted that the movement was largely artistic and found its expression in everything from music, poetry, and dance, to literature and paintings.[95] The Romantics attacked the very backbone of the Enlightenment, which, according to philosopher Isaiah Berlin, comprises of the following three propositions: (1) all genuine questions can be answered, (2) The answers are knowable, and (3) the answers must be compatible with one another.[96] The general notion of the Enlightenment was that what Newton achieved in the area of physics could likewise be applied to the ethical, political, and aesthetic domains.[97] Questions like what one should do in life, how the perfect society was to be structured and what counts as beautiful were in principle answerable by applying reason.

However, this strict rationalization of human life that leaves no room for passions and wonderment was to the Romantics questionable if not downright awful. One Romantic poem that testifies to this effect is John Keats's *Lamia*. Here he writes:

> Do not all charms fly
> At the mere touch of cold philosophy?
> There was an awful rainbow once in the heaven:
> We know her woof, her texture: she is given
> In the dull catalogue of common things.
> Philosophy will clip an Angel's wings,
> Conquer all mysteries by rule and line,
> Empty the haunted air, and gnomed mine—
> Unweave a rainbow, as it erewhile made
> The tender-personed Lamia melt into a shade [98]

Keats's antagonistic attitude toward natural philosophy understood as science and in particular the work of Newton is clear from reading the poem. Newton's success in replicating the rainbow in his studies of prisms was to Keats devastating to the poetry of the rainbow.[99] The prism was the instrument "with which the first born daughter of Wonder would be killed."[100]

Another Romantic that questions the spirit of the Enlightenment and its support of the "Nil Admirari" attitude is the poet Lord Byron. In the satirical poem *Don Juan* Byron proclaims that he "never could see the very Great Happiness of the Nil Admirari."[101] Immediately after we find not only a greeting to Horace and Pope (the first four lines) but also a powerful counterargument that challenges the reasonableness of the "Nil Admirari" attitude. It reads:

> Not to admire is all the art I know
> (Plain truth, dear Murray, needs few flowers of speech)
> To make men happy, or to keep them so;
> (So take it in the very words of Creech).
> Thus Horace wrote we all know long ago;
> And this Pope quotes the precept to re-teach
> From his translation; but had none admired,
> Would Pope have sung, or Horace been inspired?[102]

Byron's point is that if we cannot wonder we cannot be inspired. If Pope never wondered at the poetry of Horace his Horace-inspired poetry would never have taken form. In other words, Byron claims that poetry cannot rely on the cold light of reason alone but must begin in wonder.

It can be argued that Byron's dislike of the "Nil Admirari" attitude captures an important aspect of the zeitgeist of the Romantic Era. However, it has to be said that not all Romantics disliked the science of the Enlightenment. The poet Percy Shelley,[103] for example, embraced science quite passionately, and in the poem "Queen Mab" he envisions that an earthly utopia will follow the advancement of science.[104] The poet Wordsworth equally embraced science but alerted his readers to its dangers, one of them being coldness and detachment. In "A Poet's Epitaph" he writes:

> Physician art thou?—one, all eyes,
> Philosopher!—a fingering slave.
> One that would peep and botanize
> Upon his mother's grave?[105]

The Romantic Era as a whole can be seen as a countermovement to Enlightenment thought. The detachment of the scientist and her disregard of the passions was to the Romantics a fundamental mistake. The ultimate outcome of the Romantic revolt was a sharp division between science and poetry. Science would, in the name of reason, continue its exploration of the material universe, and poetry would claim rulership of the heart, beauty, imagination, spirit, and wonder.[106] It can be argued that the tension between the divided was never harmonized and as Romanticism entered its autumn years a deep chasm had opened between the two poles. Nevertheless, as the century progressed, Romanticism as a countermovement lost its momentum and its influence faded in the face of the advancement of science.

Throughout the late nineteenth century, resurgences of Romantic wonder can be found now and then. However, the successful application of science had at this time become so extensive that its value was hard to question. Furthermore, scientific thinking was colonizing other areas of learning. Jeremy Bentham's "principle of utility" or "Greatest Happiness Principle" emphasizing that happiness of the greatest number is the measure of right and wrong, is a good example.[107] The work of Charles Darwin is another example of the colonizing power of scientific thought. In *The Expression of the Emotions in Man and Animals* from 1872, Darwin explores the functionality of emotional states and their link to expressions.[108] However, as mentioned, the late nineteenth century also witnessed occasional upheavals of Romantic wonder. William Hamilton's lectures on metaphysics and logic published posthumously in 1859–1860 can be considered one such upheaval. In his lectures Hamilton draws attention to passages in Aristotle's *Metaphysics* book 1.2, 9, and in German philosopher Friedrich Heinrich Jakobi's *Werke*, volume 2. Hamilton starts with Aristotle:

> Wonder, says Aristotle is the first cause of philosophy: but in the discovery that all existence is mechanism, the consummation of science would be an extinction of the very interest from which it originally sprang.[109]

He then continues with a quotation from Jakobi:

> Even the gorgeous majesty of the heavens, the object of a kneeling adoration to an infant world, subdues no more the mind of him who comprehends the one mechanical law which the planetary systems move, maintain their motion, and even originally form themselves. He no longer wonders at the object, infinite as it always is, but at the human intellect alone which in a Copernicus, Kepler, Gassendi, Newton and Laplace, was able to transcend the object, by science to terminate the miracle, to reave the heavens from its divinities, and to exorcise the universe. But even this, the only admiration of which our intelligent faculties are now capable, would vanish, were a future Hartley, Darwin, Condillac, or Boneut, to succeed in displaying to us a mechanical system of the human mind as comprehensive, intelligible and satisfactory as the Newtonian mechanism of the heavens.[110]

Hamilton is clearly an exponent for Romantic wonder in the sense that he expresses his discontent with what he sees as wonder-less scientific inquiry. Philosopher John Stuart Mill later challenges Hamilton's viewpoint and argues that Hamilton is mistaken in his view that science is hostile to wonder. Mill writes:

> I do wonder at the barrenness of imagination of a man who can see nothing wonderful in the material universe, since Newton, in an evil hour, partially unraveled a limited portion of it. If ignorance is with him a necessary condition of wonder, can he find nothing to wonder at in the origin of the system of which Newton discovered the laws? nothing in the probable former extension of the solar substance beyond the orbit of Neptune? nothing in the starry heavens, which, with a full knowledge of what Newton taught, Kant, in the famous passage which Sir W. Hamilton is so fond of quoting (and quotes in this very lecture), placed on the same level of sublimity with the moral law? If ignorance is the cause of wonder, it is downright impossible that scientific explanation can ever take it away, since all which explanation does, in the final resort, is to refer us back to a prior inexplicable. Were the catastrophe to arrive which is to expel Wonder from the universe—were it conclusively shown that the mental operations are dependent upon organic agency—would wonder be at an end because the fact, at which we should then have to wonder, would be that an arrangement of material particles could produce thought and feeling? Jacobi and Sir W. Hamilton might have put their minds at ease. It is not understanding that destroys wonder, it is familiarity.[111]

The nineteenth century also saw a new batch of wonder advocates emerge, namely the American transcendentalists who, according to English literary scholar Tony Tanner, held central the idea that by beholding the world with the wonder of a child one would recover and retain a sense of its actual glory.[112] Tanner explains that wonder, despite its fading status in Europe, lived on in the American literature and, in particular, in the writings of Ralph Waldo Emerson, Henry David Thoreau, and Walt Whitman. Their transcendentalist writings were grounded in a particular need, namely the need to recognize and contain a new country and the "wondering vision was adopted as a prime method of inclusion and assimilation."[113]

Additionally, literary scholar Fred Nadis points out that during the 1830s and 1840s America witnessed the emergence of the American Wonder Shows, which thrived on the experience of wonder. Boosted by a robust market economy, a wealth of printed materials on science, together with a strong public interest in science as well as pseudoscience and religion,[114] wonder showmen "worked at the boundary of science and magic, relying on wonder to help their audiences suspend disbelief."[115] Furthermore, Nadis writes that to strengthen the impact of their shows the wonder showmen continually:

> Cast scientific and technological breakthroughs in magical terms and remnants of a magical worldview in scientific terms. Especially useful from a showman's point of view were electricity and other new invisible energy forms scientists were uncovering that might be regarded as part of the same spectrum as the invisible powers of the ancient world.[116]

Of notable wonder, showmen Charles C. Came, who toured New York in the 1840s and 1850s, offering patent medicines, scientific lectures, and electrical healing demonstrations, is worth mentioning.[117] Another is Harry Houdini, who in the 1880s, before he made his name as an escape artist and anti-spiritualist conducted fake séances together with his wife in the Midwest, which included "wonders" such as "floating tables, self-playing accordions and the appearances of spirit faces."[118]

In 1895 German physicist William Conrad Röntgen discovered the X-ray, which, as mentioned earlier, was later put to use in a wonder-filled existential way in Thomas Mann's *The Magic Mountain*. The X-ray soon found its way into the wonder shows and displays of the X-ray became popular at events such as the 1896 National Electric Exhibit in New York, where inventor Thomas Edison on some evenings explained the mysteries of the newfound ray to the audience.[119]

As the nineteenth century comes to an end it becomes apparent that wonder is on the wane when it comes to evoking the mysterious and the realm of science is the only place where "real wonder" emerges. Writer, journalist, and educator Arthur Mee emphasizes this in his popular 1908 publication *Children's Encyclopedia*, as it includes a section on wonders in nature as explained by science.[120] In America, realism caught up with the wonder showmen and "wonder-busting" magicians like the now older Houdini took center stage.[121] Nadis explains:

> The magicians were not precisely educating their audiences, but "wising" them up to the art of deception. From the magicians' point of view, the passion for wonder had become an appetite that could never lead to illumination but which might, if properly arranged, provide

light entertainment. Wonder was no longer located in "objects of wonder" but in the magicians' skills and craft. Recognizing the disenchantment of the world, the stage magicians were offering a variant on the wonder show: one based in natural progress that exalted ingenuity and potential.[122]

Despite the disenchantment and the public "turn" to realism, Romanticism was never fully thwarted by science and as we continue into the twentieth and twenty-first century one can still find remnants of Romantic wonder in what Quinn calls "modernist phenomena," involving occultisms, gnosticism, surrealism, symbolism, and fantasy.[123] It is not my business to depict these movements in detail here and it will suffice to say that as movements or phenomena they all promote Romantic wonder. The reason for this is that they ask us to turn away from the outer world and focus on inner personal experiences.[124] As a consequence, wonder becomes "a result of direct inner experience of some ultimate trans- or sur-reality attainable by non-rational means—Gnostic, revelation, magic, or art."[125] It can be argued that here wonder finds a function that is not easily challenged by science; however, it is also a function that, academically speaking, comes at a high price, as wonder conceptually becomes increasingly mystical and solipsistic. Some might see this as its prime strength; however, to immunize wonderment from scrutiny does not, academically speaking, promote understanding and merely prompts suspicion and skepticism.

We are now at the end of the historical exploration of wonder, but before we continue, let us briefly summarize it. By probing the history of wonder particular turning points have come to light. We began by addressing the Greek myths as described by Hesiod and learned that wonder is connected to Iris, the rainbow, who delivers tidings from the gods. From Plato it became clear that wonder is the feeling and starting point (a point shared by Aristotle) of philosophy and is bound together with an acute sense of ignorance, which altogether can be quite unpleasant. In the medieval period, Augustine informs us that it is quite possible to marvel at, for example, the mountains and the sea but that introspection will reveal that the ignorance we harbor about ourselves is most worthy of wonderment. Furthermore, we also pick up from Augustine that the created universe is a source of wonder as it surpasses the wonder of the things it contains indicating that the creator is the greatest wonder of all. Thomas Aquinas fused Aristotelian thinking with Christianity and thought that wonder was the desire to know God. Moving on to thinkers from the early Modern Period, Nicolas of Cusa believed that wonder ultimately prompts us to embrace our ignorance and rest in faith, as we cannot know God. The first humanist Pico della Mirandola offers us a chance to marvel at ourselves as free rational beings without a nature. To Francis Bacon, exponent of the new philosophy, wonder is broken knowledge. This means that when it comes to knowledge about God the study of nature provides no clue and we therefore remain in a state of wonderment about God. For Descartes, wonder was the first of all the passions situated between deficiency and excess, and so making it a passion worthy of the inquiring scientific mind. Furthermore, we learn that wonder fades as our experience of it grows in numbers. Moving on to the Enlightenment, Adam Smith brings to our attention that wonder is distinct from surprise and admiration, and arises from an encounter with what is new and singular. Kant described wonder not as a passion, but affection produced by the representation of novelty exceeding our expectations, and that this affection is altogether different from admiration or esteem. Whether it is correct to think of wonder as something completely different from a passion can of course be debated, and I shall return to this in a later chapter when I address wonder as an emotion. For now it will suffice to say that the supremacy of reason and mechanical thinking over passion proved demeaning for wonder in the time after the Enlightenment. However, the view of wonder expressed by Enlightenment scholars was not unchallenged. With its emphasis on the passions, the Romantics offered an influential countermovement and Byron pointed out that not to wonder was problematic because without wonder inspiration would not arise. However, as science continued its advancement, Romanticism, which was a largely artistic movement, retreated. Throughout the nineteenth century wonder continued to decline despite sporadic upheavals of the Romantic kind. According to Quinn these upheavals connect with occultism, gnosticism, surrealism, symbolism, and fantasy and present wonder as an inner personal experience far removed from the outside world that science had claimed as its focus. The emphasis on personal experience persists to this day.

PROVISIONAL TAXONOMY OF ALTERED STATES

Let us now explore what may be called a provisional taxonomy of altered states with the aim of highlighting some of the features that make wonder distinct from a selection of related or similar experiences that one may reasonably mistake for being wonder. The following will explore seven such altered states: awe, horror, the sublime, curiosity, amazement, admiration, and astonishment, but because of its particular importance to European philosophy and technical quality, the sublime will receive extra attention.

What is awe? What does it mean to be awestruck or to stand in awe of something? In his *The Idea of the Holy*, theologian Rudolf Otto investigates the experience that underlies all religion, which he labeled "the numinous." The numinous can be understood as the "wholly other" or "that which is quite beyond the sphere of the usual, the intelligible, and the familiar, which therefore falls quite outside the limits of the 'canny,' and is contrasted with it, filling the mind with blank wonder and astonishment."[126] According to Otto, the English phrase or word that (to a degree) encapsulates the above is "religious dread" or simply "awe."[127] This particular take on awe is somewhat echoed in Hepburn's work, who suggests that awe is "dread mingled with veneration, reverential wonder."[128] To add further texture to the notion of awe, psychologists Robert Emmons and Charles Shelton informs that awe is an experience that may arise from a variety of objects and events of majestic, vast, and powerful quality and can produce a sense of being overwhelmed.[129] In this respect it could be ventured that as a sensation awe is seldom joyous unless the object in question is of a benevolent nature. A sense of joyous awe could spring from the experience of being saved from a band of thugs by a hero of superior strength, size, and agility. Watching the sun reemerge from being overshadowed by the moon during a total solar eclipse may likewise produce awe in conjunction with joy. Despite the existence of a possible joyous sense of awe it can be argued that the traditional companions of awe are fear and terror. Observing natural objects like Rakekniven Peak found at the north end of Trollslottet Mountain, Queen Maud Land, Antarctica may easily inspire awe in conjunction with fear and terror. One need only imagine what it must be like to attempt to climb its 640-meter, almost vertical wall, amid the unforgiving and extremely hostile icy landscape. Likewise it can be argued that the swift American-led 2003 military invasion of Iraq produced awe escorted by fear and terror.[130]

Awe is sometimes evoked in connection with the divine; however, it can also be found in relation to nature, politics, and art as psychologists Dasher Keltner and Jonathan Haidt point out, and may facilitate personal change or transformation in the form of a radical alteration of a person's outlook, attitude, and system of value, or way of life.[131] One can imagine that being the sole survivor of a serious accident, like a plane crash or natural catastrophe like a tsunami, may produce a sense of awe and inspire, for example, a change in attitude in terms of how one lives. The same goes for people who have survived a heart attack, cancer, or some other serious ailment. Life altering experiences based on awe are, as indicated, also represented in the field of religion and a prime example of such is the awesome circumstances that led to the conversion of the biblical character St. Paul.[132] Initially, St. Paul, also known as Saul, was a persecutor of the early Christians, but one day on the road to Damascus something remarkable happened:

> Suddenly there shined around him a light from heaven: And he fell to the earth, and heard a voice saying unto him Saul, Saul, why persecutest thou me? And he said. Who art thou Lord? And the Lord said. I am Jesus whom thou persecutest: it is hard for thee to kick against the

> pricks. And he trembling and astonished said, Lord, what wilt thou have me do? And the Lord said unto him, Arise, and go to the city, and it shall be told thee what thou must do. And the other men which journeyed with him stood speechless, hearing a voice but seeing no man. And Saul arose from the earth: and when his eyes opened, he saw no man: but they led him by the hand, and brought him into Damascus.[133]

It seems apt to describe the experience of St. Paul as one of awe because of the terrifying majestic display of power God delivers. First, God produces a sudden heavenly flash, which causes Paul to fall to the ground and blinds him. Hereafter, God, without any introduction and in a voice without a clear point of origin, starts to interrogate St. Paul, asking him why he prosecutes. This is followed by the curious comment: "It is hard for you to kick against the pricks." Now what the latter means is uncertain but one interpretation could be that it is equivalent to "it is useless to fight against my will" or "it is useless to fight against the power of God." In any case, this display of awesome power has a huge effect on Paul, who offers his compliance. Subsequently, he was ordered to go to Damascus to await further orders, which he does without questioning. The experience has a huge impact on St. Paul, who, as the story goes, undergoes a radical transformation and becomes a devoted and god-fearing Christian.

In what sense does awe differ from wonder then? Keeping in mind that exceptions may be found,[134] one of the major differences it would seem is the notion that while wonder has a tendency to be accompanied by joy or delight, awe has a tendency to be experienced together with a sense of fear and terror. Paul's experience is clearly a case of the latter, making his experience one of awe. One could seek to counter this by pointing out that the narrative does not say anything about Paul being awestruck but only that he trembles and experiences astonishment. Furthermore, one could venture that what is meant by "astonished" could be "surprise" or even "sudden wonder," which, if true, would cast a different light on Paul's experience. However, since it is conceivable that astonishment is but a component of both the experience of wonder and awe, it can be ventured that labeling Paul's experience as one of astonishment is insufficient and that there must be more to his experience than "astonishment" can cover. In this light there is good indication that what is afoot in the case of St. Paul is awe. This is mainly because his experience involves submission to an overwhelming power and is one totally devoid of delight and joy. God seeks to dominate and succeeds via a display of power, will, and terror in the form of taking away Paul's ability to see. This leaves him quite vulnerable and completely in the hands of his comrades and it enables us to understand what philosopher Martha Nussbaum has in mind when she writes: "Wonder and awe are akin, but distinct: wonder is outward-moving, exuberant, whereas awe is linked with bending, or making oneself small. In wonder I want to leap and run, in awe to kneel."[135]

The second state of mind we shall focus on is horror. Horror sometimes appears in the literature on wonder indicating that the two are related or similar in composition. Verhoeven, for example, writes that "wonder can shade from slight, by being way of surprise, astonishment and amazement right up to way of dismay and horror."[136] Another example is Daston and Park who find that although wonder has its own history it is nevertheless a history that is closely bound to the history of horror, which is based primarily on their study of medieval monsters.[137] Regardless, there is a qualitative difference between the experience of wonder and horror and to substantiate this difference let us focus on the work of philosopher Jerome Miller, who promotes the notion that horror represents the source of our most radical questions, and to entertain a sense of horror signals a departure from the familiar and ordinary. As an underlying premise horror encompasses the assumption that the person experiencing it is comfortably situated within a universe of meaning. However, the actual experience of horror springs from the possibility that this given universe of meaning is under threat of being dismantled.[138] In this sense horror comes as a direct result of losing the center around which a given life revolves and which makes it a coherent whole.[139] For most of us, losing the center from which we gravitate is a rarity, however this does not mean that we are totally bereft of the experience of horror. We might have experienced what Miller calls "intimations" or hints of horror, which can take the form of the most insignificant interruptions in a person's life.[140] Miller gives the example of his wife being forty-five minutes late in coming home one winter evening and continues:

> As I stand musing by the window watching the snow wrap everything in an eerie silence, I find myself suddenly visited by an inexplicable inkling of horror, a hint of some unspeakable possibility. My wife's lateness, although it seems to be only an event in my world awakens in me an intimation of radical disruption of it. By virtue of her primacy in my life, by virtue of the fact that she is not simply another person in it but the centre in terms of which it is structured and focused, my wife's death would be the end of my world.[141]

It is easy to see why the mere thought of losing someone who is placed at the center of one's world can produce intimations of horror. However, such intimations need not only spring from close relations with family members. One can imagine intimations of horror emerge from reading literature or embarking on a study that challenges the order of things as one has come to perceive it or has been taught to perceive it during one's life.

In what sense is horror then different from wonder? Broadly speaking, both horror and wonder seem to be a threat to the integrity of one's universe. According to Miller, we are in a state of wonder when confronted with the limitation of our knowledge but at the same time we are filled with the urge to further our knowledge.[142] Horror is different in the sense that it is a representation of the structure of our individual universe of meaning under threat. It is different because we are very much aware of what structures our universe of meaning. We know what it looks like and so what horrifies us cannot be truly unknown. If it were wholly unknown how could we even begin to see it as a possible threat to the structure of our universe of meaning? While wonder tends to lead us from a condition of ignorance toward knowledge, horror has a tendency to lead us from the familiar world of the known toward an unknown. While wonder tempts a person to run toward its object, horror makes one run away. It can also be argued that while horror threatens to destroy our universe of meaning, wonder seems bent on expanding it. To exemplify this, one could look to the works of twentieth-century weird fiction writer H. P. Lovecraft, who is perhaps most famous for his horror/science fiction stories but also wrote stories of wonder,[143] similar in style to those of Lord Dunsany.[144]

Now Lovecraft's *Celephais* illustrates very well how wonder makes us run toward its object and how in wonder our universe is expanded (figure 1.3). Lovecraft writes:

> There are not many persons who know what wonders are opened to them in the stories and visions of their youth; for when as children we listen and dream, we think but half-formed thoughts, and when as men we try to remember, we are dulled and prosaic with the poison of life. But some of us awake in the night with strange phantasms of enchanted hills and gardens, of fountains that sing in the sun, of golden cliffs overhanging murmuring seas, of plains that stretch down to sleeping cities of bronze and stone, and of shadowy companies of heroes that ride caparisoned white horses along the edges of thick forests; and then we know that we have looked back through the ivory gates into that world of wonder which was ours before we were wise and unhappy.[145]

Quite different is the theme of Lovecraft's horror story "Dagon," where the protagonist, after drifting aimlessly for days on a small lifeboat south of the equator, encounters a huge polyphemus-like creature that "should not exist" on a vast upheaval of the ocean floor. The story ends with the protagonist committing suicide by throwing himself from a window onto the street below because the horror he uncovered simply destroyed his world. In other words, the memory of the creature he encountered effectively put an end to his universe of meaning and so he decided to commit suicide to escape or to permanently "run away" from the horror occupying his mind.[146]

Figure 1.3. Les Edwards, *Eldritch Tales: Celephaïs.* 2010. Courtesy of Les Edwards, www.lesedwards.com

The next altered state, similar to wonder and worthy of exploration, is the sublime.[147] The sublime has in many ways suffered the same fate as wonder because what is meant by the sublime in everyday speech is quite distinct from the meaning attached to the sublime within academia. According to Holmqvist and Pluciennik the sublime, in its ordinary usage, frequently addresses what is noble and morally positive[148] but within academia it remains a disputed technical term that due to its complicated history and relationship with the Roman oratory of Longinus, eighteenth-century philosophy and politics, Romantic art, psychoanalysis, and the depiction of postmodern technology is difficult to capture.[149] Thus the sublime is as it were a "shape-shifter," but to get some foothold on the subject and a starting point, let us consider a definition offered by literary scholar Philip Shaw that goes as follows:

> In broad terms, whenever experiences slip out of conventional understanding, whenever the power of an object or event is such that words fail and points of comparison disappear, then we resort to the feelings of the sublime. As such, the sublime marks the limits of reason and expression together with a sense of what lie beyond these limits.[150]

From this vantage point the sublime refers to what we feel when we face, for example, the foggy vistas in Romantic painter Casper David Friedrich's 1818 painting *Wanderer above the Sea of Fog*, and the state of mind we experience when beholding images of the collapsing Twin Towers in New York following the 2001 terrorist attack. Likewise it specifies the feeling we experience upon witnessing the scene in Francis Ford Coppola's 1979 film *Apocalypse Now*, where American helicopters obscured by the rising sun attack a Vietnamese village to the sound of Richard Wagner's "Ride of the Valkyries." Additionally, the sublime covers what we experience when we behold the ominous stream of code behind every object in the 1999 film *The Matrix* by the Wachowski brothers, and Olafur Eliasson's installation *The Weather Project* at Tate Modern in London 2003.

To further our understanding of the sublime let us now focus on three of its major contributors starting with Longinus. It is widely acknowledged that the first literary work on the sublime is *Peri Hupsous* or *On Sublimity* by Longinus, whose identity unfortunately is a matter of controversy. Written around the first century AD, this particular piece of work takes the form of an orator's guide to how one might manipulate an audience most effectively. From Longinus's text we foremost learn about the effects of the sublime but also that the sublime stands in relation to wonder and astonishment. Longinus writes:

> For grandeur produces ecstasy rather than persuasion in the hearer; and the combination of wonder and astonishment always proves superior to the merely persuasive and pleasant. This is because persuasion is on the whole something we can control, whereas amazement and wonder exert invincible power and force and get the better of every hearer. Experience in invention and ability to order and arrange material cannot be detected in single passages; we begin to appreciate them only when we see whole context. Sublimity, on the other hand, tears everything up like a whirlwind and exhibits the orator's whole power at a single blow.[151]

If one seeks to dominate an audience, one must in Longinus's view break away from traditional oratory and make the audience experience a sense of wonder and astonishment. The rationale behind this is that in comparison, oration based on controllable persuasion is simply not as effective. To Longinus, the effect of the sublime is like a tsunami or avalanche. It is an uncompromising, forceful, natural event that sweeps everything along with it defying the will of any that might oppose it. Important to Longinus's view of the sublime is that wonder and astonishment are subordinate to the sublime as they both qualify as what tears everything up and get the better of every hearer. Now it might be true that astonishment contributes to this effect but it is not necessarily the case that wonder does. Admittedly, wonder instigates a certain instability which in combination with astonishment may leave us overwhelmed or wonderstruck, but the hearer needs not be a passive recipient completely "defenseless" against Longinus's whirlwind as we can envision the hearer to be an active listener who can evaluate and moderate her wonderment.

In 1757, Edmund Burke anonymously published his *A Philosophical Enquiry into the Origin of Our Ideas of the Sublime and Beautiful*, which, like Longinus's work, stands as a landmark when it comes to inquiries into the sublime. For Burke the source of the sublime is the terrible. He writes:

> Whatever is fitted in any sort to excite the ideas of pain and danger, that is to say, whatever is in any sort terrible, or is conversant about terrible objects, or operates in a manner analogous to terror, is a source of the sublime.[152]

On the outset it appears as if the Burkean sublime is rooted in terrifying natural events like the 1755 Lisbon earthquake. The rationale behind this is the fact that the earthquake was caused by something outside human control and brought about pain and danger. Nevertheless, Burke's contribution to the notion of the sublime comes with a certain amount of ambiguity and this is due to its focus on cognition and the psychological effect of terror. Shaw points out that the ambiguity of Burke's position becomes clear if one looks to the second half of the quotation above. The word "conversant" indicates a shift from the sublime being a quality inherent in particular objects toward sublimity being a mental state.[153] This particular development is significant, as Longinus's natural whirlwind now stands challenged.

Kant's *Critique of Judgment* also contains deliberations on the sublime and takes our understanding of the topic to an entirely new level. Kant refers to the sublime as what is "absolutely large" or that "in comparison with which everything else is small."[154] This may not sound revolutionary but important to Kant's outlook is that the largeness is something that is formed in our heads so to speak. Kant writes:

> For what is sublime, in the proper meaning of the term, cannot be contained in any sensible form but concerns only ideas of reason, which though they cannot be exhibited adequately, are aroused and called to mind by this very inadequacy, which can be exhibited in sensibility.[155]

Key to Kant's understanding of the sublime is that the sublime does not reside within an object such as a vast ocean heaved up by storms, a blizzard or an icy wasteland, but is a product of the mind that judges the object as sublime and it is in this respect that Kant places the sublime within our heads.

In addition to the above it is important to point out that Kant distinguishes between two forms of the sublime: the mathematically and the dynamically sublime.[156] The mathematically sublime throws additional light on the notion of the sublime as the absolutely large as mentioned above, because to judge something as absolutely large is to address the boundlessness of the object. This is the very core of the Kantian sublime because unlike the beautiful in nature, which is concerned with the form or the boundedness of the object, the sublime can be found in the formless or that which is unbound.[157] The experience of the sublime in this regard arises not from the natural object but from contemplation of that object, and more so from the failure of comprehending the particular object in its totality.

Concerning the dynamically sublime, Kant writes: "When in an aesthetic judgment we consider nature as a might that has no dominance over us, then it is dynamically sublime."[158] To spell out what Kant has in mind, consider this example. When I was a child my family and I would spend every summer in my grandparents' beach house, which was located on a small hill on the west coast of Northern Jutland in Denmark. This meant that from time to time we had to endure powerful seasonal thunderstorms, and from those years I remember in particular one incident where my mother, during an exceptionally violent thunderstorm, evacuated my brothers and me to the car because she judged that the wooden beach house was no longer safe for us to be in. We knew that the car would provide safety from the lightning due to its rubber tires, so once we were all seated in the car the fear and terror of the storm we all harbored vanished. My experience here corresponds to Kant's dynamically sublime because from our safe haven we could watch the magnificence of the storm, knowing full well that despite the multitude of lightning strikes, the loudness of the thunder, and the distinct smell of ozone in the air, we would be safe and live to tell the tale. The storm had, in other words, no dominance over us and we were able to aesthetically judge the storm as fearful without being afraid of it, which according to Kant is an important part of the dynamically sublime.[159]

To finish this brief entry on the Kantian sublime we might say, as Shaw has pointed out, that the Kantian sublime is neither entirely materialistic nor wholly idealistic in its nature, but is born out of a structural necessity or "a supplement not belonging to the realms of either pure or practical reason, but which yet must be assumed for either to cohere."[160] In this sense the sublime comes about when we realize the transcendental dimensions of experience.[161]

In what sense does the sublime differ from wonder then? Fisher believes that "in the sublime, fear and surprise, power and danger occur in a rich blend" and that the sublime stands in sharp contrast to wonder in the sense that where the sublime could be called aestheticization of fear, wonder is the aestheticization of delight."[162] I am sympathetic to Fisher's view because the literature on wonder tends to favor the connection between wonder and joy or delight. Examples such as Boyle's glowing meat examined in the beginning of the chapter point in that direction and so does the various philosophical writing on wonder.[163] However, we have also acknowledged that wonder can be accompanied by fear as we saw in the example involving Shakespeare's Horatio, and that wonder can be associated with a wound, something traumatic or otherwise unpleasant.[164] Thus, it might be more accurate to say that wonder is mostly the aestheticization of delight despite its obvious vagueness.

The difference between wonder and the sublime may also lie in their respective relationship with knowledge. Typically a sense of wonder entails awareness of one's ignorance (lack of knowledge) and a desire to know about the object or indeed subject at hand. We find this exemplified in Mann's character Castorp who does not quite know what to make of the sight of his cousin's beating heart, inner scaffolding, and the existential thoughts it gives rise to. We may also reasonably speculate that Shakespeare's character Horatio likewise displays awareness of ignorance and a desire for knowledge as he ventures forth to gather more information about why the dead king has come back. Likewise, it is exemplified in the case of Boyle as he stayed up all night trying to figure out why the meat was glowing. In light of this, we might say that in wonder, the wonderer (unconsciously perhaps) entertains the hope that further investigation into the object of wonder will grant greater understanding or knowledge of it, but this kind of hope is not necessarily present in the sublime.

If we look to the Burkean sublime, it comes across as an experience that puts an end to our quest for knowledge, as we are overwhelmed with terror. The Lisbon earthquake, which we may call sublime in a Burkean sense, took the lives of thousands of God-fearing people and left survivors and intellectuals pondering why God would allow such an event to happen. Philosopher Daniel Speak writes that the Catholic Church explained that the earthquake and the subsequent fires and tsunami were God's way of punishing the sinful citizens, but while the earthquake took place most people were gathered in their churches, and the red light district, which one may reasonably expect would be categorized as a place of sin by the church, emerged largely unharmed from the event.[165] In a Burkean sense the Lisbon earthquake is sublime first and foremost because of the terrible destruction it brought upon the citizens of Lisbon but also because it was a dramatic blow to Christianity. It raised terrifying questions that needed an answer, such as why would God punish good God-fearing people while leaving the sinful area of the city largely untouched; was God nothing like what he had been construed to be and did the destruction of Lisbon happen for no particular reason, thus signaling that human beings are situated in a world bereft of a benevolent intervening divine caretaker?

If we focus on the Kantian mathematically sublime, the difference between wonder and the sublime also becomes visible. While the sublime is concerned with the absolutely large and boundless, wonder (although it might be associated with the vastness of space) facilitates a sense of boundness and connectedness without the wonderer really knowing why. This is exemplified by Keen's experience, as he for weeks after his experience of wonder found himself haunted by a wondering expectancy, signaling that he is connected to the world anew. Had he not been able to acknowledge this connection or enlargement of his world, it is doubtful that he would have entertained his "post taumatic expectancy" and might have felt alienated or otherwise disassociated instead. Continuing with Kant's mathematically sublime, there seems also to be a difference between wonder and this version of the sublime in terms of the hope of achieving greater understanding or knowledge of the object facilitating the experience. In Kant's mathematically sublime, the particular experience arises not from a natural object such as a blizzard but from the contemplation of that particular object and the failure of comprehending it in its unbound totality. Because of the unbound nature of a blizzard, any hope of achieving greater understanding or knowledge about it is thwarted because the blizzard is amorphous and undefined. Thus it might be ventured that the mathematically sublime, unlike wonder, is accompanied by a kind of "hopelessness," because obtaining further knowledge about the unbound object of concern is futile.

The difference between wonder and the sublime also presents itself if we focus on Kant's dynamically sublime. While the dynamically sublime does not hold any dominion over the self that is acknowledging it, the idea of having a "solid self" is not present in wonder because wonder gives way to at least a temporary displacement/diminishing of the self. Thus we might say that in wonder we are not in a "safe place" where the intellect may appreciate "the boundless ocean heaved up" [166] or a violent thunderstorm. In wonder we are at least momentarily thrown or unhinged because we find ourselves connected to a larger world, which we do not fully understand. The case of de Pasquale supports this because through the realization of his mortality he also recognized the connecting and troublesome question of how to live, to which he had no answer and which perhaps prompted his interest in philosophy.

Curiosity and wonder are sometimes used interchangeably. We see this, for example, with the cabinets of wonder[167] from Renaissance Europe, as they are also known as cabinets of curiosity. However, there is no reason to presume that wonder and curiosity are synonymous. In fact, in the High Middle Ages wonder was understood as something quite distinct from curiosity.[168] To the medieval philosopher wonder was awed reverence in conjunction with the uncomfortable realization of one's ignorance. Curiosity, on the other hand, was viewed as a morally ambiguous desire closely associated with lust, pride, and the craving of knowledge about the business of one's neighbors. All in all, curiosity was a negatively charged word as it prompted people to mingle in affairs that were not their concern.[169] As mediaeval times came to an end a shift took place that changed the face of both wonder and curiosity. The status of wonder decreased as it became associated with dull stupor and the vulgar passion of the masses rather than the refined educated feeling of the philosopher. For curiosity the shift meant an increase in status and respectability as it became associated with natural philosophy.[170] A major exponent of this interpretation of curiosity was Thomas Hobbes, who viewed desire and passion as the driving force of human life. Hobbes writes:

> Desire to know why, and how, curiosity; such as in no living creature but Man; so that Man is distinguished, not onely [only] by his Reason; but also by this singular Passion from other Animals.[171]

According to Aristotle what makes us different from other animals is our capacity for rational thought.[172] With Hobbes this notion gets supplemented with curiosity, as rationality cannot alone account for what moves the mind and body of human beings. One noticeable feature about curiosity is that it is never quenched. Associated with greed and independent from need and satisfaction, curiosity never rests and constantly yearns for what is novel and new.[173] According to philosopher Jianhong Chen, Hobbes adopted an approach to wonder similar to that of Aristotle, but at the same time he made sure that it was not at odds with the Christian outlook on wonder, emphasizing that "nothing can be called wonders except divinely wrought miracles."[174] In the eighteenth century wonder had lost much of its status and affiliation with the academic mindset and curiosity had become the prime motivator for the scientific endeavor.[175] In his 1937–1938 lectures at the University of Freiburg, Martin Heidegger addresses this development and argues furthermore that it is a mistake to think that philosophy still begins in wonder, considering that we live in times where wonder is no longer understood in the same sense as in ancient Greece. As he puts it:

> It has long been known that the Greeks recognized [thaumazein] as the "beginning" of philosophy. But it is just as certain that we have taken this [thaumazein] to be obvious and ordinary, something that can be accomplished without difficulty and can even be clarified without further reflection. For most part, the usual presentations of the origin of philosophy out of [thaumazein] result in the opinion that philosophy arises from curiosity. This is a weak and pitiful determination of origin, possibly only where there has never been any reflection on what is supposed to be determined here in its origin. Indeed we consider ourselves relieved of such reflection, precisely because we think that the derivation of philosophy out of curiosity also determines its essence.[176]

Furthermore, Heidegger's analysis of wonder informs us that wonder is quite distinct from amazement, admiration, and astonishment, which he groups under the wondrous and the marvelous, which again is linked to the appreciation of the uncommon.[177] According to Heidegger, to be amazed is to "find oneself in face of the inexplicable,"[178] understood as how when something or someone amazes us we face an inability to explain the object of amazement. However, if we find out what makes the object amazing the amazement disappears. To explain this we might turn to philosopher Brad Elliot Stone, who gives the example of a magic trick. Every magic trick is explainable and with training one can learn to imitate it. However, when the magic trick is explained it is no longer amazing.[179] In addition, Heidegger claims that once we get used to the new and amazing we begin to crave more.[180] Seeing the same magic trick over and over becomes, at length, boring and we begin to seek new vistas in order to feel amazed.

Quinn has pointed out that in the English language the word "admiration" is sometimes used as synonymous with wonder,[181] however, to Heidegger admiration is not the same as wonder. According to Heidegger, anyone who let herself be admired puts herself down or is of a lower rank.[182] We might admire the artistry, grace, athleticism, and technical skill of Cuban ballet dancer Carlos Acosta; however, the use of admiration is, according to Heidegger, not to be mistaken for wonder. Heidegger explains:

> Everyone who allows himself to be admired, and precisely if the admiration is justified, is of a lower rank. For he subordinates himself to the viewpoint and to the norms of his admirer.[183]

If I were to allow myself to be admired by someone I would have to accept this person's idea of what is admirable, but in doing so I become dependent upon her admiration in order to be admirable. Furthermore, this does not make me a wonder or wonderful but merely admirable following the measure of a particular person. In other words, the standard of admiration, which is put to use, is not my own, which means I will be subordinate to the standard of the admirer and in this sense, as Heidegger writes, admiration "embodies a kind of self-affirmation."[184] Furthermore, as Stone points out, if one was to desire a continuation of being admired it would demand hard work because there are many admirable people in history, and so the academic would have to be more prolific, and the runner able to run longer and faster than their predecessors.[185]

To Heidegger, being astonished is the same as "retreating in face of the awesome, up to what is called dumbfoundedness."[186] It is something we cannot understand nor will be able to understand, because when we are astonished we allow the unusual to grow "precisely as what is extraordinary, into what overgrows all usual powers and bears in itself a claim to a rank all its own."[187] This is because in our dull and stupefied state we have lost the ability to take up a position with regards to the thing that causes us to be astonished.[188] Heidegger continues by stating that when we are astonished we are mindful of the fact that we are "excluded from what exists in the awesome."[189] However, because astonishment is in need of the extraordinary, Heidegger categorizes it differently from wonder. Astonishment fades away as repetition sets in and the extraordinary becomes the everyday. Skiing through powdery snow may seem special and extraordinary at first, but if you do it everyday for a whole winter the extraordinary about it diminishes and becomes an everyday thing bereft of excitement.

In Heidegger's view, amazement, admiration, and astonishment are more closely linked to curiosity than wonder. The reason for this is that, like curiosity, they are in league with the extraordinary, the strange, and peculiar. Heideggerian wonder is entirely different because "in wonder what is most usual itself becomes the most unusual."[190] In other words, in wonder we see the extraordinary in the ordinary and this kind of wonderment entails a particular kind of understanding, namely, that in wonder anything whatsoever becomes the most unusual. Heidegger writes that this kind of wonder "no longer encounters anything that could offer it an escape. It no longer knows the way out but knows itself solely as being relegated to the most unusual of the usual in everything and anything: being as beings."[191] Contrary to curiosity, with its focus on the singular extraordinary object, one can in wonderment ask why is there something rather than nothing. Questions like these are questions bound to make us wonder, and uniquely so, because they make us see the extraordinary in the ordinary.

We are now at the end of what can be seen as a preliminary taxonomy of altered states of mind similar to wonder. We started by addressing the experience of awe. Awe differs from wonder in the sense that it is usually accompanied by fear and terror, whereas wonder brings joy and delight. The second altered state we focused on was horror. Both horror and wonder can be a threat to one's universe of meaning but they differ in one particular way. When we feel horror about something we tend to shun that thing because it only promises to destroy. This is in stark contrast to wonder because in wonderment we want to know more about the object that causes it because it promises to expand our understanding of things. The third altered state I addressed was the sublime. The difference between wonder and the sublime resides mainly in the company they keep and in their respective relationship to knowledge and understanding. Like awe the sublime favors the company of fear and terror; however these are seldom found in wonderment, which is mostly accompanied by delight. The sublime also differs from wonder because it is far more dramatic in its effects. Longinus speaks about the sublime as a whirlwind that tears everything up and exhibits the whole power of the orator in a single blow. To Burke the sublime is rooted in terrifying objects and to Kant the sublime can be both fear inducing and at the same time delightful. Furthermore, the Kantian view informs us that the sublime is neither a property of a given object nor a product of our thinking. It is the feeling that is visited upon us when we realize the transcendental dimensions of experience. Moving on to curiosity, Daston and Park reveals that curiosity is different from wonder in the sense that as a motivator for inquiry it is never quenched, and in the Heideggerian sense it is therefore more fitting for modern inquiries than wonder. Amazement differs from wonder in the sense that it relies on the unknown or uncovered properties of the object. Thus amazement is different from wonderment because what we find wonder-filled does not necessarily stop being wonder-filled just because we know how it functions. Admiration is likewise different from wonder because if we admire someone this person has to continuously increase her efforts for our admiration to continue. If we were to find a person full of wonder this demand would not be there. The last altered state I addressed was astonishment. Astonishment differs from wonder in the sense it fades over time and that being astonished equals being stupefied. In astonishment we lose our ability to take up a position with regards to the thing that causes us to be astonished; however, in wonderment this does not happen because, regardless of our wondrous state, we are mindful of being excluded from what the marvelous thing contains. Unlike in astonishment, we find in wonder the most usual and ordinary extraordinary. Bearing the differences between wonder and awe, horror, the sublime, curiosity, amazement, admiration, and astonishment in mind let us now move on to take a closer look at some of the enemies of wonder.

ENEMIES OF WONDER

In his book *In Defence of Wonder and Other Philosophical Reflections*, Raymond Tallis laments that despite the many wonders this world has to offer, we are rarely detained by wonder,[192] and this section aims at providing some clue as to why this is so. The first "enemy of wonder" we shall look at belongs to the category "natural enemies of wonder," which is a category borrowed from Tallis[193] that refers to the fact that we human beings are embodied and vulnerable creatures. By evoking the Shakespearian notion that there was never a philosopher who could endure a toothache patiently,[194] Tallis points out that destitution and need, hunger and thirst, illness and pain, sadness and despair—not forgetting bereavement—sense of rejection and the fear of being the cause of harm to others are all natural enemies of wonder. In addition, what he labels "entire conditions of life," understood as prison camps, war, poverty, including also the human tendency of taking on the responsibility for the welfare of others, are also to be considered natural enemies. Factors such as these simply render it impossible for most people to entertain a sense of wonder because doing otherwise would result in the neglect of an immediate and pressing unforgiving reality.[195]

Tallis also talks about something entirely different from natural enemies of wonder, which he calls "elective enemies of wonder." The elective enemies of wonder are attached to our modern way of life including its habit of rush and busyness. A modern lifestyle includes the idea of free time. I say idea because it is far from certain that the idea of free time finds its practical correspondence. According to Tallis, it is a symptom of modern living that we replicate the business of working life in our free time. In other words, we fill up our free time with demanding projects that not only demand the excellence of particular skills, but also keen attention and time. Tallis's point is that even though we have free time, which in principle could be used to wonder, we often opt for letting our business colonize our free time, leaving no room at all for wonder.[196] Furthermore, the fact that we are social creatures poses a great problem for the occurrences of wonderment. Because wondering is essentially a lonely business, whenever someone is wondering she is viewed as asocial or not committed to corporation and serious engagement with a given project or situation. Imagine sitting in a pub with a friend you have not seen for a while. Imagine further that the person you are meeting with now and then disappears into a state of wonder and that she does not enlighten you as to what makes her wonder. Classifying the meeting as outright successful would probably be an overstatement and most people would be inclined to think of the meeting as irritating and not worth repeating. Wonder signals a momentary departure from the life we share with other people and "is more often part of our solitude."[197]

I am sympathetic to Tallis's account of both natural and elective enemies of wonder; however, with regards to the latter it can be argued that wonderment, to a certain degree, can be a mutual experience, which, to an extent, would both counter the notion that wonderment is a solitary experience and that our urge to socialize makes us less likely to experience wonder. Now Tallis does not deny the existence of shared experiences of wonder and points out that we may want to communicate our wonder for the purpose of validation.[198] In addition, it seems plausible that two people may be inspired by the same source of wonder and experience wonder at the same time. Some years ago my wife and I climbed Mt. Fuji in Japan. As we watched the sunrise together from the summit we both noted that time somehow seemed different. We both became aware of an intense yet calm focus on the rising sun together with openness toward the world and a readiness for change. We both noted in silence the array of colors filling the sky, and with it came a feeling of delight and joy together with certain bafflement about what the world is. Now I am not claiming that our experiences of wonder were identical but during the conversations we had afterwards the above mentioned seemingly shared experiences came up. It can be argued that we are merely constructing them as we engage in conversation and at the bottom line they are nothing but social constructs or products of convention. However, I find it important to mark that before we entered a discussion we sat with an individual experience, which found resonance in the other during our conversation. This perhaps indicates that the sunrise on Mt. Fuji was of a particular kind, and given that our respective experiences seem to overlap with regards to some basic elements of wonder, such as displacement, openness, and joy, I think this sufficiently proves that it is at least not unthinkable that an experience of wonder can be shared. Based on this I claim that wonderment needs not be an exclusively lonely business and that through shared experiences of wonder (which still needs to be experienced individually) one may weaken the impact of elective enemies of wonder.

"Well-tempered curiosity" can also be seen as an enemy of wonder. This is a notion favored indirectly by the scientifically minded Adam Smith, who claims that wonder is merely anxious curiosity from which we seek to rid ourselves by extending our knowledge.[199] In this sense wonder is not an experience to be savored or treasured but an experience we should root out by engaging in scientific inquiry. Once knowledge of the object of wonder is obtained the anxiety of not knowing will disappear and all will be well. However, if we, in all matters, were to be guided by a sense of tempered curiosity, it would demand absolute faith in the scientific method understood as the idea that natural science, given time, would be able to explain every phenomenon that currently might give rise to a sense of wonder. There are, nonetheless, questions about our being and the very existence of the universe that seem to defy such an attitude and Heidegger's notion that it is a wonder that there exists something rather than nothing confers support on this.

Continuing with the thinking of Heidegger "evolutionary social progress" might also be an enemy of wonder. This was Heidegger's point in his 1937–1938 lectures at the University of Freiburg, in which he claims that wonder is no longer a viable starting point for philosophy. Heidegger explains that we have moved on since philosophy was conducted in ancient Greece and we have now committed ourselves to curiosity to the extent of being obsessed.

"The urge for contentment and stability" is also an enemy of wonder. Whenever we encounter something we do not understand or have insufficient information about, we can try to do away with the uncomfortable sensation by obtaining knowledge or understanding about the unknown. This would relabel the unknown to known, or at least frame the unknown in such a way that it no longer interferes in an uncomfortable way. Alternatively, a far more irrational and psychologically loaded reaction may take place where we shun or refuse to have anything to do with what makes us wonder because it makes us uncomfortable. In such circumstances one might seek to deem wonder irrelevant, unimportant, uninteresting, or otherwise downgrade in order to justify the neglect of it. This is a notion explored by philosopher Trevor Norris who is engaged in education. According to Norris, wonder can be a source of transformation and education.[200] However, as a teacher he has experienced what he calls students' "refusal to wonder," and alerts us to a most brilliant example of that very phenomenon. Norris writes:

> In a lesson on consumerism in a Business Ethics course I recently taught, we researched the third world labor practices of the students' favorite shoemaker. At one point many students were fuming and attacked me with "what's wrong with my Nikes?" Others in the class suggested that people like working in sweatshops. This encounter with the new and difficult knowledge did not provoke wonder, but aggressive and often personal attacks, creating a palpable classroom tension. We will do well to remember the fate of Socrates at the hands of the Athenian demos. At times I feel lucky to have escaped the classroom unscratched.[201]

In Plato's *Theaetetus*, the namesake of the dialogue declares himself lost in wonder as Socrates's "torpedo fish" strikes him. Violence and aggression is very much missing from the scene. However, according to Norris, because human beings are political creatures, situations may arise where too much personal investment is at play for a person to become wonderstruck. In such a case a person may display a refusal to wonder and turn aggressive.[202] In the example above we find the students in a defiant and aggressive position submitting Norris to personal attacks. Norris clarifies that the students do not feel the need for change despite their ability to see that their support of Nike is generating sweatshops in third world countries.[203] Furthermore, he claims that what we have here is a perfect case of what is called "Calvin's refusal," which is a term coined by philosopher Megan Boler after Bill Watterson's cartoon character Calvin, who returns a library book loaned by his mother with the comment "It complicates my life. Don't get me any more."[204] In the light of the example, it is safe to say that due to the destabilizing impact of wonder, it is plausible that some politically engaged people of whom it can be said they live to defend particular interests, could display a downright refusal to wonder. Furthermore, we might say that it is important to acknowledge that a sudden expansion of one's perspective, following an experience of wonder, can, as chemist and philosopher Catherine Hurt Middlecamp argues, induce pain,[205] which most people would seek a quick escape from. Middelcamp illustrates her point by referring to an old Sufi tale, which goes like this:

> "Old woman, how much for that rug in the stall?" the man in horseback called. "One hundred rupee, sir" the old woman answered. "It is a fine rug and I will not sell it for a single rupee less." "One hundred rupee, woman?" the man said. "Why on all my travels I have never seen a rug so fine. Why in the name of Allah are you asking only one hundred rupee?" And the old woman paused in wonder and in pain

and said: "because, sir, until now I never knew that there were any numbers above one hundred."[206]

The tale clearly depicts that learning something new can be wonder-filled and exhilarating but also painful, and we can imagine that for some people the painful, part is so overwhelming that they will turn aggressive just like Norris's students to get rid of the pain as quickly as possible. Alternatively, it can also be argued that what we are dealing with here is largely a matter of psychology and, ultimately, it boils down to an urge for contentment and stability that override perfectly logical and empirically sound arguments that otherwise would make a strong case for personal change, transformation, and behavioral modification.

TOWARD A PRELIMINARY UNDERSTANDING OF WONDER

Let us now add to our preliminary understanding of wonder by considering the outlooks on wonder by a selection of contemporary writers on wonderment.

Bringing Raymond Tallis into focus once again, he argues that wonder should be the proper state of humankind.[207] Now the reason for this is that there are a number of things about our existence and the world we live in that are simply wonder-filled. One may start by pointing out that the fact that human beings exist is quite a wonder. That we are fleshly creatures endowed with conscious thought, which can be used to ponder our existence, formulate ideas, and contemplate whether a balanced sense of wonder is a major contributor to our flourishing, is a feature of our existence that speaks toward the idea. However, when it comes to how wonder is to be conceptualized and how and in what situations we should use the word "wonder," there is a fine line to tread. A notion of wonder that encompasses merely childish wonderment easily collapses into sentimentalism and is undesirable in the sense that it will not achieve much support from scientists and other "unweavers of the rainbow." Likewise a notion of wonder synonymous with curiosity would prove unsatisfactory for the artist, poet, and the philosopher. Just because we can explain the appearance of the rainbow scientifically does not take away the impact a rainbow has on the aesthetically, poetically, and philosophically inclined. A rainbow in the sky can render us wonderstruck and indeed make hearts leap up to put it poetically. In this light it would seem that a preliminary understanding of wonder would have to take into account the achievements of both science and the arts. From the literature that has come to my attention, Robert C. Fuller's understanding of wonder might suit these "demands." In Fuller's view, "wonder excites our ontological imaginings in ways that enhance our capacity to seek deeper patterns in the universe."[208] Furthermore, he thinks that experiences of wonder can dramatically change perception and are morally helpful in the sense that they provide us with a second chance to choose what kind of people we want to be, and can inspire us to become true individuals, and true cosmopolitans.[209] In this sense, Fuller's take on wonder is both descriptive and normative, and with regards to the latter, one may say that although Fuller claims that he does not have ethical or theological aspirations concerning his take on wonder,[210] one can venture that his approach is not far removed from the ethical. In fact, it seems quite in tune with the writings of ethicist and philosopher Philo H. Hove, who writes:

> Wonder lies at the heart of what it is to be human: it places us directly and transparently in the face of the world in which we live with others. Wonder reveals things in a new light and tends to promote mindful and gentle regard for their inherent worth [. . .] Wonder is associated with a wide range of experiences and it is possible that it may arise in regard to anything; but a deep level of wonder seems to reveal, or put into question, certain fundamental features of human experiences; among other things, wonder can expose our vulnerability.[211]

That we, through wonderment, may give ourselves a second chance to be who we want to be, to become true individuals, true cosmopolitans, and to face the world in which we live with others, directly and transparently promoting mindful and gentle regard for the inherent worth of others, are statements not far removed from one another and hints to us that wonder may indeed be a source of ethical transformation.

According to Fuller, wonder is an emotion that has the power to transform, and not only makes us sensible to an unseen order of life but also develops in us an enduring reverence for it.[212] Like Tallis, Fuller is for a life in wonderment, although he acknowledges that it is possible to live a life without a sense of wonder. Fuller also points out that "a life shaped by wonder is attuned to the widest possible world of personal fulfillment,"[213] and here he opens up to the notion that wonder may have a significant impact on our lives as flourishing human beings. Hove seems to suggest something along the same lines as he emphasizes the possibility of entertaining a deep sense of wonder that may reveal fundamental features of our human life such as our vulnerability.

As mentioned earlier, Seneca has pointed out that it is by the toils of others that we are being let into the presence of things, and here, at the end of the introduction, we have reached a plateau where we, thanks to those who came before us, have some overview of wonder and may, to a greater extent, appreciate why it is an alluring phenomenon and subject. Iris, the rainbow and daughter of Thaumas (wonder) displays seven colors and because we began by looking at seven colorful examples gathered from real life experiences and fiction, we have honored her by suggesting that the experience of wonder contains seven constituents. The experience of wonder is (1) sudden, extraordinary, and personal. It (2) intensifies the cognitive focus and (3) the use of the imagination. It (4) instigates awareness of ignorance or lack of knowledge and causes (5) temporary displacement or diminishing of self. Additionally, it (6) connects us to a larger world and (7) brings about emotional upheaval which is mostly joyful. A brief survey of the etymological meaning of wonder clarified the root of the word "wonder" and how wonder can be seen as a noun, verb, adjective, and an adverb. Engaging with the history of wonder made it clear that our conception of the subject changes over time. This was followed by a preliminary taxonomy of altered states, similar to wonder, where an attempt was made to distinguish wonder from awe, horror, the sublime, curiosity, astonishment, admiration, and amazement. Furthermore, we considered some possible enemies of wonder in order to find out why we sometimes forget or opt not to wonder. Through these investigations the connection between wonder, emotion, and imagination has again emerged and this connection is reinforced in the philosophy of wonder advocated by contemporary philosophers Robert C. Fuller and Philo Hove. However, their complementary accounts leave certain questions unanswered including whether it is possible to view wonder exclusively as an emotion and what is the exact role of imagination in wonder? Furthermore, what are we to make of the notion of deep wonder that Hove speaks of and in what sense wonder contributes to fulfillment or human flourishing? These questions will be dealt with in what is to come, alongside a continuing exploration of the components and effects of wonder. Likewise, efforts to mount evidence in favor of the idea that cultivating a balanced sense of wonder is a strong contributor to human flourishing will be made.

NOTES

1. Seneca, *On the Shortness of Life*, trans. C. D. N. Costa (New York: Penguin, 1997), p. 34.
2. Samuel Rogers, *Autobiography of Elder Samuel Rogers*, ed. E. J. I. Rogers (Cincinnati: Cincinnati Standard, 1880), 133–134.
3. Juan De Pasquale, "A Wonder Full Life," *Notre Dame Magazine*, 2003, https://magazine.nd.edu/news/a-wonder-full-life/
4. William Shakespeare, "Hamlet," in *Tragedies* Vol. 2, (London: Everyman's Library, 1992), i.i. 40–50.
5. Thomas Mann, *The Magic Mountain*, trans. H. T. Lowe-Porter (New York: Vintage, 1927), 217–218.
6. This is asserted later when Castorp has his own hand X-rayed and describes it as "he looked into his own grave," ibid., 218. Interestingly Mann might have based the skeletal-hand-as-a-reminder-of-death device on a real event. Wilhelm Conrad Röntgen discovered the X-ray in 1895 and shortly after the discovery he subjected his wife, Anna Bertha Ludwig, to the wonders of the ray. Upon seeing her skeletal hand, which bore her wedding ring she exclaimed: "I have seen my death." See Arati S. Panchbhai, "Wilhelm Conrad Röntgen and the Discovery of X-rays: Revisited after Centennial," in *Journal of Indian Academy of Oral Medicine & Radiology*, Vol. 27, Issue 1, 2015, 92.

7. Robert Boyle, "Some Observations about Shining Flesh, Both of Veal and Pullet, and That without Any Sensible Putrefaction in Those Bodies" [1672], in *The Works of the Honourable Robert Boyle*, 6 vols., ed. Thomas Birch, vol. 3 (Hildesheim: Georg Olms, 1772), 651.

8. Lorraine Daston and Katharine Park, *Wonders and the Order of Nature* (New York: Zone Books, 1998), 13.

9. Sam Keen, *Apology for Wonder* (New York: Harper & Row, 1969), 211.

10. See Ludwig Wittgenstein, *Philosophical Investigations*, trans. G. E. M. Anscombe, in *Philosophical Investigations*, ed. G. E. M. Anscombe and G. H. von Wright (Oxford: Blackwell, 1983), 194.

11. French painter and art theorist Charles le Brun (1619–1690) depicts astonishment in combination with admiration as the widening of the eyes and gaping of the mouth. See John Onians, "'I Wonder . . .': A Short History of Amazement," in *Sight & Insight: Essays on Art and Culture in Honour of E. H. Gombrich at 85*, ed. J. Onians (London: Phaidon Press Limited, 1994), 17; Ann Sutherland Harris, *Seventeenth-Century Art and Architecture* (London: Laurence King Publishing, 2004), 307. In Lorraine Daston and Katharine Park's work, le Brun's depiction of astonishment combined with admiration is labelled "wonder." See Daston and Park, *Wonders and the Order of Nature*, 319. In *The Expression of Emotions in Man and Animals*, Charles Darwin points to the idea that surprise and astonishment are expressed in human beings by the elevation of the eyebrows, the opening of the mouth, and the protrusion of the lips. See Charles Darwin, *The Expressions of Emotions in Man and Animals* (New York: HarperCollins, 1999), XII. Of course one might say that astonishment or admiration does not correspond with wonder, but since these different states of mind are hard to separate with certainty one might agree with the idea that the depictions by le Brun and Darwin do hold some value and at least give us an idea of the face of wonder.

12. Plato, *Cratylus*, vol. 6, trans. H. N. Fowler, ed. E. Capps, LCL (Cambridge: Harvard University Press, 1926).

13. See Howard L. Parsons, "A Philosophy of Wonder," in *Philosophy and Phenomenological Research*, 30(1), 1969, 85; Mary-Jane Rubenstein, *Strange Wonder, The Closure of Metaphysics and the Opening of Awe* (New York: Columbia University Press, 2008), 9.

14. See Eric Partridge, *Origins: A Short Etymological Dictionary of Modern English*, 4 ed. (New York: Macmillan, 1966).

15. See Philip Fisher, *Wonder, the Rainbow and the Aesthetics of Rare Experiences*, (Cambridge and London: Harvard University Press, 2003), 11.

16. See Daston and Park, *Wonders and the Order of Nature*, 16.

17. See Dennis Quinn, *Iris Exiled—A Synoptic History of Wonder* (Lanham, MD: University Press of America, 2002), 4; Robert M. Theobald, *Shakespeare Studies in Baconian Light* (Whitefish, MT: Gay and Bird / Kessinger Legacy Reprints, 1901), 83.

18. Quinn, *Iris Exiled*, 6.

19. Ibid., 6.

20. Daston and Park, *Wonders and the Order of Nature,*, 16.

21. Fisher, *Wonder, the Rainbow*, 121.

22. See Sylvana Chrysakopoulou, "Wonder and the Beginning of Philosophy in Plato" in *Practices of Wonder, Cross-Disciplinary Perspectives*, ed. S. Vasalou (Eugene, OR: Pickwick Publications, 2012).

23. Onians, *I Wonder*.

24. Daston and Park, *Wonders and the Order of Nature,*.

25. Frank Nadis, *Wonder Shows, Performing Science, Magic and Religion in America* (New Brunswick, NJ: Rutgers University Press, 2005), 263.

26. Theogony translates into "birth of the gods" and is a poem written in Homeric Greek, addressing the origin and genealogy of the Greek gods.

27. Hesiod, *Theogony. Works and Days. Testimonia*, ed. and trans. Glenn W. Most, LCL (Cambridge: Harvard University Press, 2007), 266.

28. Ibid., 780, 784.

29. Onians, *I Wonder*, 32.

30. Anders Bæksted, *Nordiske Guder og Helte* (Copenhagen: Politikkens Forlag, 1990), 40. In Norse mythology the rainbow Bifrost is the bridge guarded by Heimdal connecting the divine realm of Asgard with Midgard, the world of humans.

31. British Romantic poet William Wordsworth wrote on the night of the 26th of March 1802 the poem "My Heart Leaps Up" also known as "The Rainbow." The poem contains the famous lines: "My heart leaps up when I behold a rainbow in the sky." See William Wordsworth, *Poems in Two Volumes*, vol. 2, 1850, 33. Retrieved from https://itun.es/gb/wDVkE.l.

32. Plato, *Theaetetus*, trans. H. N. Fowler, LCL (Cambridge: Harvard University Press, 1989), 155d.

33. Ibid.

34. Aristotle echoes parts of the *Theaetetus* passage in book alpha in the *Metaphysics*. See Aristotle, *Metaphysics*, trans. Hugh Tredennick (Cambridge: Harvard University Press, 1933), I. II. 6–11.

35. The example from Plato's *Theaetetus* exposes the idea of wonder as destabilizing and causing one's head to swim and in this respect it ties very well into the idea of wonder as a wound. Sylvana Chrysakopoulou is supportive of this notion as she suggests that the Greek word "thauma" (wonder) is connected with the Greek word "trauma" (wound or injury), Chrysakopoulou, "Wonder and the Beginning of Philosophy," 88.

36. Quinn, *Iris Exiled*, 87.

37. Epicureanism is based on the thinking of Epicurus (341–270 BC) who founded "the Garden" in Athens functioning both school and circle of friends. Important to the Epicurean was materialism and a rational hedonistic ethics urging one to strive toward pleasure in order to gain a state of well-being. This is an entirely individual enterprise and should be cultivated preferably in a garden remote from the noisy world of humans and political intrigues.

38. Stoicism refers to a Greek and Roman philosophical school of thought emphasizing on personal transformation and fortification of the mind. The idea is that an upcoming sage must transcend emotions and reach for moral and intellectual perfection. In Stoic thought the virtuous sage is thought to be totally immune to misfortune and would in effect be happy, which has given rise to the idea of "Stoic calm," which may translate into having the ability not to give in to irrational behavior even in the most dire or epic situations.

39. Seneca, "Epistle VIII: On the Philosopher's Seclusion" in *Epistles 1–65*, trans. Richard M. Gummere (Cambridge: Harvard University Press, 1917), 5.

40. Quinn, *Iris Exiled*, 105.

41. Ibid., 137.

42. In Book XXI of *The City of God* Augustine informs us that the bodies of the damned would be tormented in the eternal fire.

43. Augustin, *Om Guds stad* (Aarhus, Denmark: Århus Universitetsforlag, 2002) 14.

44. The original Latin title is: *De Civitate Dei contra Paganos*, meaning The City of God contra the Pagans.

45. Augustin, *Om Guds stad*, 15.

46. Augustine, *Confessions*, trans. William Watts (Cambridge: Harvard University Press, 2006), Book X, VIII.

47. "Mekhanemata" is a Greek word in which the English word "mechanics" originates and it refers to artificially made inventions, constructions, and machines. See Augustin, *Om Guds stad*, Book XXI, VI.

48. In the time of Augustine the fire salamander was thought to live in fire. It has been speculated that because fire salamanders have a habit of residing in wooden logs and that the burning of such was common in ancient and medieval times this has contributed to the rise of the myth of the fire salamander. One can imagine that some would marvel at the sudden appearance of a salamander in their fireplace but not all would realize that the poor creature was merely trying to escape its burning refuge. See Yechiel Szeintuch, Daniella Tourgeman and Maayan Zigdon, "The Myth of the

Salamander in the Work of Ka-Tzetnik" in *Partial Answers: Journal of Literature and the History of Ideas*, 3(1), 2005, 102.

49. Mt. Etna is a volcano in Italy that was highly active during ancient and medieval times. It is plausible that its activity during these times contributed to the notion that not everything is destroyed by fire because despite its subjection to fire, i.e., frequent eruptions, Mt. Etna remained largely unchanged. See Augustin, *Om Guds stad,* op. cit., XXI, IV.

50. Ibid.

51. Ibid., Book XXI, II.

52. Ibid., Book XXI, VI.

53. Ibid., Book XXI, VII.

54. Daston and Park, *Wonders and the Order of Nature*, 40.

55. Aristotle offers his thoughts on the soul or psyche in *De Anima* and largely it reads as an alternative to Plato's ideas on the eternal soul. However, the case may not be as clear cut, for in the third chapter of *De Anima*, Aristotle puts forth the distinction between "active intellect" and "active mind" of which the latter can be taken as eternal. See Aristotle, *On the Soul, Parva Naturalia, On Breath,* trans. Walter Stanley Hett (Cambridge: Harvard University Press, 1957), III, V.

56. Quinn, *Iris Exiled*, 167.

57. Thomas Aquinas, *Summa Contra Gentiles,* trans. Anton C. Pegis, (Evanston, IL: University of Notre Dame Press, 1976), Book III, XXV.

58. See Aristotle, *Metaphysics,* I.

59. Ibid., I. II. 6–11.

60. By "scientia" is meant that one come to know some truth P, where P is logically deduced from premises, which are universal and therefore necessary. Another way of explaining this is by putting forth the following syllogism: If premise 1 reads—all men are mortal; and premise 2 reads—Socrates is a man, the conclusion has to be Socrates is mortal. The conclusion is scientific knowledge as the conclusion is logically demonstrative.

61. Thomas Aquinas, *Summa Theologica,* trans. Fathers of the English Dominican Province (New York: Benziger Brothers, 2006), Part I, p. 10.

62. J. N. Hays, *Epidemics and Pandemics: Their Impacts on Human History* (Santa Barbara, CA: ABC-CLIO, 2005), 43.

63. Neo-Platonism refers to the thoughts of Plato seen through the eye of his disciples. One such disciple is Plotinus (ca. 204/5–270 AD).

64. Nicolas of Cusa, *Complete Philosophical and Theological Treaties of Nicolas of Cusa,* vol. 1, trans. J. Hopkins (Minneapolis, Minnesota: The Arthur Banning, 2001), 46.

65. Quinn, *Iris Exiled*, 168.

66. Ibid.

67. Giovanni Pico della Mirandola, *Oration on the Dignity of Man,* trans. A. R. Caponigri (Chicago: Henry Regnery Company, 1956), 3.

68. Quinn, *Iris Exiled*, 170.

69. Elisabeth Blum and Paul Richard Blum, "Wonder and Wondering in the Renaissance" in *Philosophy Begins in Wonder: An Introduction to Early Modern Philosophy, Theology and Science,* ed. Michael Funk Deckard and Peter Losonczi (Cambridge, UK: James Clarke & Co., 2011), 6.

70. Quinn, *Iris Exiled*, 171.

71. Ibid. Aristotle points out that human beings harbor a rational component. See Aristotle, *Nicomachean Ethics,* trans. H. Rackham (Cambridge: Harvard University Press, 2003), I, xiii, 15.

72. Francis Bacon, *The Advancement of Learning* (Project Gutenberg, 1971), I.

73. Ibid.

74. Ibid., 17.

75. Quinn, *Iris Exiled*, 197.

76. See Aristotle, *Meteorologica,* trans. H. D. P. Lee (Cambridge: Harvard University Press, 1951), III, 4–5.

77. Fisher, *Wonder, the Rainbow*, 42.
78. Rene Descartes, "The Passions of the Soul," trans. John Cottingham, in *The Philosophical Works of Descartes*, vol. 1. (Cambridge, UK: Cambridge University Press, 1985), LIII.
79. According to Descartes there are a total of six primitive passions and they are wonder, love, hatred, desire, joy, and sadness. However, this does not mean that these are the only passions and in *The Passions of the Soul* Descartes mentions a multitude of other passions such as hope, fear, jealousy, remorse, gratitude, anger, and disgust to name a few. These other passions are all composed of some of the six primitive passions. Ibid., LXIX.
80. Descartes uses the French word *l'étonnement* which has connotations to being thunderstruck.
81. Fisher, *Wonder, the Rainbow*, 48.
82. Descartes, "The Passion of the Soul," LXXVIII.
83. Adam Smith, *Essays on Philosophical Subjects*, ed. W. B. Wightman, J. C. Bryce and L. S. Ross (Oxford: Oxford University Press, 1980), 33.
84. Quinn, *Iris Exiled*, 240.
85. Immanuel Kant, *The Critique of Judgement*, trans. Werner. S. Pluhar,(Indianapolis/Cambridge: Hackett Publishing Company, 1987), 133.
86. Quinn, *Iris Exiled*, 243.
87. Alexander Pope, *The Poetic Works of Alexander Pope*, ed. A. W. Ward (London: Macmillan and Co., 1885), 59.
88. Ibid., 300.
89. Horace, *Satires, Epistles, Ars Poetica*, trans. H. R. Fairclough (Cambridge: Harvard University Press, 1955), Epistle VI.
90. Cicero, *Tusculan Disputations*, trans. J. E. King (Cambridge: Harvard University Press, 2001), III, 30.
91. This particular attitude has survived to this day and is depicted in the 2008 HBO TV series *Generation* which focuses on a *Rolling Stone* reporter, who, together with the US 1st Recon Marines, experience the American-led assault on Baghdad in 2003. In episode 4, entitled "Combat Jack" Lt. Fick utters: "Observe everything, admire nothing." The phrase is used to keep the marines alert and resistant to wonderment. The idea is that wonderment makes you less alert to potential hostiles. I am grateful to my brother Kim B. Pedersen for pointing this out.
92. V. G. Kiernan, *Horace: Poetics and Politics* (New York: St. Martins's Press, 1999), 25.
93. Cicero, *Tusculan Disputations*, III, 30.
94. Daston and Park, *Wonders and the Order of Nature*, 343.
95. Christopher John Murray, *Encyclopedia of the Romantic Era: 1760–1850*, Vol. 1 (Cambridge, UK: Polity Press, 2004), ix.
96. Isaiah Berlin, *The Roots of Romanticism*, ed. Henry Hardy (Princeton, NJ: Princeton University Press, 2001), 21–22.
97. Ibid., 22.
98. John Keats, "Lamia" in *The Complete Poems of John Keats*, 3rd edition, ed. J. Bernard (New York: Penguin Books, 1988), II, 229–238.
99. Quinn, *Iris Exiled*, 270. Richard Dawkins's book *Unweaving the Rainbow* borrowed the title from Keats and is a book that aims to show that scientists can retain a sense of wonder despite their methods and discoveries.
100. Onians, "I Wonder," 32.
101. Lord Byron, "Don Juan" in *The Works of Lord Byron* (London: John Murray, 1833), Canto V, C.
102. Ibid., Canto V, CI.
103. Mary Shelley was the wife of Percy Shelley and her attitude to science was very different from her husband's. In her famous novel *Frankenstein* she expresses her aversion to the arrogance of science and points out possible dangers with the enterprise by

creating Frankenstein's monster—a man-made creature bereft of bodily beauty and destined to become one of the loneliest creatures ever imagined in English literature.

104. Quinn, *Iris Exiled*, 269.

105. William Wordsworth, *Wordsworth's Poetical Works*, Vol. 2., Ed. W. Knight, (Project Gutenberg, 1896), 20.

106. Quinn, *Iris Exiled*, 272.

107. Jeremy Bentham, *A Fragment on Government* (Cambridge: Cambridge University Press, 1988), vii.

108. Charles Darwin, *The Expression of Emotions in Man and Animals* (New York: HarperCollins, 1999).

109. William Hamilton, *Lectures on Metaphysics and Logic*, Vol. 1, *Metaphysics*, ed. H. L. Mansel and John Veitch, (Boston: Could & Lincoln, 1860), 26–27.

110. Ibid.

111. John Stuart Mill, *An Examination of William Hamilton's Philosophy and of the Principal Philosophical Questions Discussed in his Writings* (London: Longmans, Green, Longman, Roberts & Green, 1865), 544–45.

112. Tony Tanner, *The Reign of Wonder: Naivety and Reality in the American Literature* (Cambridge: Cambridge University Press, 1965), 22.

113. Ibid., 10.

114. Fred Nadis, *Wonder Shows: Performing Science, Magic and Religion in America* (New Brunswick, NJ: Rutgers University Press, 2005), 10.

115. Ibid., 14.

116. Ibid.

117. Ibid., 29.

118. Ibid., 122.

119. Ibid., 14.

120. Quinn, *Iris Exiled*, 275. The encyclopedia inspired the publishing company Ward Lock & Co in 1911 to start publishing the Wonder Book series. The target group were children, and filled with quality photographs, the books depicted a sense of wonder that was entirely orientated toward science and technology.

121. Nadis, op. cit.,*Wonder Shows*, 135–36.

122. Ibid., 137.

123. Quinn, *Iris Exiled*, 293. Fantasy refers to art set in imaginary worlds. In the beginning of the twentieth-century fantasy was mostly communicated in books and magazines such as *Weird Tales* created in 1923. Today the vehicles for fantasy are many and can include everything from films to graphic novels, TV series, table-top and video games.

124. Ibid., 294. American weird fiction writer Howard Phillips Lovecraft is important in this matter and especially his poetry and works involving the dreamlands. See Jan B. W. Pedersen, "Lovecraft's Lifelong Relationship with Wonder" in *Lovecraft Annual* No. 11., ed. S. T. Joshi (New York: Hippocampus Press, 2017) and Jan B. W. Pedersen, "Howard Phillips Lovecraft: Romantic on the Nightside" in *Lovecraft Annual* No. 18, ed. S. T. Joshi (New York: Hippocampus Press, 2018).

125. Quinn, *Iris Exiled*, 293.

126. Rudolf Otto, *The Idea of the Holy*, trans. J. W. Harvey (Eastford, CT: Mertino Publishing, 2010), 26

127. Ibid., 14.

128. Ronald W. Hepburn, "Landscape and the Metaphysical Imagination" in *Environmental Values*, 5 (3), 1996, 201.

129. Robert A. Emmons and Charles M. Shelton, "Gratitude and the Science of Positive Psychology" in *Handbook of Positive Psychology*, ed. C. R. Snyder and S. J. Lopez (Oxford: Oxford University Press, 2002), 240.

130. The 2003 invasion of Iraq seemed executed on the basis of a "shock and awe strategy" designed not to facilitate extermination but crush all hope of resistance. See the introduction of Harlan K. Ullman and James P. Wade, Jr., "Shock and Awe:

Achieving Rapid Dominance" (Vienna, VA: Defense Group Inc. for The National Defense University, 1996).

131. Dasher Keltner and Jonathan Haidt, "Approaching Awe, a Moral, Spiritual, and Aesthetic Emotion" in *Cognition and Emotion*, 17 (2), 2003, 297.

132. Ibid., 298.

133. *The Holy Bible* (London: Tophi Books, 1994), Acts 9, 3–8.

134. Philosopher Jerome Miller points out that "wonder includes awe within it, and can even be indistinguishable from it" See Jerome Miller, *In the Throe of Wonder: Intimations of the Sacred in a Post-modern World* (State University of New York Press, 1992), 189. He furthermore states that what may prevent a distinction is if "the beings which awaken wonder are experienced as, and identified with, being itself. For if we make that identification, we will worship what we love as ultimately sacred—until we begin to realize that it is liable to nothingness" Ibid., 189. In his later work philosopher Sam Keen also emphasizes on the close connection between wonder and awe. In his understanding we perceive the mystery of existence as "at once awesome-terrifying-majestic-overpowering and fascinating-wonderful-promising-desirable." See Sam Keen, *In the Absence of God: Dwelling in the Presence of the Sacred* (New York: Harmony Books, 2010), 87.

135. Martha Nussbaum, *Upheavals of Thought*, 8th ed. (Cambridge: Cambridge University Press, 2008), 54.

136. Conelis Verhoeven, *The Philosophy of Wonder* (The Macmillan Company, 1972), 27.

137. Katharine Park and Lorraine Daston, "Unnatural Conceptions: The Study of Monsters in the Sixteenth and Seventeenth-Century France and England" in *Past & Present*, No. 92 (Oxford University Press, 1981), 35.

138. Miller, *In the Throe of Wonder*, 130.

139. Ibid., 126.

140. Ibid., 125.

141. Ibid.

142. Ibid., 130.

143. For more information on H. P. Lovecraft and his works involving wonder see Jan B. W. Pedersen "On Lovecraft's Lifelong Relationship with Wonder in *Lovecraft Annual* no. 11, ed. S. T. Joshi (New York: Hippocampus Press, 2017).

144. Lord Dunsany, also known as Edward Moreton Drax Plunkett, was the 18th Baron of Dunsany in Ireland and a fantasy writer. Among his many publications *The Book of Wonder* and *Tales of Wonder* are most relevant to the student of wonder.

145. Howard Phillips Lovecraft, "Celephais" in *Eldritch Tales*, ed. Stephen Jones (London: Gollancz, 2011), 149.

146. For more information on Howard Phillips Lovecraft's writings on wonder see Jan B. W. Pedersen, "On Lovecraft's Lifelong Relationship with Wonder" in *Lovecraft Annual* No. 11, ed. S. T. Joshi (New York: Hippocampus Press, 2017).

147. It derives from the Latin sublimis, which is a complex word combining sub meaning "up to" and limen, which refers to the top piece of a door. See Philip Shaw *The Sublime* London: Routledge, 2006), 1.

148. Kenneth Holmqvist and Joroslaw Pluciennik, "A Short Guide to the Theory of the Sublime" in *Style, Resources in Stylistics and Literary Analysis*, 36(4), 2002, 718.

149. Angela Woods, *The Sublime Object of Psychiatry: Schizophrenia in Clinical and Cultural Theory* (Oxford: Oxford University Press, 2011), 25.

150. Shaw, *The Sublimes*, 2.

151. Longinus quoted in Shaw, *The Sublime*, 18–19.

152. Edmund A. Burke, *A Philosophical Enquiry into the Origin of Our Ideas of the Sublime and Beautiful*, ed. A. Philips (Oxford: Oxford University Press, 1990), 36.

153. Shaw, op. cit., 49.

154. Immanuel Kant *The Critique of Judgment*, trans. W. S. Pluhar (Indianapolis, IN: Hackett Publishing Company, Inc., 1987), §25.

155. Ibid., §23.

156. Ibid., §24.
157. Ibid., §23.
158. Ibid., §28.
159. Ibid.
160. Shaw, *The Sublime*, 88.
161. Ibid.
162. Fisher, *Wonder, the Rainbow*, 2.
163. See Aristotle, *Poetics*, trans. S. Halliwell (Cambridge: Harvard University Press, 1955), XXIV, 17–18; Martyn Evans "Wonder and the Clinical Encounter" in *Theoretical Medicine and Bioethics*, 33(2), 2012, 6; Robert Fuller, "From Biology to Spirituality", 380; Sam Keen, *Apology for Wonder* (New York: Harper & Row, 1969), 29; and Derek Matarvers, "Wonder and Cognition" in ed. S. Vasalou, *Practices of Wonder Cross-Disciplinary Perspectives* (Eugene, OR: Pickwick Publications, 2012), 166.
164. See Sylvana Chrysakopoulou, "Wonder and the Beginning of Philosophy in Plato" in *Practices of Wonder, Cross-Disciplinary Perspectives*, ed. S. Vasalou (Eugene, OR: Pickwick Publications, 2012), 88; Howard L. Parsons, "A Philosophy of Wonder" in *Philosophy and Phenomenological Research*, 30(1), 1969, 85; Mary-Jane Rubenstein, *Strange Wonder, The Closure of Metaphysics and the Opening of Awe* (New York: Columbia University Press, 2008), 9; Paul R. Fleischman, *Wonder* (Amherst, MA: Small Batch Books, 2013), 368.
165. Daniel Speak, *The Problem of Evil* (Hoboken, NJ: John Wiley & Sons, 2014), 94.
166. Kant, *Critique of Judgment*, §28.
167. Cabinets of wonder, cabinets of curiosity also known as "Wunderkammern" contained according to sixteenth-century scholar, physician, and pioneering connoisseur Samuel Quicchelberg, both man-made works of art (artificialia) and objects from nature (naturalia). See Adriana Turpin "The New World Collections of Duke Coismo I de'Medici and Their Role in the Creation of a Kunst- and Wunderkammer in the Palazzo Vecchio" in *Curiosity and Wonder from the Renaissance to the Enlightenment*, ed. R. J. W. Evans and A. Marr (Farnham, UK: Ashgate, 2006), 63 and Elizabeth M. Hajos, "The Concept of an Engravings Collection in the year 1565: Quicchelberg, Inscriptions vel Tituli Theatri Amplissimi" in *The Art Bulletin*, 40(2), 1958, 156. Common to these objects were their "wondrous nature" and cabinets of wonder could include everything from the horns of supposed unicorns, stuffed crocodiles, ostrich eggs, rare plants, miniatures, bones, feathers, fossils, anatomical deformities in preserving jars, phosphorescent minerals, and ethnographic objects. See Jeronimo Arellano, Jeronimo. "From the Space of the Wunderkammer to Macondo's Wonder Rooms: The Collection of Marvels in Cien anos de solodad" in *Hispanic Review*, 78(3), 2010, 271–72 and Stephen Greenblatt, "Resonance and Wonder" in *Bulletin of the American Academy of Arts and Sciences*, 43(4), 1990, 29. A famous Wunderkammer is Museum Worminanum, belonging to the sixteenth/seventeenth-century Danish physician and antiquary Olaus Wormius or in plain Danish, Ole Worm. For a depiction of Museum Wormianum see Jan B. W. Pedersen "On Lovecraft's Lifelong Relationship with Wonder" in *Lovecraft Annual* No. 12, ed. S. T. Joshi (New York: Hippocampus Press, 2017), 31.
168. Lorraine Daston and Katharine Park, *Wonders and the Order of Nature*, 15.
169. Ibid., 305.
170. Ibid.
171. Thomas Hobbes, *Leviathan*, ed. R. Tuck (Cambridge: Cambridge University Press, 1992), I, 6.
172. Aristotle, *The Metaphysics*, Book I.
173. Daston and Park, *Wonders and the Order of Nature*, 307.
174. Chen, Jianhong. "On Thomas Hobbes's Concept of Wonder" in *Philosophy begins in Wonder: An Introduction to Early Modern Philosophy, Theology, and Science*, ed. M. F. Deckard and P. Losonczi (Cambridge, UK: James Clarke & Co, 2011), 130–32.
175. Daston and Park, *Wonders and the Order of Nature*, 305.
176. Martin Heidegger, *Basic Questions of Philosophy*, trans. R. Rojcewicz and A. Schuwer (Bloomington, IN: Indiana University Press, 1994), §36 [155–56].

177. Heidegger, *Basic Questions of Philosophy*, §37 [156–57].
178. Ibid., §37 [162–63].
179. Brad Elliot Stone, "Curiosity as the Thief of Wonder, An Essay on Heidegger's Critique of the Ordinary Conception of Time" in *Kronoscope*, 6(2), 2006, 209–10.
180. Heidegger, *Basic Questions of Philosophy*, §37 [157–58].
181. Quinn, *Iris Exiled*, 4.
182. Heidegger, *Basic Questions of Philosophy*, §37.
183. Ibid., §37 [163–64].
184. Ibid., §38 [163–64].
185. Stone, "Curiosity as the Thief," 210–11.
186. Heidegger, *Basic Questions of Philosophy*, §38 [165–66].
187. Ibid.
188. In *The Passions of the Soul* Descartes formulates a similar idea about astonishment. To Descartes astonishment is wonder in excess and in his view astonishment is always bad because it leaves us immobile and prevents us from "perceiving more of the object than the first face which is presented" Descartes, *Passions of the Soul*, LXXIII. In other words, because of our astonished state we are unable to learn more about the source of our astonishment.
189. Heidegger, *Basic Questions of Philosophy*, §38 [163–64].
190. Ibid., §38 [165–66].
191. Ibid., §38 [167–68].
192. Raymond Tallis, *In Defence of Wonder and Other Philosophical Reflections* (Durham, UK: Acumen, 2012), 6.
193. Ibid.
194. The line "For there was never yet philosopher that could endure the toothache patiently" can be found in Shakespeare's play *Much Ado about Nothing*. See William Shakespeare, "Much Ado About Nothing" in *Comedies*, Vol. 2 (London: Everyman's Library, 1996), V. i. 35.
195. Tallis, *In Defense of Wonder*, 6–7.
196. Ibid., 8.
197. Ibid., 9.
198. Ibid.
199. Adam Smith, "The History of Astronomy," in *Essays on Philosophical Subjects*, ed. W. P. D. Wightman and J. C. Bryce (Oxford: Oxford University Press, 1980), II, 5.
200. Trevor Norris, "The Refusal of Wonder" in *Philosophy of Education Yearbook*, 2001, 223.
201. Ibid., 222–23.
202. Ibid.
203. Ibid., 223.
204. Megan Boler, "Taming the Labile Other" in *Philosophical of Education Yearbook*, ed. S. Laird (Philosophy of Education Society, 1997).
205. Catherine Hurt Middlecamp (2009). "The Old Woman and the Rug: The Wonder and Pain of Teaching (and Learning) Chemistry" in *Feminist Teacher*, 19(2), 134.
206. Ibid.
207. Tallis, *In Defense of Wonder*.
208. Fuller, *Wonder*, 2
209. Ibid., 158.
210. Ibid. 2.
211. Philo H. Hove, "The Face of Wonder" in *Journal of Curriculum Studies*, 28(4), 1996, 437.
212. Fuller, *Wonder*, 158.
213. Ibid.

TWO

Wonder and Emotion

The possibility that wonder is related to the realm of emotions and feelings has been known since the time of the ancient philosophers.[1] However, even though it is reasonable to think of wonder as an emotion or feeling, it is not possible to label it exclusively so.

The idea that wonder is an emotion seems evident when we look to the examples of wonder mentioned in the opening section of chapter 1. Recall from Shakespeare's *Hamlet* that Horatio, upon seeing the ghost for the first time, remarks, "it harrows him with fear and wonder."[2] This particular utterance can be seen as a report on Horatio's emotional life, indicating that he is experiencing two, or a mixture of two, different emotions, namely, fear and wonder.

Likewise, Keen's recollection of being given a knife by a mysterious stranger in Maryville, Tennessee, evokes the idea of wonder being an emotion. It is entirely reasonable to think that the pervasive sense of gratitude and wondering expectancy he experienced in the weeks following the event was prompted by an initial emotion of wonder produced by the extraordinary handover of the knife. When we read his description one certainly gets the sense that there is a particular emotional quality to his experience, which should not be underestimated.

The wonder Boyle experienced upon witnessing the luminous meat brought to him from the larder by his servant again qualifies as an emotion. What points to this notion is that as we may recall from the introduction that wonder in general is joyful, and to think of joy as an emotion seems reasonable. In further support of Boyle's wonder being an emotional response stands the fact that he finds within him an urge to share his experience, which leaves one with the impression that he is being moved by something from within. One might, of course, object to this notion and argue that what Boyle is doing is merely seeking to validate his experience of wonder, and thus what is at play is perhaps not so much an emotional response but in fact Boyle's rationality. Given Boyle's scientific profile this counts as highly probable, but to push back one could say that the argument is weakened by the fact that at least one of his servants had already experienced the same luminous quality of the meat, and that should provide all the validation Boyle requires. In this light it seems odd to suggest that Boyle's urge to share his experience rests merely on a wish to validate his experience. One could argue that Boyle might not have thought very highly of his servants and therefore it did not cross his mind to ask any of them to validate what he saw, which is why he penned his urge to share his experience with someone he deemed worthy. This is indeed a possibility but also difficult to verify, and thus it is far more plausible to say that the joyful wonder Boyle experienced in connection with his discovery was what made him want to share it. We are attracted to wonder because it brings joy. It makes our hearts leap up, as Wordsworth would say, and because of this feature, displays of wonder, such as eighteenth-century Prussian showman Gustave Katterfelto's[3] Wonder of Wonders Show,[4] which took place at Spring Gardens in London in 1780, were popular. The same feature is behind the popularity of modern IMAX films in the beginning of the new millennium, depicting, for example, the wonders of climbing Mount Everest or what it is like to live on the International Space Station.[5] The popularity of such attractions is correlated with our attraction to wonder, which, besides being enjoyable in some cases, also compels us to share the wonder we are experiencing.

To add to our collection of examples depicting wonder as an emotion, let us turn to the wonder-provoking activity of stargazing, or to be precise, meteor spotting, which we have touched on earlier in connection with Rogers's experience of wonder brought forth by the 1833 Leonid meteor shower. The following three reports sparked by the Leonid meteor shower, visible in certain parts of America in 1966, will help mount further support in favor of the idea that wonder is an emotion.

The first report comes from Dr. Gerald Kuiper, who observed the meteor shower together with a number of his students on November 17, 1966. The next day Dr. Kuiper put the following entry in the *New York Times*:

> The students . . . noted the time, brightness and trajectory of each meteor. As hours passed it was dull work. At most only about two a minute were seen. Then about 5 A.M . . . , the rate suddenly began to increase. Within a few minutes the meteors were raining down so fast that further recording was hopeless. The students simply stood and gazed in wonder. They estimated that, during the 15-minute peak of the shower, the "stars" were falling at the rate of 40 a second.[6]

In his report to Leonid MAC[7] on November 19, 2002, Robert Gleaves recalls his experience of the 1966 meteor shower and gives this description:

> I was sound asleep when I was awakened by someone shaking me and telling me to get up quick. It was my mother and she seemed to be very excited about something, not telling me at that moment what it was, only asking me to hurry up and come outside with her. I had no idea that what I was about to see would burn a picture in my mind that would be with me to this day. There in the sky was the most incredible vision I have ever witnessed. It was if every star was falling from this north Texas sky, arcing the earth's dome of atmosphere in every direction. I watched with my mouth wide open for 30 to 45 minutes and the show never seemed to slow up! It almost brings tears to my eyes when I stop and really think of how incredible that morning really was, but the thing that really made it special for me was the date—Nov. 17th, 1966 . . . my 17th birthday. What a wonderful gift.[8]

Pam Clemmer also witnessed the event in 1966 and her Leonid MAC report filed on November 18, 1998, reads:

> It wasn't a dark and stormy night. I was 14, and living in a small house in Shawnee Mission, Kansas. That's eastern Kansas. I got up in the middle of the night to make my scheduled trip to the bathroom and as I glanced out the bathroom window, streaks of light from the moonless dark sky caught my eye. I moved to the south facing bathroom window, and what I saw as I approached that window is indelibly etched in my memory, even though it has been some 30 odd years. Odd indeed. I'm sure my mouth gaped open in wonder as I watched the navy sky rain stars. It truly was a constant shower of stars. At first, I was frightened. I didn't understand what was happening. Then, the beauty of it took over. I must have stood there 30 minutes or more waiting for the rain to stop. It never did. I finally went back to bed feeling as if I had witnessed something that no other person on the planet had seen . . . or would ever see again. I live in Colorado now . . . and won't be able to see the shower this time. I saw it once though a long time ago . . . and I won't ever forget. It was SPECTACULAR![9]

All of the above descriptions seem to suggest that the implicated "stargazers" experienced a peculiar arresting emotion during the meteor shower. Furthermore all three descriptions connect the experience to wonder. Kuiper observes that his students simply stood and gazed in wonder. Gleaves calls the meteor shower a wonderful birthday gift and Clemmer is sure that her mouth "gaped open"[10] in wonder when she watched the sky rain stars.

Further support for depicting wonder as an emotion can be found in the literature on wonder. Toward the end of the introductory chapter it was pointed out that contemporary wonder-theorist Robert C. Fuller thinks of wonder as an emotion that may give rise to personal transformation and makes us sensible to what he refers to as an unseen order of life and facilitate in us a lasting reverence for it. Fuller's contribution to the understanding of wonder is praiseworthy because it synthesizes and widens our understanding of the phenomenon of wonder through an evolutionary-adaptive perspective.[11] Furthermore, it paves the way for thinking of wonder, understood as an emotion, as "one principal source of adult spirituality,"[12] which supports Fuller's idea that "a life shaped by wonder evidences the very existential and cognitive sensibilities that would seem indispensable to humanity's search for religious meaning."[13]

That wonder is an emotion is not unique to Fuller. In fact, the first significant hint of wonder being an emotion comes from Plato who views wonder as the feeling experienced by the philosopher.[14] Later on in the history of wonder Descartes found wonder to be the first of all the passions[15] and Adam Smith called wonder a sentiment. Now, many other wonder-theorists besides Fuller, Plato, Descartes, and Smith support the idea of wonder being an emotion, and to establish a clearer view of just how popular this idea is among different academics hailing from a variety of disciplines, we might begin by turning our attention to literary scholar James Vincent Cunningham. In his *Woe and Wonder: The Emotional Effect of Shakespearian Tragedy* he argues that:

> [Wonder is] an emotion less discussed in connection with tragedy than either fear or sorrow and one that the literary person today does not easily think of as an emotion, but it is a commonplace in the Renaissance especially in connection with the deaths of notable persons and with the effects of drama and fiction.[16]

Cunningham clearly states that wonder is an emotion yet an emotion that is rarely discussed in comparison to the emotion of fear and sorrow when it comes to tragedy, and particularly so in 1964 compared to the Renaissance period.

Contemporary philosopher Jesse Prinz also thinks of wonder as an emotion and argues that it is perhaps our most important emotion because it has inspired humanity's greatest achievements in science, art, and religion. According to Prinz we wonder at scientific discoveries because they take us beyond the world of appearances and "with it we discover endless depths, more astounding that we could have imagined."[17] We wonder or stand in awe (which according to Prinz is an intense form of wonder) at places of worship, such as temples and cathedrals, as they have a way of making us feel small yet elevated. We wonder at art because art often depicts religious outlooks and so it is that we can wonder at everything from the limestone idol Venus of Willendorf to the depiction of animals in the Chauvet cave in France, thought to have been utilized in shamanistic rites.[18]

Quinn acknowledges that "wonder is a human emotion and not an idea or concept" but it is "the passion that arises from consciousness of ignorance."[19] Additionally, Quinn points out that wonder is a species of fear or the most rational form of fear that is, the fear of ignorance.[20]

Philosopher Sophia Vasalou likewise supports the idea of wonder as an emotion and in her introduction to the anthology *Practices of Wonder* she writes that:

> The appearance of wonder at so many important locations in our practices serves, on the one hand, as a testimony to the inherent complexity of this emotion. For if, in many of our philosophical, scientific, and other intellectual inquiries, wonder has often been cast as the passion of inquiry and connected with the desire to know and understand, its presence in other practices as in spiritual or aesthetic contexts—if indeed we may draw these boundaries with sufficient distinctness— brings to the fore its character, not merely as questing or inquisitive, but more importantly, as an appreciative response.[21]

Vasalou clearly points out that wonder is an emotion connected with inquiry and the quest for understanding, but to her it may also pass as an appreciative response to something. Recall that when Boyle experienced the luminous meat his wonder facilitated an all-night inquiry into the nature of the strange phenomenon, however, we can also say that Boyle's wonder was an appreciative response, that is, he understood full well that before him was something extraordinary and mysterious.

Philosopher Marguerite La Caze is another patron of the idea that wonder qualifies as an emotion and she argues in her *Wonder and Generosity* that wonder, and indeed generosity, plays important roles in both ethics and politics and that wonder is a passion that enables a particular response to others that "accepts their differences."[22] Furthermore, she puts forwards that wonder "involves recognizing others as different from ourselves in that it is a response to what is unfamiliar and a way of finding the unfamiliar in the familiar."[23]

That wonder is an emotion is additionally advocated by philosopher Martha Nussbaum, who in her opus on emotions *Upheavals of Thought* writes that wonder is the emotion that responds:

> To the pull of the object, and one might say that in it the subject is maximally aware of the value of the object, and only minimally aware, if at all, of its relationship to her own plans. That is why it is likely to issue in contemplation, rather than in any other sort of action toward the object.[24]

Additionally, she states that wonder is the emotion that makes it possible for human beings to transcend selfishness and respond to and recognize the inherent worth of others because, as she writes, it "helps move distant objects within the circle of a person's scheme of ends."[25] In this sense wonder is an inclusive emotion that as Fuller would argue encourages "'empathy and compassion' [and] redraws our world of concern, establishing true mutuality with a wider sphere of life."[26] The idea that wonder can be complex, which we saw in connection with Quinn's view of wonder as a species of fear, can also be found in the of philosophy of Nussbaum who stipulates that:

> Wonder is sometimes an important ingredient in other emotions. In grief there is, I think, often a kind of wonder—in which one sees the beauty of the lost person as a kind of radiance standing at a very great distance from us.[27]

This speaks of the complexity of wonder and that as much as wonder may be a species of fear it can also be a part of grief.

That wonder is an emotion likewise comes natural to theologian Celia Deane-Drummond, who in her book *Wonder and Wisdom* explores what wonder, understood as the destabilizing yet "innocent feeling of amazement so common in little children,"[28] has to do with wisdom, which to her aims at presenting "a picture of the whole that enlightens rather than fragments knowledge from disparate sources."[29]

Additionally, wonder, understood as an emotion to an extent, finds support in the work of psychiatrist Paul R. Fleischman, who in his book *Wonder* argues that wonder might qualify as an emotion but that wonder can also be thought of as a thought-pattern or the absence of such.[30] Additionally, Fleischman writes that when we wonder "something about the world itself awakens in us" and in this sense "wonder is a type of complex awareness which participates in complex knowing and feeling."[31] To begin appreciating the emotional aspect of wonder, Fleischman suggests that we begin pondering what life is because as he writes "if you put an effort into understanding what life is you will feel wonder."[32] Thinking about what life is can indeed provoke wonder because what constitutes life is an elusive matter, understood as it is not merely something we do not completely understand, but also a matter we perhaps do not even understand how to approach once we begin to think about it.

So far we have paid attention to a variety of examples supporting the notion that wonder is an emotion and we have addressed some of the wonder-theorists in favor of the idea. Of all the theorists, Fleishman deserves special attention, because as much as he is an exponent of the idea that wonder qualifies as an emotion, he also serves as a reminder that it is far from certain that wonder can be pigeonholed exclusively as an emotion. To continue to explore in what capacity we may call wonder an emotion, it will be prudent to address what actually makes up an emotion and this we shall turn to now.

WHAT IS AN EMOTION?

Quinn points out that the word emotion comes from the Latin "emovere," meaning "to move out," and that it entered into the English vocabulary at some point in the eighteenth century.[33] As a word it has to an extent replaced older expressions such as the Greek word "pathos" and the later Latin translation "passio," which we know in English as passion. The rendition "to move out" gives us a hint in terms of what emotions do, namely, that they move or urge us to act or behave in a particular way. Nussbaum expresses this elegantly:

> Emotions shape the landscape of our mental and social lives. Like the "geological upheavals" a traveler might discover in a landscape where recently only a flat plane could be seen, they mark our lives as uneven, uncertain, and prone to reversal.[34]

To Nussbaum, emotions are what give our mental life color or nuance as they shape our mental lives. Furthermore, they can be cultivated and qualify as intelligent responses to the perception of value.[35] This means that to Nussbaum emotions are relevant in matters of ethical judgment because as she writes: "we cannot plausibly omit them, once we acknowledge that emotions include in their content judgments that can be true and false, and good and bad guides to ethical choice."[36]

Nussbaum's contribution to the understanding of emotions is important and the idea that emotions can be cultivated links up to her work in political philosophy and ethics. Nevertheless, her approach is but one among many and the nature of emotions, and indeed the nature of their expression, is a complicated and controversial matter. To begin to appreciate this complexity one could begin by pointing out that there are two distinct ideas, which I shall label the "cultural approach" and the "natural approach" that have long troubled and divided scholars working on the subject.

The cultural approach signifies that human emotions are social constructs, understood as philosopher Ian Hacking puts it that, "emotions and their expressions are quite specific to a social and linguistic group."[37] In this sense "culture" is everything and human behavior, including our most intimate emotions, preferences, or experiences are fabricated by culture. The cultural approach is inspired by the idea that human behavior varies across cultures and to get some hold on the scope of this idea let us turn to philosopher Robert C. Solomon who explains that:

> The repertoire of emotions in a culture (or a subculture) depends not only on the cultural background and the environment but on the way people talk and think about emotions. In our society, conversations often tend to focus on outrage, resentment, and, in a very different mood romantic love. We talk very little about grief, very little about gratitude, although these two emotions form the foundation of a great

many extended conversations and so are "basic" emotions in other cultures. Among the Kululi of Papua, New Guinea, for example, grief and gratitude form two of the central themes of the entire culture, while American males to be very specific, seem to feel very uncomfortable with both of them.[38]

Solomon clearly points out that there are vast differences in the way emotions such as grief and gratitude are thought and talked about across cultures, which speaks to the importance of culture and subculture in the making of emotions.

For further clarification of what it means that emotions are linked to social and linguistic groups, one can also turn to psychologist Vivian Burr, who in her book *Social Constructionism* gives voice to the social constructionist view of emotions. She writes:

> Psychoanalysts take the view that there are discrete and identifiable emotions, such as anger, envy and hatred, which are innate in all human beings. They are a part of the way human beings are constructed, and the words we have attached to them are simply the labels we have chosen to refer to these emotional entities. A social constructionist view, by contrast, would say that, in English-speaking cultures, the words "anger," "hatred," and "envy" and the concepts to which they refer pre-date any one person's entry into the world as an infant, and in the process of learning to talk we have no choices but to come to understand ourselves in terms of these concepts. This view would suggest that our experience of the world, and perhaps especially of our own internal states, is undifferentiated and intangible without the framework of language to give it structure and meaning. The way language is structured therefore determines the way that experiences and consciousness are structured.[39]

To the social constructionists there are no innate emotions as such, which we may label universal. From the very beginning of our lives we become socialized into a particular context and thus to put it bluntly we are taught what to think and feel by the members and language of the society in which we are situated.

To exemplify the idea that the culture we are situated in determines how our emotions develop we might turn to anthropologist Catherine Lutz, who in her book *Unnatural Emotions* reveals her study of the people inhabiting the island Ifaluk in the South Pacific and their particular emotion "fago," which she translates into compassion/love/sorrow.[40] Lutz writes that to really understand what "fago" means "requires an understanding of the way the Ifaluk conceptualize positive relationships with others,"[41] and this indicates that in order to grasp or understand "fago" one has to submerge oneself into the culture of the Ifaluk. Again we see the importance of culture in the development of emotions.

To provide another example highlighting emotions as social constructs we might turn to the Japanese psychiatrist Takeo Doi. His study on the Japanese concept of "amae" prompted him to argue that it qualifies as a key to understand the Japanese personality and that "amae," which we may translate into "indulgent interdependence"[42] or "sweet dependence,"[43] in reality is completely untranslatable because it has many meanings in Japanese and is an emotion that "intrinsically avoids verbalization."[44] If, for arguments sake this is true, those outside Japanese society will have no clue as to what "amae" refers to in full and if one were to acquire such understanding it would depend entirely on one's ability to submerge oneself into Japanese culture. Only through being a part of Japanese culture could we understand the true meaning of "amae."

As mentioned earlier, there is another idea that influences thinkers on emotion, which I have labeled the natural approach. Now, in the earlier quotation from Burr, it was pointed out that psychoanalysis builds on the idea of innate human emotions and thus the practice of psychoanalysis represents an outlook on human emotions quite different from that of the social constructionist. The idea is that emotions are a part of our human makeup and that no matter what culture, social group, or language group we belong to, we all are equipped with a particular set of emotions. This idea can be traced back to ancient times and in support of this stands Aristotle's *de Anime* or *On the Soul* as it is also called, where Aristotle deliberates if some of the conditions of the soul (anger, courage, desire, sensation) can be attributed to the soul only or if all of them are bodily things and happenings.[45] Aristotle's conditions of the soul are useful for our understanding of emotions because they can be viewed as precursors for what we today would call "basic emotions." Now, according to philosopher Peter Goldie, the idea of basic emotions involves that:

> Our concept of emotions are organized hierarchically, with the non-basic emotions falling under one or more of the basic emotions. So, for example, if anger is a basic emotion, then less basic species of anger might be annoyance, fury, rage, indignation and so forth. Other non-basic emotions could then be comprised of a cocktail of basic emotions: jealousy, for example, might include fear and anger. According to this view, then basic emotions are themselves common to all humans, and other sorts of emotion need not be.[46]

That there might be such a thing called universal emotions is an interesting notion because if true it effectively points out a human communality. However, it has to be said that what qualifies as basic emotions is not quite as fixed as some perhaps would like to think and that the "list of basic emotions" has virtually changed over time and is still a matter of controversy. To substantiate the Indian treatise *Natyashastra*, a Sanskrit text dating back to the third century BC committed to the investigations into the nature of consciousness distills nine principal emotions: sexual passion, amusement, sorrow, anger, fear, perseverance, disgust, wonder, and serenity.[47] A different list can be found in the *Li Chi*, a Chinese encyclopedia dating back to the first century BC, which describes the seven feelings of men as: joy, anger, sadness, fear, love, disliking, and liking.[48] By contrast, Cicero's work highlights only four emotions namely lust/desire, delight, fear, and distress[49] and Descartes names six simple and primitive passions, namely, wonder, love, hatred, desire, joy, and sadness.[50] The philosopher Baruch Spinoza found there to be three primary emotions, which are pleasure, pain, and desire[51] and philosopher Thomas Hobbes listed the following simple passions: appetite, desire, love, aversion, hate, joy, and grief.[52] Lastly Darwin identified seven emotional expressions including low spirits (anxiety, grief, dejection, and despair), high spirits (joy, love, tender feelings, and devotion), reflection (meditation, ill-temper, sulkiness, and determination), hatred (anger), disdain (contempt, disgust, guilt, pride, helplessness, patience, affirmation, and negation), surprise (astonishment, fear, and horror), and self-attention (shame, shyness, modesty, blushing).[53] Now this montage of discrepancy over basic emotions clearly is brought together from older sources and thus one might be inclined to think that contemporary psychology can offer a conclusive vision of what counts as innate human emotions. Alas, this is in a strict sense not the case, which becomes obvious when we consult the work of psychologist Robert Plutchik, who in *Emotions and Life: Perspectives from Psychology, Biology and Evolution* informs us about the variations in the lists of basic emotions advocated by a number of modern scholars.[54] That we cannot say for sure what makes up the set of basic emotions is naturally a problem and a serious challenge to advocates of the natural approach to emotions. Having said that, this does not mean that the cultural approach prevails. The natural approach endures within the philosophy of emotions because, although theorists cannot completely agree on a list of basic emotions, most theorists recognize that fear, sadness, and anger are basic emotions and consensus is almost within reach when it comes to emotions such as joy, love, and surprise.[55]

Now settling which of the two ideas is the correct one is beyond the scope of this book and given our present focus not at all a necessity. For our purposes it is profitable to keep both ideas in mind because both may help us understand wonder better. To elaborate one might say that the cultural approach is merited, because to say that emotions are socially constructed can help cast light on why the conception of wonder has changed over time, and why it is that, for example, the feeling of wonder celebrated in Plato's *Theaetetus* as the beginning of philosophy is so readily dismissed by the eighteenth-century English poet Alexander Pope, who we recall voiced that fools admire, but men of sense approve. One possible explanation is that changes in the social climate and the general conception of the order of things discredited wonder, and from being the feeling of the philosopher it became the feeling associated with naivety. In other words, we can say that given the seemingly wonder-friendly culture of ancient Athens, an upstart philosopher would have been encouraged to see wonder in a positive light, while a student during the less wonder-friendly Enlightenment period with its emphasis on reason, in all likelihood, would have been cultivated to think and speak of wonder in a much more reserved and negative way. A further merit of the cultural approach is that it will help us remain critical toward whatever conclusions about wonder the natural approach might provide us, and not to be led astray by what could be nothing but social trends in the current research climate on emotions, attempting to pigeonhole wonder merely as a complex emotion too muddled for serious attention, or explain away its significance by describing it as synonymous with, for example, surprise or fear.

Now keeping this in mind, together with the uncertainties surrounding the list of basic emotions, it has to be said that the approach to emotions and indeed wonder (which I shall elaborate on later in this chapter), drawing on the natural approach to emotions, does offer a fruitful way forward when it comes to understanding what emotions are. This is because the "war" between social science and natural science is not as prominent as it was in the twentieth century and that since the 1980s genetics have established the strong influence of biology on human behavior. Likewise, the disciplines of evolutionary psychology aiming at explaining why "natural selection favors the kinds of mental activity that we discern in organism today,"[56] and sociobiology, which is concerned with "why humans and other social organisms evolved particular behavior patterns,"[57] have emerged and advanced our understanding of what human emotions are. The advancement of our understanding of emotions that these new movements have brought forth can partly be found in the insistence of researchers advocating the natural approach to "get to the 'bottom of things,' to identify the basic building blocks of emotions, the basic emotions."[58] To an extent these new fields and disciplines have successfully merged the cultural approach and the natural approach recognizing that emotions are grounded in biology, but social factors are also important in the generation of particular emotions and their expression.[59]

THE COGNITIVE APPROACH

Let us now break away from the big lines in the philosophy of emotions and focus on a particular approach to understanding emotions, namely the cognitive approach that gained momentum after the publication of psychologist Ulric Neisser's 1967 book *Cognitive Psychology*.[60] The cognitive approach advocates the notion that emotions are intentional states of mind, meaning that they are "directed at or toward some object"[61] and this approach is quite suitable for an investigation into wonder because when we wonder, we wonder about something meaning that our wonderment is directed toward a particular object or event. The cognitive approach has in this respect a certain explanatory power as it allows emotions to become part of a larger affective realm, and emotions to be broken down into smaller subcategories, which consequently will increase the level of detail and thus we stand a better chance of advancing our understanding of wonder, if indeed it is an emotion. Now, before we engage further with the cognitive approach it has to be said that as an approach it is not unrivalled or immune to criticism. The cognitive approach is an alternative to the approach to emotions pioneered by psychologist William James, arguing that emotions equal feelings and are connected with bodily states. James writes:

> Without the bodily states following on the perception, the latter would be purely cognitive in form, pale, colourless, destitute of emotional warmth. We might see the bear, and judge it best to run, receive the insult and deem it right to strike, but we could not actually feel afraid and angry.[62]

James's idea is that without bodily feelings there is no such thing as emotions and that bodily changes are responsible for emotions. Rooted in ancient Greek thought the cognitive approach treats emotions as cognitive, thought-centered, and directed toward the world.[63] This challenges James's view and insists that his approach emphasizes too much on bodily states and too little on the cognitive aspect of emotions.[64] For this reason the cognitive approach is popular, but in our endeavor to understand in what sense wonder is an emotion, we must exercise caution because as philosopher Simon Blackburn argues, emotions are not as cognitive as some might think and the cognitive approach is far too Apollonian[65] and far less Dionysian[66] leaving out as Nussbaum has stated, "what is messy and ungovernable in the life of the passions."[67] Blackburn's criticism is insightful and important but pursuing it further lies outside the scope of our current inquiry.[68] Pushing forward we shall adopt the cognitive approach because it seems most promising with regards to clarifying in what sense wonder is an emotion.

To continue and present a more in-depth account of the cognitive approach let us turn to contemporary philosopher Arron Ben-Ze'ev who finds that a typical emotion:

> Is generated by perceived significant changes; its focus of concern is personal and comparative; its major characteristics are instability, great intensity, partiality and brief duration; and its basic components are cognition, evaluation, motivation and feelings.[69]

According to Ben-Ze'ev, emotions call for our attention when we encounter significant positive or negative changes in personal matters or the state of affairs of those connected to us. We respond to the unfamiliar but the attention called for does not persist, and after a while the change is viewed as a normal state of affairs and ceases to excite us. Emotions exist to protect our personal concerns and in the event of an emotional change its importance, or meaning, is comparative in the sense that it is against a personal referential framework or background that the importance or meaning of the change can be evaluated and assessed.[70] In addition he explains that a typical emotion has four characteristics: instability, great intensity, partiality, and brief duration; and four basic components: cognition, evaluation, motivation, and feelings.[71]

The first characteristic, instability, relates to the notion that emotions are unstable states and indicators of change or transition. Born out of a changing context "they signify some agitation, they are intense, occasional, and limited in duration."[72] The second characteristic, great intensity, is called for due to the notion that significant change requires the "mobilisation of many resources."[73] The third characteristic, partiality, is highlighted because emotions are partial in the sense that they can focus on a narrow target, such as a person or a limited number of people and express a personal and interested standpoint. Ben-Ze'ev explains that emotions in this sense are similar to heat-seeking missiles since their only concern is to find the heat-generating target.[74] The fourth characteristic of emotion is brevity. Ben-Ze'ev states that typical emotions are relatively short-lived since a person cannot mobilize all her resources to remain focussed on a particular event for a prolonged period. If so she would rapidly lose her ability to function adaptively.[75] A mental system simply cannot be unstable for long and still function normally and at some point it will "construe the change as a normal and stable situation."[76] Thus emotions are transient states, however, from that, it does not follow that their impact on a person mirrors this particular quality. Ben-Ze'ev finds that "a brief emotional state can have profound and long-lasting behavioral implications."[77]

One might object to the idea of brevity as a constituent of an emotion and challenge Ben-Ze'ev's idea of what an emotion is by pointing out that the emotion of sorrow linked to bereavement need not be brief but may last for a long time. The famous British actor Peter Cushing, who lost his wife Helen on January 14, 1971, experienced such long-term sorrow. Biographer Christopher Gullo writes that "Cushing often stated that he was born in 1913 but died in 1971," and that in the decade following Helen's death, most of Cushing's roles portrayed "loners and widowers"; some of these "were so close to his real-life pain that he had trouble getting through them."[78] I am sympathetic to the objection of brevity being a constituent of emotion, but in defense of Ben-Ze'ev's outlook we can say that long-lasting sorrow connected to bereavement may correspond more to a mood rather than an emotion (discussed further below) and perhaps, in cases such as Cushing's, a condition made up by a series of sorrowful moods interrupted from time to time by various other moods and emotions. Thus Ben-Ze'ev's approach to emotion still stands.

As mentioned, Ben-Ze'ev also informs us that emotions contain four basic components that "express a conceptual division of the elements of this experience."[79] The first three components: cognition, evaluation, and motivation are intentional, meaning they refer to a subject-object relation or they are all about "being about something."[80] In other words, the matter at hand involves our ability to ignore the constant flow of stimuli in our surroundings so that we may form, for example, a meaningful relationship to another person. The final basic component is feeling, which Ben-Ze'ev ascribes to what he calls "the feeling dimension." Feelings are hard to describe and people often turn to the use of metaphors in the attempt to convey a particular feeling. He furthermore explains that feelings reveal the subject's state of mind in form of a primitive mode of consciousness. They are not intentional and one cannot demand a reason why one is feeling something in particular. "We cannot reason people out of their toothache as we might reason them out of their hatred [and thus] feelings are not subject to normative appraisal."[81] According to Ben-Ze'ev the intense feeling dimension may have a positive and negative influence on the mind. On the positive side, being aroused can be cognitively advantageous since it might aid one in (a) understanding particular aspects of a given situation, (b) heightening one's attention, and (c) increasing memory. On the negative side it can be said that if one harbors intense feelings the intellectual faculties of a person might be compromised, meaning that sound cognitive assessment in a given situation is impossible.[82]

Returning to the intentional dimension and the component of emotion called cognition, Ben-Ze'ev claims that it delivers the needed information about a particular situation or context. However, this information is often distorted due to the influence of (a) partiality, (b) closeness, and (c) an intense feeling dimension.[83] Ben-Ze'ev explains that partiality compromises knowledge since distorted claims may be adopted due to lack of vision or perspective. According to Ben-Ze'ev, partiality is similar in effect to that of great closeness, which disrupts the cognitive part in emotions and keeps us from seeing multiple facets of a given object. To illustrate this point he gives the example of looking at someone from a very short distance. In such a situation our vision is distorted and in order to gain a more collected and encompassing sight of the person in front of us distance is a requirement. Likewise, intense feeling can cause distortion because when one harbors such feelings our intellectual faculties are compromised "and no longer functions normally."[84]

With regards to the evaluative component of emotion, Ben-Ze'ev considers it of the utmost importance as it assesses the merits of the information delivered by the cognitive component in terms of its impact on the well-being of a person.[85] Imagine a tired student walking into her favorite coffee bar with the intention of spending a few hours on reading Heidegger's *Being and Time* over a cup of coffee. She learns that unfortunately the coffee bar is out of coffee beans meaning that she cannot enjoy her much-needed "cognitive enhancer" while reading Heidegger. Evaluating this information up against her idea of her well-being she would decide either to stay and read Heidegger over, for example, a cup of tea or simply decide that the coffee is too important to be missed and that she will have to take her business elsewhere.

The final component in the intentional dimension is, according to Ben-Ze'ev, motivation. Motivation is concerned with a person's eagerness to "maintain or change present, past or future circumstances."[86] A motivated person might defy a considerable amount of obstacles in order to change her circumstances. Imagine an upcoming ballet dancer bent on being hired by a major ballet company. She might defy the advice of her parents, the pangs of poverty or anxiety provoked by the intense competition in order to fulfill her dream.

So far we have engaged with the notion of changes and we have found that emotions are personal and the importance of emotional change is measured against a personal background. Furthermore, we have explored the major characteristics of emotion together with the basic components. However, Ben-Ze'ev's description of emotion does not stop here. He continues by stating that the intensity of a typical emotion depends on variables like the event's strength, reality, and relevance.[87] An event's strength determines the intensity of an emotional experience, so if I am angry the intensity of my anger is measured against the level of damage I have suffered because of the event. An event's reality refers to what degree we believe the event to be real, which is to say that the more we believe an event to be real the more intense our emotions will be. The relevance of an event is likewise important because the greater the relevance an event has the more important and intense it will be. A deadly tornado hitting us right here, right now, is more relevant to us than a tornado hitting an uninhabited area in Oklahoma because our lives are in danger and thus our emotions would be more intense.

Our accountability, readiness, and deservingness in relation to the event also influence the way emotions work because they form the "constituting background circumstances of the emotional event."[88] By accountability Ben-Ze'ev highlights responsibility and agency, which is to say that a higher degree in accountability results in greater emotional intensity. By readiness Ben-Ze'ev points to the cognitive change that takes place in our minds during an event. If something happens unexpectedly it generates intensity because as he writes: "we are angrier if we happen to be expecting a contrary result, just as the quite unexpected fulfilment of our wishes is especially sweet."[89] Concerning deservingness

Ben-Ze'ev points out with reference to Aristotle that we all seek fair treatment and despite that we might disagree on what counts as just and unjust we all think "the self is a worthwhile person."[90]

Furthermore, contextual and personality variables are influential as well when it comes to emotional intensity.[91] What is at play here is that "personal traits, world views, cultural background, and current personal situation" are factors that may fuel the intensity of an emotion.

As a last entry Ben-Ze'ev claims that emotions belong to a greater affective realm, which includes sentiments, moods, affective traits, and affective disorders,[92] meaning that it is a very versatile approach that provides a rich and explanatory description of emotion.

THE COGNITIVE APPROACH AND EPISTEMIC EMOTIONS

Earlier we encountered the notion of basic emotions and the predicate "basic" suggests there are other kinds of emotions to consider, which we, for the sake of argument, could term non-basic emotions. Given that we do not have a complete list of the basic emotions naming non-basic emotions is naturally problematic, but granted Plutchick is right in his view that a consensus has been reached stating that fear, sadness, and anger are basic emotions then emotions such as, for example, love, jealousy, hate, joy, gratitude, awe, grief, dread, reverence, hope, trust, humility, and (perhaps) wonder can be classified as non-basic emotions. To advance our understanding of wonder let us now focus on a particular subgroup of non-basic emotion labelled epistemic emotions by following philosopher Adam Morton who classifies wonder as an epistemic emotion.[93]

To begin, we might say that Morton is interested in how we acquire beliefs correctly and in this respect he identifies epistemic emotions that are directed especially toward knowledge or epistemic ends. In this respect he has devised a list of possible candidates for epistemic emotions: "Curiosity, intellectual courage, love of truth, wonder, meticulousness, excitement and humility."[94] It can be ventured that these particular candidates do not represent emotions but are, in truth, virtues, yet Morton remains open to the existence of epistemic emotions. The reason for this is in part to be found in his distinction between virtue, character, and emotion.[95] For example, Morton claims that "generosity" can refer to three different things. To harbor the virtue of generosity one has to be generous—that is, one displays generous actions, however in order for a generous action to be virtuous it needs to be balanced: neither giving too little nor giving too much. Morton gives the example of a person in academia whose generous character and insistence on incorporating the work of an incompetent coworker slows down a research project. This person harbors generosity as a character trait but she cannot be viewed as virtuous since her generosity is excessive.[96] Emotion contrasts both virtue and character. It is quite possible to imagine a person who, after exhibiting great generosity, may say, "I did not feel generous" but this does not nullify her generosity.[97] The opposite is also possible as one can imagine a person posts displaying no generosity whatsoever claims that she feels enormously generous. In either case, feelings do not define whether an act is generous nor do they define whether it is virtuous.

Morton also offers an alternative argument to distinguish virtue, character, and emotion through the concept of longevity. Virtues are normative concepts since they "pick out dispositions to profitable, correct, or admirable patterns of action or thought."[98] Furthermore, it can be said of virtues that just like one swallow does not make a spring, one virtuous act does not make one a virtuous person. Virtue, it seems, appeals to longevity. Concerning the notion of character, it can be said that just because a person loses her temper momentarily during a discussion it does not make her an angry character. Likewise, just because a cowardly character experiences a brief moment of courage, it does not follow that she is no longer a coward. In this light the idea of character, like the notion of virtue, demands certain durability. Emotions on the other hand are, according to Morton, different since they are occurrent and "happen at particular moments and through determinate stretches of time, during which they have causal influence on the person."[99] Furthermore, Morton explains that emotions can be associated with conscious affect, meaning we can have a feeling of being generous just as we can have conscious awareness about a particular thought formation or pressing desire. In addition, emotions can also be motives since they can "cause behavior by making particular desires and beliefs salient."[100]

With regards to how we human beings acquire beliefs, it is nevertheless still possible for the skeptic to deny the existence of epistemic emotions. First of all it is, as Morton argues, quite plausible that an inquiring mind does not rely on emotions at all in the process of obtaining knowledge, because it can be argued that all one needs is the virtues of being careful, curious, imaginative, and responsible. Secondly, even if one accepts that emotions have a say in virtuous behavior, it still leaves room for the skeptic because feeling curious at a key moment in time does not mean that the emotion functions epistemically.[101] Nevertheless, Morton argues that there are occasions where virtues are not enough and where emotions play a key role when it comes to acquiring knowledge. He claims that an inquiry based on emotion-less virtues would be shallower or somewhat lighter in its constitution.[102] To illustrate this, Morton first points to the notion of motivation and gives the example of a young scientist, whose qualifications are unquestionable if it was not for the fact that she does not care about her subject, and is completely devoid of curiosity. She wants a career and she knows that by pushing a particular line of inquiry she will be successful in getting precisely that. According to Morton it is quite possible that the scientist will succeed in producing excellent scientific work, however, it is unlikely that she will revolutionize her field or take a chance and dedicate her working life to a line of inquiry that for her seems important.[103] In order to be a scientist par excellence one has to harbor certain motivating epistemic emotions and in this respect he mentions wonder, curiosity, and skepticism.[104] Without wonder the scientist would never wonder at an emerging pattern in her pool of data. Without curiosity she would never ponder how scientists view her field centuries into the future. Without skepticism she would never stop and think whether her inquiry would benefit from an alternative, perhaps less supported, method.[105]

Secondly, Morton argues that the epistemic emotions answering to curiosity, worry, concern, and interest are linked to obtaining knowledge and how we consider relevant alternatives to a given belief. If one is curious about a particular matter one is interested in knowing the truth and would not just settle with a belief.[106] Knowledge is what satisfies curiosity and obtaining knowledge "requires exploration of a maze of possibilities, some consistent with the fact that is known and some incompatible with it."[107] Refraining from exploring alternative possibilities would induce epistemic worry or concern about the truthfulness about one's knowledge.

Thirdly, Morton investigates the notion that the emotion of responsibility is linked to epistemic worry. He argues that if one feels responsible for knowing something about a particular subject one would experience epistemic worries about possible unexplored avenues.[108] To illustrate this he asks the reader to imagine a scientist in charge of a research project seeking to establish if the chemicals used in the making of a particular brand of baby bottles are carcinogenic. The scientist might have established that the chemical is harmless in itself but when it comes to contact with plastic, normal food acidity, or with digestive enzymes things are no longer certain. The scientist may have cleared a wide range of these combinations, however, it is doubtful that she has cleared all possible combinations. Therefore, according to Morton she has to remain alert. In fact Morton argues she has to be worried, be haunted and the whole affair has to nag her.[109] Harboring the epistemic virtue of worry is simply not enough in such a situation. The scientist needs epistemic emotions to be a responsible scientist.

IS WONDER AN EMOTION?

Let us now attempt to cast light on the stargazers' peculiar arresting experiences by making use of the insights into emotion from a cognitive perspective provided by Ben-Ze'ev and Morton. It may be prudent to start by asking if it is reasonable to think that the stargazers are experiencing an emotion in the arresting moment. According to Ben-Ze'ev and his take on emotions, it seems the answer is yes. All the stargazers are facing something extraordinary, unexpected, and very real, and their reaction fits very well with Ben-Ze'ev's description of an emotion. Ben-Ze'ev lists that an emotion contains four characteristics and four components and the first characteristic is instability. In this respect it can be said that the arresting moment is a moment of transition or transfiguring for all the implicated stargazers. All the implicated parties have to face and cope with the extraordinary and unexpected as the normal appearance of the night sky is suspended. The second characteristic is great intensity. In relation to the stargazers it can be argued that the arresting situation for them is a situation of great intensity due to the visual onslaught of the meteor shower. The students from the first example seem to testify to this effect since they simply stop their work and gaze at the sky. In the second example, Gleaves's excited mother hurries him out of bed and the fact that he describes the meteor shower as the most incredible vision he has ever witnessed speaks of great intensity. In the third example, Clemmer describes herself as frightened and ignorant of what is going on when she first encounters the meteor shower. This speaks of great intensity. The third characteristic partiality is also called for in the three examples. All the involved people focus in the situation on a specific target, namely the meteor shower. Nothing else seems to matter. The fourth characteristic is brief duration and I shall argue this is also honored by the provided examples. For the students the event is arresting for fifteen minutes while the shower is at its peak. Gleaves reports that he was held captive by the shower for thirty to forty-five minutes and Clemmer reports that she stood and watched the shower for thirty minutes before her ability to focus declined and she went back to bed.

According to Ben-Ze'ev, emotions also have four components that we need to consider before we can say that the stargazers are dealing with an emotion. The first component is cognition and is supposed to deliver information about a given situation; however, in all the examples this function is hard at work but fails to deliver a complete picture of what is going on. Relying on their observational skills and counting ability the students action quickly comes to a halt as the intensity of the meteor shower overwhelms them. Gleaves's statement "I had no idea that what I was about to see would burn a picture in my mind that would be with me to this day," speaks of a person who was oblivious as to what was coming and was swept away by what he encountered. Clemmer reports that when she first saw the unusual streaks of light in the sky she set out to investigate but was filled with fright when she finally saw the navy sky rain stars and found that she did not understand it.

The second component is evaluation, and in relation to the stargazers it seems all the involved evaluate the situation as not dangerous. The students gaze at the phenomenon while standing still, Gleaves merely watches the sky, and when Clemmer overcomes her initial fear she focuses entirely on the beauty of the shower.

The third component is motivation. For all the stargazers it can be said that they had an interest in observing the shower. Other needs, such as sleep, were suspended, and in Clemmer's case it might also have interrupted her scheduled visit to the bathroom.

The last component is feeling, and it seems that all the stargazers are experiencing an arresting feeling. The students just gaze at the meteors, not doing anything else, and Gleaves and Clemmer report that they had their mouths open for thirty to forty-five minutes while they were watching the sky. In addition, judging from Gleaves and Clemmer's reports, it can be argued that they both experienced increased attention and memory since they both handed in their reports many years after the event took place and still recall the event as wonderful and spectacular. Clearly the event in the case of Gleaves and Clemmer had a long-lasting effect.

Based on this it seems plausible that the stargazers are experiencing some kind of emotion during the peak of the shower but does this emotion correspond to wonder? Morton says little about the epistemic emotion of wonder in particular; however, from his work we learn that if wonder indeed is an epistemic emotion it must be directed toward knowledge or some epistemic end. Would it be fitting to say that the stargazers are experiencing the epistemic emotion of wonder? In the case of the students it seems a plausible option. We know that the students set out on a scientific mission in order to learn how the particular meteor shower works. We know they relied on observation and planned to note the frequency, trajectory, and brightness of the meteors. We also know that they had to give up their endeavors when the rate of meteors increased dramatically. It can be argued that the students at this point became stunned or flabbergasted by the intensity of the meteor shower, which effectively ended their initial epistemic pursuits. Alternatively, it can be argued that the students experienced a transition in their epistemic focus. It is thinkable that the students initially were motivated by curiosity and focused on collecting facts about the meteor shower. Furthermore, it can be argued that the students, at the peak of the event, were pushed to exchange the scientific outlook with a more wondering philosophical line of questioning. This could include exchanging desires to know about frequency, trajectory, and brightness with reflections on, for example, the beauty of the event to thoughts of their own existence in relation to the vastness of space or why there is something rather than nothing. Taking this into account it is quite plausible that the students are experiencing the epistemic emotion of wonder.

Considering Gleaves and Clemmer's witness reports it seems they also could have experienced an epistemic shift. From the time Gleaves's mother woke him up and ushered him to follow her outside he must have been curious about what was afoot. The same goes for Clemmer when she saw the first streaks of light outside her window. Seconds later they both faced the full force of the meteor shower and it is quite plausible that they, in that very moment, both experienced a transition from being motivated by the emotion of curiosity to that of being motivated by the epistemic emotion of wonder.

OTHER FACES OF WONDER

So far it seems possible that wonder can be viewed as an emotion or more specifically an epistemic emotion. However, this does not imply that wonder is only an emotion and in the following three different aspects of wonder based on the work of Ben-Ze'ev, Parsons, and Evans, suggesting that wonder is perhaps best viewed as not merely an emotion but multifaceted will be depicted.

To begin, let us consider the possibility of wonder being a mood. A mood differs from an emotion in the sense that emotions have specific intentional objects whereas moods have general or diffuse intentional objects. Furthermore, moods differ from emotions in relation to the time they occupy because they can last for seconds to days but typically last for a few minutes to a few hours. Moods on the other hand typically last longer and their lifespan ranges from hours, over days, to weeks and months.[110] From this vantage point it seems quite possible that one can be in a mood of wonder. Imagine a person who for most of her adult life has advocated a particular philosophy. Suppose then that the person enrolls in a philosophy course and during the course she encounters a teacher who successfully argues against the philosophy she, until this very day, has built her life around. Furthermore, imagine that the teacher also offers the starting point of a new promising philosophy, which the student has the option of exploring further. Now it is quite possible that the student experiences the epistemic emotion of wonder at the moment her philosophy is refuted. Given her particular status as a philosophy student it is also possible that her newfound emotion of wonder can evolve into a long-lasting mood that fuels her future inquiries into a new promising philosophy. To exemplify we might draw attention to de Pasquale who experienced an episode of wonder following the funeral of his good friend. It is quite possible that the episodic wonder that revealed to him the fragility of human life contributed to the development of a "wonder-filled mood" that, in the long run, encouraged his philosophical attitude and pursuit of a professional philosophic career and a viable answer to the question of how to live.

Moving on, let us now consider wonder as a value. The work of Parsons acknowledges the emotional aspect of wonder but adds to the complexity of wonder by introducing it as a value. According to Parsons, wondering is an essential characteristic of the human being who, poetically speaking, is a product of the stars and at the bottom line a citizen of the cosmos.[111] He argues that when thinking about wonder one cannot avoid taking into account our relationship with the universe. He furthermore claims that wonder:

> Suggests a breach in the membrane of awareness [and resembles] a sudden opening in a man's system of established and expected meanings, a blow as if one were struck or stunned.[112]

Parsons explains that to be wonderstruck is to be wounded by the sword of a peculiar event in such a way that it renders one open to a reformation of one's current outlook. Furthermore, Parsons writes that: "The excitation of wonder ranges from the sudden and intense to the gradual and moderate, until it shades into ordinary emotion."[113] Parsons seems to advocate a notion of wonder that has many features. Toward the end of "A Philosophy of Wonder" he laments the separation of science, aesthetic and humanistic values. Furthermore, he believes that all three cultures are fuelled by wonder yet the humanistic side is being neglected and that without the humanities one cannot guarantee the advancement of human value.[114] In order to achieve a world of value one must, in Parson's view, first of all guarantee a sufficient supply of basic material goods and services for all. Secondly, and perhaps most interesting for our purposes is his idea that we must encourage the will to create—the will to wonder. Parson elaborates:

> The will to wonder which comes easily for the well fed and well loved and well taught child, is a readiness to explore and hold one's mind open. [. . .] Philosophy begins in wonder but wonder begins in the child. And while philosophy in the full sense cannot be taught to the child, the philosopher who sets not just a professional but also a human value on wonder will be concerned about a society that inhibits wonder in the child and adult and thus inhibits the very reconstruction of society called for.[115]

Parsons's idea of wonder as a value is interesting since it promotes a new aspect of wonder. His insight into wonder encourages us to ask the question if wonder is something that we should value and cultivate in our citizens. Without touching the emotional aspect of wonder, this brings wonder onto the moral and political scene, and encourages us to view wonder as multifaceted.

To continue our exploration of wonder being something other than an emotion, let us now consider the idea that wonder is an attitude. Philosopher Martyn Evans points out that wonder can be viewed as an attitude.[116] According to Evans wonder arises within us. It grows out of possible ordinary circumstances yet it is something that entertains a focus in which the ordinary is changed or submerged with the extraordinary.[117] If one were to apply this notion to the three examples with the stargazers it can be said that their wonderment grew out of quite ordinary circumstances. The night sky is not unfamiliar to them nor are shooting stars or meteors. In the case of the students it is plausible to presume that this is, in part, the reason why their night out under the stars until 5:00 a.m. was fairly mundane. After 5:00 a.m. things changed, and with the sudden rise in the frequency of incoming meteors the extraordinary found its way on to the scene. Ultimately it overwhelmed the students and wonder as a special attitude arose. Evans explains further that wonder is of a curious intensified nature. What induces it can be unexpected, hard to comprehend, but nevertheless we attach significance to it and seek to understand it.[118] Mirrored against the case of the meteor-seeking students this highlights the significance of the sentence: "the students simply stood and gazed in wonder." The same goes for the case of Gleaves and Clemmer, who describe themselves as gaping in wonder at the intense meteor shower. To either gaze or gape in wonder does not mean that one has given up the enterprise of obtaining knowledge or to reach understanding. It is an intense experience which underlines that one knows and understands so very little about the object at hand and its relation to the rest of the world.[119] If a student was to stand and gaze in wonder at an extraordinary shower of meteors she would only do so if she had cultivated a particular attitude that appreciates the grandeur of the world and human existence, and that we human beings are, to use a biblical term, looking at the world through a glass darkly. From such an attitude a disposition to wonder may spring understood as a willingness to be open to it and not to shun, dismiss, downgrade, or otherwise fear it as a state of mind. In other words, to have an attitude to wonder is to become willing to suspend at least for a while what we take for granted, get in wonder's way, allow it into our lives and through it take an extra look at the ordinary.

We have come far enough now to see that it is possible to view wonder as an emotion and even an epistemic one but to claim that wonder is exclusively an emotion is an overstatement. Wonder is best viewed as multifaceted and there are at least four possible avenues one could explore in order to paint wonder on a broader canvas. In addition to classifying wonder as an emotion, or, more specifically, an epistemic emotion, wonder could be looked upon as a mood, a value, and an attitude, and even though these candidates were only explored briefly they sufficiently flag the importance of keeping an open mind when it comes to depicting wonder. In all likelihood wonder is more than one thing. With the notion of wonder being multifaceted in mind, let us now take a closer look at the role of imagination in wonder in order to continue our exploration of this peculiar state of mind.

NOTES

1. Plato, *Theaetetus*. trans. H. N. Fowler (Cambridge: Harvard University Press, 1989), 155 C-D.
2. William Shakespeare "Hamlet," in *Tragedies*, Vol. 1, (Everyman's Library, 1992), I. i. 40–50.
3. According to Fred Nadis, Katterfelto was one of the first wonder showmen to operate in London during the eighteenth century, however, some of the greatest wonder shows took place in nineteenth-century America. Wonder showmen worked on the knife-edge between science and magic utilizing wonder to help their audience suspend belief. They strengthen their position by addressing scientific and technological advances in magical terms and by using scientific language to flag fragments of a magical worldview. Among the more notable wonder showmen in America are Nicola Tesla, who marvelled people by sending a million volts of alternating current through his body and suddenly burst into flames on stage, and Harry Houdini, also known as the Handcuff King, who amazed the crowds by escaping from leg irons and handcuffs. See Fred Nadis, *Wonder Shows, Performing Science, Magic and Religion in America* (New Brunswick, NJ: Rutgers University Press, 2005), 14, 70, 123.
4. Katterfelto's show was essentially a performance that mixed magic and science and addressed topics such as "the powers of the four elements" or the mechanism behind "thunder, lightning, earthquakes and different winds." Ibid., 3. In addition, Katterfelto's shows would include everything from the exhibition of a solar microscope "that projected enlarged images of the 'insects' he insisted caused the influenza then devastating Londoners [to the sudden appearance of black cats called the Doctor's Devils that at different moments] would lose and gain tails and emit electrical sparks." Ibid.
5. Eric Crosby, "An Aesthetic of Wonderment: IMAX and Affect" in *Journal of Moving Image Studies*, 6, 2007, 1–2.
6. Quoted in Howard Parsons, "A Philosophy of Wonder" in *Philosophy and Phenomenological Research* 30(1), 1969, 88.
7. Leonid MAC is short for Leonid Multi-Instrument Aircraft Campaign and is led by the SETI Institute, Aerospace Corporation, and NASA Ames Research Center. One of the activities of Leonid MAC involves collecting witness reports on the 1966 Leonid meteor shower. More information can be found at http://leonid.arc.nasa.gov/index.html
8. Robert Gleaves, "The Perfect Storm" (Nov. 19, 2002) in *Leonid MAC, NASA* Available from: https://leonid.arc.nasa.gov/1966-gleaves.txt. [Accessed Sept. 19, 2018].
9. Pam Clemmer, "Toto, We're Not in Kansas Anymore" (Nov. 18, 1998), in *Leonid MAC, NASA*. Available from: https://leonid.arc.nasa.gov/1966clemmer.txt [Accessed Sept. 19, 2018]. The opening line "It wasn't a dark and stormy night" seems somewhat odd but it may not necessarily be without a deeper meaning. This becomes clear upon realising it could be a twist on the famous atmospheric phrase "It was a dark and stormy night" featuring in the opening sequence of English novelist Edward Bulwer-Lytton's 1830 suspense novel *Paul Clifford*. See Edward Bulwer Lytton, *Paul Clifford* (Whitefish, MT: Kessinger Publishing, 2010), 13. Stipulating that it was *not* a dark and stormy night could be Clemmer's way of telegraphing that she was not "emotionally charged" prior to her extraordinary experience, which adds credibility to her report. Speculating along the same lines her particular formulation could alternatively be an attempt to flag that her report is concerned with an experience of a particular kind of wonder, i.e. natural wonder, because the phrase "It wasn't a dark and stormy night" could be a tribute to Rachel Carson (an important exponent of the wonder of nature) who opens her famous *The Sense of Wonder* with "one stormy autumn night when my nephew Roger was about twenty months old I wrapped him in a blanket and carried him down to the beach in the rainy darkness." See Rachel Carson, *The Sense of Wonder* (New York: HarperCollins, 1984), 8. If indeed this is the case the formulation adds

credibility to her report because to evoke the notion of natural wonder in relation to something as extraordinary as the 1966 meteor shower seems perfectly appropriate.

10. This particular expression finds support. Recall that my daughter's mouth gaped when she encountered the duck-rabbit for the first time and that it is possible to view le Brun's depiction of astonishment in combination with admiration and Darwin's description of surprise and astonishment as the expression of wonder. See John Onians, "'I . . . Wonder': A Short History of Amazement" in *Sight & Insight: Essays on Art and Culture in Honour of E. H. Gombrich at 85*, ed. John Onians (London: Phaidon Press Limited, 1994), 17; Ann Sutherland Harris, *Seventeenth-Century Art and Architecture* (London: Laurence King Publishing, 2004), 307; Lorraine Daston and Katharine Park, *Wonders and the Order of Nature* (New York: Zone Books, 1998), 319; and Charles Darwin, *The Expression of Emotions in Man and Animals*, (New York: HarperCollins, 1999), XII.

11. What this means is that emotions are thought to have functions, i.e., they facilitate adaptation and contribute ultimately to our survival. Ibid., 365. According to Fuller the function of wonder as an emotion in an evolutionary aspect is that it leads to "sustained attention to one's surroundings." Ibid., 11.

12. Ibid., 365.
13. Ibid., 384.
14. Plato, *Theaetetus*, 155d.
15. Rene Descartes, "The Passions of the Soul" in *The Philosophical Works of Descartes*, vol. 1, trans., Elisabeth S. Haldane and G. R. T. Ross (Cambridge: Cambridge University Press, 1986), LIII.
16. James Vincent Cunningham, *Woe or Wonder: The Emotional Effect of Shakespearean Tragedy* (Swallow Paperbooks, 1964), 20–21.
17. See Jesse Prinz, "How Wonder Works" in *Aeon Magazine*, 2012.
18. Ibid.
19. Dennis Quinn, *Iris Exiled: A Synoptic History of Wonder* (Lanham, MD:University Press of America, 2002), xii, 11.
20. Ibid., 17–18.
21. See Sophia Vasalou, "Introduction" in *Practices of Wonder: Cross-Disciplinary Perspectives* (Eugene, OR: Pickwick Publications, 2012), 2.
22. Marguerite La Caze, *Wonder and Generosity: Their Role in Ethics and Politics* (New York: SUNY Press, 2013), 1.
23. Ibid.
24. Martha Nussbaum, *Upheavals of Thought*, 8th ed. (Cambridge, UK: Cambridge University Press, 2008), 54.
25. Ibid., 55.
26. Fuller, "Wonder and the Religious," 384.
27. Nussbaum, *Upheavals of Thought*, 54.
28. Celia Deane-Drummond, *Wonder and Wisdom* (London: Darton, Longman and Todd Ltd.), 2006, 1.
29. Ibid., 152.
30. Paul R. Fleischman, *Wonder* (Amhesrt, MA: Small Batch Books, 2013), 109.
31. Ibid., 14.
32. Ibid., 150.
33. Quinn, *Iris Exiled*, 11.
34. Nussbaum, *Upheavals of Thought*, 1.
35. Ibid.
36. Ibid.
37. Ian Hacking, *The Social Construction of What?* (Cambridge: Harvard University Press, 2001), 18.
38. Robert C. Solomon, *True to Our Feelings* (Oxford: University Press, 2007), 257–58.
39. Vivien Burr, *Social Constructionism* (London:Routledge, 2003), 48.
40. Catherine Lutz, *Unnatural Emotions* (University of Chicago Press, 1998), 12.
41. Ibid., 121.

42. See Solomon, *True to Our Feelings*, 258.
43. See Rom Harre, "An Outline of the Social Constructionist Viewpoint" in *The Social Construction of Emotions*, ed. Rom Harre (Oxford: Basil Blackwell Ltd., 1988), 10.
44. H. Morsbach and W. J. Tyler, "A Japanese Emotion: Amae" in *The Social Constructions of Emotions*, ed. Rom Harre (Oxford: Basil Blackwell Ltd., 1988), 290.
45. See Aristotle, *On the Soul, Parva Naturalia. On Breath*, trans. W. S. Hett (Cambridge: Harvard University Press, 1957). Aristotle develops his view of emotions in the *Art of Rhetoric* where he focuses on emotions such as pity, anger, and fear so one might learn how to manipulate them in one's audience. See Aristotle, *The Art of Rhetoric*, trans. J. H. Freese (Cambridge: Harvard University Press, 1926). Likewise in the *Nicomachean Ethics*, Aristotle works on emotions and particularly "anger" and the notion of having the correct emotions as a part of being virtuous. See Aristotle, *Nichomachean Ethics*, trans. H. Rackham (Cambridge: Harvard University Press, 2003).
46. Peter Goldie, *The Emotions* (Oxford: Oxford University Press, 2000), 87.
47. Richard. A. Shweder and Jonathan Haidt, "The Cultural Psychology of the Emotions: Ancient and New" in *Handbook of Emotions*, 2nd edition, ed. Michael Lewis and Jeanette M. Haviland-Jones (New York: The Guilford Press, 2000), 399.
48. James Russell, "Culture and the Categorization of Emotions," *Psychology Bulletin*, vol. 110, (American Psychology Association, 1991), 426.
49. Cicero, *Tusculan Disputations*, trans. J. E. King (Cambridge: Harvard University Press, 2001), IV, 13–15.
50. Descartes, "The Passion of the Soul," 362.
51. Baruch Spinoza, *Ethics*, trans. R. Elwes (London: J. M. Dent, 1989), III, prob. 59.
52. Thomas Hobbes, *Leviathan*, ed. R. Tuck (Cambridge: Cambridge University Press, 1992), I, ch. 6.
53. Charles Darwin, *The Expression of Emotions*, VII-XIII.
54. Robert Plutchik, *Emotions and Life: Perspectives from Psychology, Biology and Evolution* (American Psychological Association, Washington, DC, 2003), 73.
55. Ibid.
56. Fuller, *Wonder*, 21.
57. Ibid.
58. Robert C. Solomon, "Back to Basics: On the Very Idea of 'Basic Emotions'" in *Journal for the Theory of Social Behaviour*, 32 (2), 2002, 115.
59. Fuller, *Wonder*, 26–27.
60. See Ulric Neisser, *Cognitive Psychology* (London: Psychology Press, 2014).
61. John Deigh, "Concepts of Emotion in Modern Philosophy and Psychology" in *The Oxford Handbook of Philosophy of Emotion*, ed. Peter Goldie (Oxford: Oxford University Press, 2010), 17.
62. William James, "What is an Emotion?" in *Mind*, 9(34), 1884, 190.
63. See Deigh, "Concepts of Emotions," 26.
64. Matthew Ratcliffe, "William James on Emotion and Intentionality" in *International Journal of Philosophical Studies*, 13 (2), 2005, 179.
65. The term is derived from the Greek god Apollo who, as Sam Keen puts it, "incarnates the ideals we associate with Classical Greek thought [and he represents] ego, light, youth, purity, reasonableness, order, discipline, and balance." See Sam Keen *Apology for Wonder* (New York: Harper and Row, 1969), 152.
66. Keen explains that the term derives from the ancient Greek god Dionysus who is god of fertility and resembles the energy of nature. The Greeks associated him with wine, metamorphosis, and worshipping Dionysus was an enthusiastic enterprise involving "ecstasy, license, revelry, and direct participation, by eating, in the life of the dying and reborn god. In the ecstasy induced by wine and dancing the worshippers lost their own personalities and were merged with Dionysus. Thus the boundaries separating man, nature, and the divine were erased." See Keen, *Apology for Wonder*, 154.
67. Nussbaum, *Upheavals of Thought*, 16.

68. Interested parties can read more about Blackburn's criticism of the cognitive approach in his book *Ruling Passions* (Oxford University Press, 1998) and the article "Précis of Ruling Passions" in *Philosophy and Phenomenological Research, LXV*(1), 2002, 122–35.

69. Aaron Ben-Ze'ev, "The Thing Called Emotion" in *The Oxford Handbook of Philosophy of Emotion*, ed. Peter Goldie (Oxford: Oxford University Press, 2010), 61.

70. Ibid., 42–44.
71. Ibid., 42.
72. Ibid., 45.
73. Ibid.
74. Ibid.
75. Ibid., 46.
76. Ibid.
77. Ibid.
78. Christopher Gullo, *In all Sincerity . . . Peter Cushing* (Bloomington, IN: Xlibris, 2004), 203.
79. Ben-Ze'ev, "Thing Called Emotion," 47.
80. Ibid.
81. Ibid., 49.
82. Ibid., 48.
83. Ibid., 47.
84. Ibid., 48.
85. Ibid.
86. bid.
87. Ibid., 50–51.
88. Ibid., 52.
89. Ibid., 53.
90. Ibid. For a closer look at Aristotle's view of the matter see Aristotle, *Nicomachean Ethics*, op. cit., V. ix. 4–7.
91. Ben-Ze'ev, op. cit., 54.
92. Ibid., 61.
93. Adam Morton, "Epistemic Emotions," in *The Oxford Handbook of Philosophy of Emotion*, ed. Peter Goldie (Oxford: Oxford University Press, 2010), 389.
94. Ibid., 386.
95. Ibid.
96. Ibid.
97. Ibid., 387.
98. Ibid., 388.
99. Ibid.
100. Ibid.
101. Ibid.
102. Ibid.
103. Ibid., 386.
104. Ibid., 389.
105. Ibid.
106. Ibid., 391.
107. Ibid., 394.
108. Ibid., 396.
109. Ibid., 394.
110. Ben-Ze'ev, "Thing Called Emotion," 55.
111. Parsons, "Philosophy of Wonder," 84–85.
112. Ibid., 85.
113. Ibid., 85–86.
114. Ibid., 100.
115. Ibid., 101.

116. H. Martyn Evans, "Wonder and the Clinical Encounter" in *Theoretical Medicine and Bioethics*, 33(2), 2012, 128.

117. Ibid.

118. Ibid.

119. Wonder in relation to ignorance is not a novel notion. In Plato's *Theaetetus*, a dialogue on the nature of knowledge, the character Theaetetus confesses that he remains ignorant about the nature of knowledge and that it has produced in him a sense of wonder. See Plato, *Theaetetus*, 155 C-D.

THREE
Wonder and Imagination

Imagination serves as an important component in the experience of wonder. It is what animates it, makes it intense, and sometimes a conveyer of what is universally important and true. Thanks to the workings of the imagination in wonderment, we see the world anew when we wonder, which may have a positive impact on our flourishing. Unfortunately, it is also what makes wonder "dangerous" and potentially a hazard to our flourishing, because it is owing to the activity of the imagination in wonder that we sometimes wonder inappropriately.

The incitement to pay attention to imagination in connection with wonder mounts from what has been explored so far. The case of de Pasquale reminds us of our wonder-filled ability to envision our own mortality and its significance. The survey of the etymology of wonder indicated that wonder has something to do with visualization or the imaginings of the mind's eye and how we come to understand or know things. From our dealings with the history of wonder we are encouraged to think that there is a connection between wonder and imagination. Augustine, for example, reminds us that our ability to call up sights such as mountains and rivers from memory within ourselves is a wonder-filled feature of our nature. The connection between wonder and imagination is also expressed in the contemporary philosophy of wonder. Fuller thinks that "wonder excites our ontological imaginings in ways that enhance our capacity to seek deeper patterns in the universe,"[1] which points to the idea that in wonder we put before ourselves depictions of how the world fundamentally is. Furthermore, he thinks that experiences of wonder can change perception, are morally helpful and may inspire us to become true individuals and true cosmopolitans.[2] Hove believes wonder reveals things in a new perspective (which hints that we put something new before our mind's eye) and makes us mindful of the inherent worth of others and that a deep level of wonder helps us become aware of fundamental features of our condition such as our vulnerability.[3] To better understand the role of imagination in wonder, how wonder can change perception or help us gain perspective, how wonder can enhance our moral scope, and in what capacity it is possible to say that a person who entertains a vivid imagination also harbors a deep sense of wonder; it is important to cast some light on what imagining or imagination means.

An investigation into how imagination is a part of the wonder-filled experience can also be grounded in the notion that it follows naturally from how wonder has been presented so far. In the introduction "wonder" was defined as a sudden experience that intensifies the cognitive focus and awareness of ignorance about a given object. This definition communicates an idea of wonder that is flexible and does not pigeonhole wonder or narrow it down to be, for example, exclusively a passion or emotion. The definition is inclusive and supports the idea that wonder can also be classified as an attitude or a virtue. In wonder there is a gathering of attention; a sharpening of the focus, and the realization that one is ignorant about the object of one's wonderment. These are all qualities of the wonder-filled experience that are supported by other scholars of wonder such as philosopher Sophia Vasalou, who speaks of wonder as "attention arresting";[4] it links to Fisher's work as he defines wonder as "a sudden experience of an extraordinary object that produces delight";[5] and the definition pays homage to Miller's emphasis on the notion that "were there no given, wonder could never spring on us its unpredictable surprise, would never be able to sneak up and startle us into realizing that we do not know what lies right here in front of us."[6] My definition of wonder claims no originality but it is useful as it allows further investigation into wonder and, in particular, in relation to imagination. To elaborate one might start with pointing out that just because one is experiencing wonder as something sudden, arresting, attention gathering, and as something that produces awareness of one's ignorance about a given object, does not mean that one's mind has come to a complete standstill. If this were indeed so, the state of the mind in question would be more attuned to that of astonishment perhaps. It is true that an experience of wonder can be astonishing but in the pure or distilled case it is perfectly possible to depict wonder as an experience that springs solely from the initial inability of the mind to produce satisfying cognitive schemata, that is, to come up with depictions of the perceived object of wonder that would make sense to the wonderer and integrate with her knowledge and understanding about the order of things without introducing problems or dissonance. The idea is that when a person is wonderstruck, she actively seeks to understand and attach meaning to what is perceived but does so without completely succeeding. Such a process is highly imaginative but for this notion to be worth its salt we must establish a clearer idea of what is actually meant when we use the word "imagination."

THE RANGE AND SCOPE OF IMAGINATION

According to philosopher Eva T. Brann the word "imagination," connecting with the word "image," entered the European vocabulary via Augustine in the fifth century AD[7] and derives from the use of the Latin term "imaginatio,"[8] "imaginem," or "imago."[9] Furthermore, and to paraphrase Brann, we might say that imagination is associated with the Latin word "imitatio," indicating that imagination has a mirroring or copying aspect.[10]

The topic of imagination is complex and difficult to approach, which rests on the fact that it covers a vast territory.[11] This is supported by Brann's magnum opus *The World of the Imagination*, which, despite its impressive handling of the history of imagination, is selective in its coverage and does not consider aspects of imagination, such as hallucinogenic imagery or non-visual image-formation.[12]

Furthermore, the topic of imagination cannot be allocated exclusively to a particular field or discipline. Imagination is important to philosophy where it plays a part in ideas about perception. This is noticeable in the works of philosopher David Hume, where the imagination is considered the power that enables our minds to repeat ideas before itself.[13] Imagination also plays a role in philosophical ideas about personal identity and in this regard Warnock states that imagination aids us "in making sense of, or interpret, the past."[14] Furthermore, imagination is important to the philosophy of education, and philosopher Ron Norman informs us that this is so because imagination helps us transcend conventional thinking.[15]

Imagination is also important in the field of psychology, where it plays a part in relation to having imagery. This becomes clear if we look to the phenomenon of hypnagogic imagery, which refers to the images acknowledged by a person transitioning between being asleep and being awake.[16] Imagination is likewise important with regards to dreams where McGinn argues that dreams are made of images.[17] Within psychology pretend play also involves the imagination, and according to psychologist Paul L. Harris to engage in pretend play "offers a way to imagine, explore and talk about possibilities inherent in reality."[18]

Imagination is likewise crucial to the production and apprehension of works of art.[19] In this respect we might say it took the imaginary power of nineteenth-century illustrator Gustave Dore to depict the scenes from Dante's *The Divine Comedy*, because the surroundings in which we find Dante have an air of otherworldliness that have very little resemblance if any to our ordinary world.[20]

Furthermore, imagination is important to the field of religion. In this regard McMullen points out that the idea of image is significant to all of the monotheistic religions in the sense that the supreme deity cannot be imagined.[21] Philosopher Aaron Hughes suggests, "the imagination is responsible for translating the incorporeal divine world into corporeal, material images."[22] In this sense the imagination plays a part in what we might call the mystical experience of the divine.

To complicate matters, there is a trend in the literature to qualify imagination with another word in order to narrow down the kind of imagination in question. To give an example let us focus on historian Robert Muchembled's idea of "collective imagination,"[23] and that the devil as we know him in the West is a product of such. To Muchembled, our current idea of the devil is the synthesis of simple rumors, folklore, literature, paintings, religion, politics, and films, which we may group as "hidden players" that generate explanatory systems which in turn motivate individual as well as group behavior.[24] In this sense our conception of the devil is contextual or socially constructed, meaning that he owes his "solidification" to cultural forces. In support of this view stands the fact that conceptions of the devil change over time and that "older versions" in all likelihood would seem ridiculous to people living a modern life. This becomes apparent when we consider the devil-sightings of medieval monk Raoul Glauber, who describes him as a small, scrawny manikin in dirty clothing,[25] and the depiction of the archfiend given in Dante's *The Divine Comedy*, where he is presented as a three-faced, sinner-devouring giant with batwings.[26] By contrast, we may acknowledge the depiction of the devil by English poet John Milton, where he is not so much described as beastly and inhuman, but takes the form of a beautiful fallen angel with a rebellious streak, not far removed from the heroic and iconoclastic intellectual. Likewise, we would perhaps more readily accept variations on Milton's Satan like the one we find in Taylor Hackford's 1997 film *The Devil's Advocate*, where the devil takes the form of a shrewd and exploitive male manager of a New York law firm ("curiously" named Milton).[27] Now we might agree or disagree with Muchembled's view of the devil as a product of our collective imagination, but regardless of which stand we take we can appreciate the rationale behind affixing the word "collective" in order to fine-tune the quality of imagination depending on the nature of inquiry.

Imagination is difficult to grasp because the range and scope of the subject is vast and connects with a multitude of different fields of inquiry such as philosophy, psychology, art, and religion. Imagination comes across as an individual cognitive capacity or quality that is involved in matters such as perception, personal identity, and the ability to transcend conventional thinking. Likewise, it plays a part in generating images and enables, for example, pretend play and the production and apprehension of works of art. The subject of imagination is further complicated by the fact that one might encounter "imagination" combined with another word indicating a particular kind of imagination. In this respect we looked at Muchembled's "collected imagination," which enriches our conception of imagination by pointing out that imagination is not merely an individual capacity or quality but can also be seen as a mass phenomenon that can give life to particular ideas or imaginings such as the devil.

Our engagement with imagination so far has provided us with a somewhat broad understanding of the subject, but to take this further and build a richer conception of imagination that can help us understand the role of imagination in wonder let us now turn to examine Warnock's Romantic approach to imagination.

MARY WARNOCK AND IMAGINATION

Warnock's Romantic approach to imagination, including her views on imagination in relation to education, has been developed over the course of three books: *Imagination*, from 1996, her 1992 book *The Uses of Philosophy*, and *Imagination and Time* published in 1994.

Her approach is perhaps not so much an original position as a positive appraisal of a particular view of the imagination, namely the Romantic. Warnock thinks we ought to take the Romantic perspective on imagination seriously because even though it is not the only available view on the subject she thinks it impossible to grasp what imagination truly is without at least trying to understand the Romantic version.[28]

To begin to articulate Warnock's approach in more detail let us look at the concluding remarks of her book *Imagination* where she states that imagination is:

> A power in the human mind which is at work in our everyday perception of the world, and is also at work in our thoughts about what is absent; which enables us to see the world, whether present or absent as significant, and also to present this version to others, for them to share or reject. And this power, though it gives us "thought-imbued" perception [. . .] is not only intellectual. Its impetus comes from the emotions as much as from the reason, from the heart as much as from the head.[29]

According to Warnock, imagination is a quality of the mind that not only influences our everyday perception of the world but also how we perceive the world in the absence of things. The latter point is important because the ability to perceive absent things is what enables a person to hold before her mind's eye a vision of the world that contains, for example, her family and friends living far away and attach importance to them, despite the fact that they are out of her sensory reach. Warnock furthermore insists that imagination is fuelled not merely by our intellect understood as our capacity for reason, but also our capacity for having emotions. This makes sense because our ability to put before the mind's eye visions of absent relatives and friends might also encompass or even be fuelled by the feelings we have toward such people including, for example, that we long to be with them. To Warnock the Romantic approach to imagination is true because we all have the capacity to transcend what is immediately in front of us. Our use of language supports this because when we describe and classify things we look beyond what is immediately present. We relate the present to the past and to the future. We relate the present to past experiences and what we expect to experience again.[30]

Warnock goes on to stress the necessity of imagination, as it is responsible for the application of thoughts or concepts to things. Without such application we would not have human discourse nor would goal-directed activity be impossible and we would not be able to see into what she calls the life of things.[31]

To better comprehend what Warnock has in mind it would be helpful to take a closer look at the Romantics and their outlook and one way of doing that is to begin by rehearsing some of the pivotal points of the philosophy of transcendental idealists,[32] such as Kant and reactionaries to Kantian philosophy including philosopher Friedrich Schelling, who we might say in part inspired the Romantic outlook. Kant divided the world into the "world for us" and the "world in itself," insisting that we do not have access to the latter and that it would forever be beyond our reach and that we are situated in a world of appearances.[33] Now in Warnock's view this particular notion became the center of gravity for post-Kantians such as Schelling, who rebelled against the Kantian division between the world in itself and the world for us by insisting that:

> There are not two kinds of stuff in the world, mind-stuff and matter-stuff: there is only one. The Kantian mystery of the thing-in-it-self, lying behind the phenomena which we perceive and reduce to law-abiding order in the world, has been moved by the simple expedient of denying that there is any such mystery. What we order by means of the categories of our understanding is not mere appearances, it *is* the things themselves. For the things are also our own ideas. And therefore it can be said that the categories or rules of the mind do more than order; they create.[34]

In this light the imagination has a "world-creating function," which is tied up not only with creativity but also in some sense with truth because in that view there is nothing beyond what we perceive.

The notion of the imagination as "world-creating" is important to the further development of the Romantic conception of imagination advocated especially by Coleridge. According to Warnock, Coleridge's travels in Germany made him aware of the thoughts of imagination expressed above and he sought to include them in his own approach to imagination.[35] The influence of German philosophy on Coleridge becomes clear by reading his 1802 poem *Dejection: an Ode*. The poem speaks of the loss of the shaping spirit of imagination and the joy that comes with using the imagination. Without the joy, Warnock writes, we only see, and even though we may see things that qualify as beautiful we do so without feeling that they are so.[36] Warnock explains that joy according to Coleridge is synonymous with the soul or, to put it differently, the inner power that animates us—which gives us life. Joy transforms perception into feeling, and it is precisely that which is lost in the loss of the shaping power of imagination.[37]

From this Warnock distills that the Romantic position on imagination initially has two functions, which by means of some inner power allow us to shape and feel.[38] Feelings and indeed emotions are important to the Romantic conception of imagination because they link the person experiencing them with what is universal.[39] According to Warnock, Coleridge writes:

> On Friday night 8th February 1805 my feeling, in sleep, of exceeding great love for my infant seen by me in the dream, yet so that it might be Sara, Derwent or Berkeley, and *still it was an individual babe and mine*. Of love in sleep—a sort of *universal-in-particularness* of Form seems necessary—*vide* the note preceding, and my lines "All look or Likeness caught from Earth, All accident of Kind or Birth, Had passed away: there seemed no trace of Aught upon the brighten'd face Upraised beneath the rifted stone, Save of one Spirit, all her own. She, she herself and only She, shone in her body visible." This abstract self is indeed in its nature a Universal personified ... will not this prove it (sc. Love) to be a deeper feeling, and with such intimate affinity with ideas, so to modify them and become one with them, whereas the appetites and the feelings of revenge and anger coexist with the ideas, not combine with them; and alter the apparent effect of the forms, not the forms themselves. Certain modifications of fear seem to approach nearest to this love-sense in its manner of acting.[40]

Warnock's interpretation of this rather obscure passage goes as follows:

> Here Coleridge [says] two things. First, that if, in the absence of a real object, one has a very vivid image of it (a Form) then there is a necessary connection between feeling love for it (or fear of it) and seeing the form as somehow standing for a universal or general thing, as well as the particular thing of which it is the form or image. Secondly he suggests that love and some sorts of fear are the *only* emotions which have this universalizing power. Which make us feel, that is, that the image before us has a general significance beyond itself, though still retaining its particular character.[41]

Warnock condenses her interpretation into three elements, which makes up what she calls the combining power of the imagination. The combining power of the imagination connects the power to conjure up an image with the ability to see the image as universally significant and the power to bring forth deep feelings in us in the presence of the image.[42]

When addressing the Romantic conception of the imagination it is important to consider the more "systematic" writings on imagination from Coleridge's *Biographia Literaria*. In this work Coleridge divides imagination into two kinds: the primary and the secondary imagination. Coleridge writes:

> The primary imagination I hold to be the living power and prime agent of all human perception and as a repetition on the finite mind of the eternal act of creation in the infinite I AM. The secondary I consider as an echo of the former, coexisting with the conscious will, yet still as identical with the primary in the *kind* of its agency, and differing only in degree and in the mode of its operation. It dissolves, diffuses, dissipates, in order to recreate; or where this process is rendered impossible, yet still at all events it struggles to idealise and unify. It is essentially vital, even as all objects (as objects) are essentially fixed and dead.[43]

Warnock informs us that Coleridge's idea of primary imagination mirrors the philosophy of both Kant and Schelling. When it comes to speaking about the imagination as a function and its role in perception and knowledge of the world, we are clearly in the territory of Kant because this theme is central to his *Critique of Pure Reason*.[44] Things begin to deviate from Kant's outlook and toward that of Schelling when Coleridge begins to address creativity, but according to Warnock it is unclear to what extent Coleridge embraces the outlook of Schelling. She acknowledges that he is not fully committed to idealism because the labors of actual creation ascribed to the deity and human imagination are simply a repetition of divine activity. Thus, she thinks that there is no clear answer to the question about whether Coleridge thought that imagination creates the world or not.[45]

Moving on to Coleridge's secondary imagination, it is Warnock's view that it originates in the writings of Schelling and his notion of the poetic faculty.[46] In Warnock's view the activity of Coleridge's secondary imagination is the re-creation of something out of that which we initially acquired from perception,[47] and it is here that we find room for the artist—the poet as someone special who has the ability to consciously make use of her special ability that is her particular fine tuned imagination to tie things together or shape things into one in a work of art such as a poem.

Warnock's work on the imagination signals not merely that it is important to take the Romantic conception of imagination seriously but also that educating the imagination is worthy of our attention, which in light of her view would entail an education not merely for intelligence but also for feelings.[48] It is important to Warnock that we develop a sense that there is more to our experiences than we think and that we try to understand these very experiences. Without it she claims we will simply experience human life as futile, pointless, and boring.[49]

The importance of educating the imagination and the view of it as a ward against ennui is also promoted in the chapter entitled "Educating for Pleasure" in her book *The Uses of Philosophy*. Here Warnock argues that using the imagination is pleasurable because it deals with the possible as well as the actual, the underlying as well as the superficial, or the obvious.[50] Additionally, Warnock writes that the imagination is the faculty that allows us to think of things, which are not there. It is the faculty that enables us to plan for the future—it is the faculty that "makes us feel that there exists an infinity of possibilities [or that] we shall never come to an end of that which we are interested in."[51]

In her book *Imagination and Time* Warnock likewise puts forth the importance of educating the imagination. She writes:

> If we can educate a child's imagination, we will give him a place in time. We will allow him to stretch his sense of the present back to the past, both his own individual past, and the past of the world as a whole. But we shall also free him to contemplate his future, his own, and that of the world.[52]

In this citation Warnock stresses the importance of educating the imagination because it will set a person free and give her a sense of context and an idea of who she is, what she has been, and how she might develop further. To put it differently, we might say that having a sense of past, present, and future is essential to sporting a personal identity or entertaining a sense of continuity in one's life. If one did not have the ability to put before the mind's eye these temporal aspects of life, it might well be said that one would never rise above the level of the wanton who unconsciously and without her say is pushed around by a variety of factors such as personal appetites, the will or actions of other people, and trends instigated by and promoted by society.

To recapitulate the gravitational points of Warnock's approach to imagination we can say that, according to Warnock, imagination: (1) plays a role in our everyday perception of the world and absent things; (2) is fuelled by our rationality and our emotions; (3) is universal because we all have the capacity to go beyond what is in front of us; (4) makes it possible to apply thought and concepts to things and "see into the life of things" meaning, that when we use it, we participate in creating the world we partake in; (5) has a combining power that enables us to put before our mind's eye an image, see it as universally significant, and entertain deep feelings in the presence of it; (6) must be educated and not merely for the intelligence but also feelings; and (7) is pleasurable because it deals with the possible as well as the actual, meaning that it enables us to grasp past, present, and future and thus sets us free to form a conception of context and to build our own personal identity.

Warnock's view of imagination broadens our understanding of the subject and, in this light, let us now turn to the role of imagination in wonder.

The first aspect of Warnock's approach worthy of addressing is "imagination as animator" and its relation to wonder. Warnock proclaims that imagination is a power of the human mind that gives life to our everyday perception of the world and our thoughts about absent things. Additionally, it is what enables us to attach significance to what we perceive and (drawing on our rational as well as our emotional capacities) to communicate it. Now in light of this aspect of Warnock's approach to imagination, is it possible to elaborate on the notion of wonderment? I think the answer is yes because it is the activity of the imagination in wonder that enables us to perceive, communicate, and behold what is significant about a concrete object of wonder. To exemplify, we might recall Boyle's experience of wonder prompted by his encounter with a piece of luminous meat brought to him from the larder. First it is reasonable to suggest that Boyle, through the use of his imagination, perceived the object of wonder for what it was, that is, a piece of luminous meat. Second, it is reasonable to say that it was due to his active use of the imagination that he realized the uncommon quality of the object of wonder and thus attached significance to it. Third, we might say that because he had no prior experience of meat that glows in the dark, it would be natural for him to give thoughts to its nature and put before his mind's eye a variety of possible explanations or theories, and perhaps even thoughts on the consequences of there being such a thing as luminous meat in the world. In this sense it is the activity of imagination in wonder that makes our experience of wonder come alive. In wonder we actively use our imagination to seek a satisfying cognitive schema of what we experience but fail to obtain, such that the object of concern is never fully beheld or understood. This explains why an experience of wonder is "life-giving," invigorating, or otherwise intensely moving, because in wonder we are not only animated by the activity of the imagination but we are also animated by the realization that despite our imaginative efforts, a complete and satisfactory picture of the object of wonder simply does not arrive. In this light we can also say that wonder here distinguishes itself from Kant's dynamically sublime, because in wonder there is no feeling of superiority of the rational intellect's ability to harness nature. Instead we are left with an awareness of our ignorance. Now one could object by insisting that such realization is not life-giving at all but merely frustrating. However, it is also possible to experience the frustrating part as life-giving because although our lack of knowledge or understanding about the object of wonder may frustrate us, it also compels us to continue to broaden our knowledge or gain better understanding of the object in question.

The next aspect of Warnock's approach to imagination we should address is concerned with "the universality of imagination" and its relation to wonder. Warnock holds that we must recognize the universality of imagination as a function, that is, that imagination is connected to our rational as well as our emotional capacities; is exercised by everyone; a part of everyone's experience and should be educated. Warnock's position is interesting but one might have reservations as to what extent the imagination can be educated. Recall that Opdal is of the view that children have a capacity for wonder, which over time might turn into philosophical reflection.[53] Reading Opdal encourages us to think that wonder, like imagination, is universal and can be educated and thus we may ask if educating the imagination will help transform childish wonder into philosophical reflection. An argument for this view can be made because in order for philosophical reflection, which we may reasonably say involves the exercise of traditional academic virtues such as criticality, clarity, rigor, and richness of perspective in one's thinking to emerge something has to generate it, and a suitable candidate could very well be the imagination. This supposition is in line with Warnock's view of education and supports the view that educating the imagination may lead to wonderment equal to philosophical reflection. However, it might also be supposed that we do *not* all start with the same talent or capacity for imagination and wonder, and that it is *not* at all a given that everyone will emerge as highly imaginative and as wonderers of the philosophically reflective kind from a formal education. In this sense education is not merely a question of input/output and thus just because one is educated does not guarantee an elaborate ability to wonder and imagine. This signifies a crucial point in the philosophy of education where attitudes toward how we start out as human beings differ, but it is not our business to defend any of these attitudes here. However, it seems reasonable to think that although it cannot be guaranteed that education brings about an elaborate ability to wonder and imagine, it is safe to say that certain forms of education or training encourage the development of a sense of wonder and the use of imagination more than others. An education that is "wonder full" or an education that at least in part introduces the student to wonders, and the activity of wonder could prompt not only the development of particular skills, but could potentially also allow for the cultivation of the student in a way that heightens her imaginary power and deepens her sense of wonder.

Moving on, let us now consider "wonder as conveyer of the universal." In Warnock's view a core feature of the Romantic account of imagination is that it has a combining power that enables us to call up an image, attach universal significance to it while entertaining certain feelings in the presence of it. Warnock elaborates on the connection between imagination and the affective realm by highlighting Coleridge, who claims that there are only two universalizing emotions, namely fear and love which "makes us feel, that is, that the image before us has a general significance beyond itself, though still retaining its particular character."[54] Now, given that the imagination is active during an experience of wonder and that in wonder we deal with emotional upheaval mostly in the form of joy but in some cases perhaps in the form of something closer to fear,[55] we might be inclined to think that wonder can give rise to the idea that the object of wonder has a general significance beyond itself—that it is universally important. In support of such an inclination stands the case of de Pasquale. Through his experience of wonder de Pasquale confronted not just his own mortality but also human mortality, and thus his experience revealed not merely something important about himself but a general feature of what it is to be human.

To further support the idea that the experience of wonder can convey something generally significant beyond itself let us return to Rogers and Clemmer's wonder at the 1833 and 1966 Leonid meteor showers, respectively. Rogers labels the 1833 meteor shower the grandest and most beautiful sight he ever saw and Clemmer mentions that at first she was afraid because she did not understand what was going on, but then a sense of beauty of the scene took over and she just stood there watching the sky for thirty minutes or more. It can be argued that these examples convey something significant beyond itself, namely, that we live in a world of grandeur and beauty and that it is possible to perceive that from time to time.

Now as much as we might think that wonder can be a conveyer of the universal or general it is important not to get too carried away. Not all that wonder may reveal to the wonderer is universal and there is a danger in venturing too far in one's generalizations. To explore this further, let us now turn to the work on imagination by philosopher Ronald Hepburn.

RONALD HEPBURN AND IMAGINATION

Ronald Hepburn's contribution to the philosophy of imagination as presented here is based on his article "Landscape and the Metaphysical Imagination."

Hepburn opens his article by posing the question, "What is it to appreciate a landscape aesthetically?"[56] He then proposes three different levels of aesthetic landscape appreciation, of which the first is concerned with what he calls "purely sensory components," such as "colours, shapes, sounds, tactile sensations [and] smells [which rarely] if ever exists on its own."[57] In appreciating landscapes we take these components and "conceptualise, we recognise, we add context, background, seek out formal relationships—reflectively."[58] The first layer of appreciation is about taking raw sensory data and making some sort of meaning out of it. For example, in our appreciation of a distant mountain we may identify a patch of green corresponding to the grassland at the bottom of the mountain. In addition, we may identify a number of red dots on the steep mountain's walls as mountain climbers wearing red jackets, and the warm, prickly, soothing sensation we experience on our faces while perceiving these climbers as the burning effect of the sun shining bright in the sky.

A second layer reveals "expressive properties, and the thought of changes over time—even of drama."[59] A thin cascade of glittering white snow and ice coming down the mountainside could be thought of as a harbinger, warning us that an avalanche is imminent, and this endangers what otherwise would be a pristine and tranquil appreciation of a mountainous landscape.

A third and final layer may convey how the world fundamentally or ultimately is.[60] Flying over the icy wastes of Svalbard, Norway, might suggest to us that the world is fundamentally harsh and inhospitable, in contrast to our viewing of more temperate and cultivated landscapes from above, such as Oxfordshire in England. Alternatively, as Hepburn points out, a particular landscape may bring about an experience of nature as loaded with "poignant beauty [that] on some occasion seems to speak of a transcendent Source for which we lack words and clear concepts."[61] Hepburn's view in these last two instances is illustrative of what he calls "metaphysical imagination."[62] In other words, when we behold a particular landscape our metaphysical imagination may be exercised to the extent that:

> We see the landscape as ominous, cosmically ominous, or as revealing—concealing a still greater beauty than its own. In a word then, the many-levelled structure of aesthetic experience of nature can include great diversity of constituents: from the most particular—rocks, stones, leaves, clouds, shadows—to the most abstract and general ways we apprehend the world—the world as a whole.[63]

Hepburn elaborates by stating:

> Metaphysical imagination connects with, looks to, the "spelled out" systematic metaphysical theorising which is its support and ultimate justification. But also it is no less an element of the concrete present landscape-experience: it is fused with the sensory components, not meditation aroused by these.[64]

To Hepburn there are clearly different dimensions to appreciating a landscape aesthetically, and the metaphysical one allows for the apprehension of the world as a whole or the development of a conception of how the world is structured. In addition, Hepburn acknowledges that the metaphysical imagination is not merely a lofty add-on, signaling a hierarchical structure to the aesthetic appreciation of a given landscape. The metaphysical imagination is to be understood as an integrated part in the total appreciation of a landscape, drawing on both metaphysical theorizing about the ultimate structure of the world and the sensory components that landscape-experiences also consist of.[65]

Although Hepburn appreciates the metaphysical imagination he makes it clear that there is a danger of over-valuing it or yielding to its authority without question. In this respect he positions himself as a critic of Warnock's conception of imagination. Hepburn writes:

> While not unaware of its limitations, she [Warnock] accepts an essentially Romantic conception of imagination and its products as "in some sense" true. Imagination is "that by which, as far as we can, we see into the life of things"; or, it is "ability to see through objects . . . to what lies behind them." It is through the power of imagination that we have "intuition of the infinite and inexpressible significance of the ordinary world." These remarks, intriguing though they are, leave me uneasy, since they do seem to invite us to give metaphysical-religious imagination too much independent authority, and they carry a risk of losing from sight its ability to render equally vivid quite incompatible views of the world.[66]

To illustrate what Hepburn has in mind, imagine an astrophysicist and a theologian standing on a hill in the early morning hours observing the rising sun. As the light slowly but surely transforms the night sky into a pristine collage of light blue and pink and later transfigures the misty landscape below the hill into a sea of gold, the metaphysical imagination of the astrophysicist produces an experience of overwhelming beauty and a conviction of nature as utterly materialistic and devoid of divinity. The very same scene may also give rise to an experience of overwhelming beauty in the theologian, but unlike the astrophysicist, her metaphysical imagination informs her that the beauty of the sunrise is the handiwork of God and that her ability to recognize this very beauty confirms that she, as a human being, is created in the image of God. Now both claims are valid, vivid products of metaphysical imagination but they are also incompatible because, logically speaking, they contradict each other. To an onlooker, it must seem that only one of them can be true because either God exists or he does not.

The danger of becoming a victim of the illusory, the fantastic, or the fanciful, while engaging in metaphysical imaginings concerning the "true" structure of the universe is ever present. To establish a more sustainable vision of nature as it really is, additional support in favor of a particular revelation courtesy of the metaphysical imagination must be brought to light. If, for argument's sake, we were to support the theistic view expressed in the example above, Hepburn would say that in order to pledge our confidence in it we would at a minimum have to rely on "a background of sound theistic metaphysical argument and theory."[67] Bypassing such would, as Hepburn argues, render us incapable of making the leap from the noetic quality of our metaphysical imaginings to "noesis in the full sense—a knowledge-claim about how the world ultimately is."[68] Now to fully comprehend what Hepburn is talking about we have to understand what is meant by the word "noetic." According to the Institute of Noetic Sciences (IONS) noetic derives from the Greek word noēsis/noētikos, meaning inner wisdom, direct knowing, or subjective understanding.[69] Additionally philosopher and psychologist William James explains that when things have a noetic quality:

> It seems to those who experience them to be also a state of knowledge. They are states of insight into depths of truth unplumbed by the discursive intellect. They are illuminations, revelations, full of significance and importance, all inarticulate though they remain; and as a rule they carry with them a curious sense of authority for after-time.[70]

To experience something having a noetic quality is powerful but the authority of the experience does not go beyond the individual experiencing it. It simply does not cut it as a knowledge-claim and whatever authority the experience exercises over the person having it is confined to that person only. Returning to the example with the astrophysicist and the theologian I focused on the theologian and her claim that the sunrise is a sign of God's presence in the world, but let us now pay attention to the astrophysicist's materialistic view of the universe. For somebody to express surety about the notion that everything is essentially materialistic and devoid of spirit, let alone a divine one, demands further support if it is to pass as a knowledge-claim. If this cannot be provided the surety is undermined and the expressed view as it were is nothing more than a questionable personal belief.

To continue our exploration of Hepburn's approach to imagination let us now take a closer look at his idea of "layered imagination" and how that may relate to wonder. In Hepburn's view, when we appreciate a landscape aesthetically the imagination is at work on three different levels, the sensory, the expressive, and the metaphysical. Granted that Hepburn is right about this and that imagination has a role to play in wonderment we can say that the wondering or wonder-filled experience likewise is layered. Suppose we witness something wonderful like the Leonid meteor shower that Elder Samuel Rogers was so lucky to see in 1833. It could be argued that during what we may call first layer wonderment, the imagination is providing us sensory data, which enables us to begin appreciating the wonder before us or in this case above. The second layer of wonderment is concerned with revealing expressive properties of the object of wonder, and, in this case, it is fair to say that it reveals to us that the meteor shower is extraordinary and significant in light of its magnitude, rarity, and beauty. The third layer of wonderment is concerned with the metaphysical and so we may ask what could experiencing a wonderful event like the 1833 Leonid meteor shower possibly have on our current metaphysical outlook? One possibility is that the natural or materialistic world is grand and beautiful. Rogers knew about the natural phenomenon of meteor showers and he links his wonder to the grandeur and beauty of the event, which he struggles to describe. Another possibility is to link the event to a religious view. Rogers's biography mentions that some religious people saw the meteor shower as a sign that judgment day was near and that they dropped to their knees confessing their sins and prayed for mercy. Likewise, Rogers reports that some people conjectured that the event was the first in a series of fearful calamities that God would bestow upon them because he was displeased with them.[71] The layered approach to imagination advances our understanding of wonder because it helps us get closer to what we can agree upon when it comes to a shared experience of wonder. Whereas we might agree on, for example, the first two layers, we might not agree on the third layer, and thus we can say that the layered approach may help us flesh out individual interpretations of the wonderful, which qualifies as advancement. Likewise, it complicates Warnock's position in the sense that Hepburn's view prompts us to be mindful about what we, courtesy of the imagination, hold significant and especially about what we grant significance beyond itself.

Continuing in this same spirit, the next aspect of Hepburn's approach to imagination, important to the inquiry, is concerned with "imagination as conveyer of truth." Given that imagination has a role in wonderment, is it plausible to think that wonder gives us access to the truth of things? On the one hand, one could argue yes because there is a revelatory and noetic quality to wonder in the sense that it does make us aware of our ignorance and in some cases, like in those of de Pasquale and Castorp from Mann's *The Magic Mountain*, wonderment reveals something universal, that is, our mortality. On the other hand we must exercise great caution because just because one person judges her experience as a conveyer of truth it may not necessarily qualify as such. To elaborate let us return to Hepburn's view of imagination. A merit of Hepburn's work is that he notices and expands Warnock's Romantic view of imagination by highlighting the dangers involved with that position. For Hepburn, the key problem with Warnock's approach to imagination is that it might lead us to think that the use of imagination alone can lead to truth. According to Hepburn this is to venture too far because it seems to grant too much independent authority to the imagination, and especially imagination of the metaphysical-religious kind.[72] The danger with this sort of imagination is, as Hepburn writes that we easily overlook, "its ability to render equally vivid quite incompatible views of the world."[73] This is an important point because as Hepburn writes:

> If, for instance the theistic metaphysical imagination is to be taken as true, may we not also require, as a condition of our confidence in it, a background of sound theistic metaphysical argument and theory? Can anything less than that justify the move from noetic quality to noesis in the full sense—a knowledge-claim about how the world ultimately is?[74]

If a background of sound theistic metaphysical argument and theory cannot be provided, chances are that what is at play is but fancy and that the image we think of as truth revealing is but deceptive or false, or that our interpretations of it are one-sided or simply wrong. My grandfather was born in 1910 and during his lifetime the world saw its first jet engine and the first contrails (short for condensation trails) appear in the sky. One day he observed such a trail in the sky and while he beheld what he knew to be the sign of technological advancement and the promise of a more "airborne" future for human kind, he noticed two elderly ladies close by watching the contrails while excitedly folding their hands and loudly praising God for writing to them. To make sense of the view that the contrails were, in fact, the handwriting of God would demand a fair amount of theistic metaphysical argumentation evoking the idea that human beings are created in God's image and that, for instance, technological advancement is the manifestation of divine power or creativity. So Hepburn's suggestion about having noetic insight "cleared" up by further metaphysical argumentation seems good advice also when it comes to experiences of wonder. It prevents us from being led astray by wonderment and from becoming victims of unreflected interpretations.

Moving on let us now address what we may call the "commensurability" in Hepburn's outlook. It is a merit of that outlook that it ties in well with Fuller's idea that "wonder excites our ontological imaginings in ways that enhance our capacity to seek deeper patterns in the universe."[75] With Hepburn's explanation of metaphysical imagination we may arguably be better equipped to understand this particular capacity and some of its potential shortcomings: for instance, consider this quote from Fuller:

> A life shaped by wonder is thus more likely to steer a middle course between a purely secular life and a narrowly religious life. On the one hand wonder prompts us to diverge from a purely secular outlook on life. It entices us to entertain the possibility that our highest fulfillment might require adapting ourselves to a metaphysical reality. Yet, on the other hand, wonder encourages an open-ended or heuristic approach to life. It thus imbues personal spirituality with a fresh quality, making

it unlikely that we will reduce our basic belief in the existence of something "more" to narrow doctrines or creeds.[76]

Fuller's approach to wonder is a positive one, as he clearly speaks of the merits of wonder, its link to spirituality and how a life shaped by wonder will prevent us from adopting narrow doctrines and creeds. This is believable if the imagination prompted is akin to that of Hepburn's metaphysical imagination because, according to Hepburn, the credibility of such imaginings depends on whether we can render them sustainable and coherent. If left unchecked the imagination involved is more akin to that of fancy and we face an increased likelihood of deluding ourselves. To understand this in depth it is necessary to explore what we mean when we use the word "fancy." Fancy appears in Milton's poem *Paradise Lost*, where Milton refers to it as his "internal sight."[77] Having sight indicates the ability of the mind to visualize, generate internal images or, to put it simply, to imagine. This speaks of a correspondence between fancy and imagination, but as Brann has pointed out during the seventeenth century, a preference for imagination arose and a certain devaluation of the fancy took place.[78] An exemplification of this devaluation can be found in Coleridge, who in his *Biographia Literaria*, made a distinction between imagination and fancy, categorizing fancy as something "lower" than the imagination. Of the fancy Coleridge writes:

> Fancy, on the contrary, has no other counters to play with, but fixities and definites. The Fancy is indeed no other than a mode of Memory emancipated from the order of time and space; while it is blended with, and modified by the empirical phenomenon of the will, which we express by the word *choice*. But equally with the ordinary memory, the Fancy must receive all its materials ready made from the law of association.[79]

Coleridge's description of the fancy is cryptic but what he seems to say is that the fancy is nothing more than a form of memory—mechanical, rigid, and uncreative in fashion.

A touch of devaluation of the word "fancy" can also be found in poet Babette Deutch's remarks on the topic. She states:

> Fancy. As noun as "a whimsical notion or the mental faculty responsible for it"; as adjective, the property of being pretentiously fine; as verb, the pursuit of a frivolous preference. In some texts fancy is the specific faculty whose product is the fantastic.[80]

According to Deutch "fancy" can be used in different connections; however, the idea that fancy is whimsical or refers to a mental faculty that is responsible for whimsical behavior carries with it a slight negative connotation. The notion that fancy as a verb signals the pursuit of a frivolous preference or that fancy highlights the product of the fantastic, points in the same direction.

To explore this further we might say that to be whimsical is to display a certain unpredictability or erratic behavior that in some instances fosters amusement. If true, this supports the notion that fancy carries with it a certain negative connotation in the sense that a person giving herself up to the fancy or who is fanciful is someone easily led astray or deceived. To illuminate this in a better way we might say that Jane Austen's character, Mrs. Bennet, from *Pride and Prejudice*, qualifies as a whimsical character or a person endowed with a fanciful mind due to her excitable behavior, together with her imagined susceptibility to tremors and palpitations.

The lady in Michel de Montaigne's essay *Of the Force of the Imagination*, who thought she swallowed a pin also carries an important message about the whimsical and deceptive aspect of fancy. Montaigne writes:

> A woman fancying she had swallowed a pin in a piece of bread, cried and lamented as though she had an intolerable pain in her throat, where she thought she felt it stick; but an ingenious fellow that was brought to her, seeing no outward tumour nor alteration, supposing it to be only a conceit taken at some crust of bread that had hurt her as it went down, caused her to vomit, and, unseen, threw a crooked pin into the basin, which the woman no sooner saw, but believing she had cast it up, she presently found herself eased of her pain.[81]

One can argue that the lady in Montaigne's example is fanciful because her imaginings of the pin inside herself made her experience excruciating pain, which is wholly imaginary in origin and which disappeared upon her witnessing the crooked pin in the basin in which she vomited.

Returning again to Fuller, we can say that his account of wonder may be in need of modification because it becomes hard to see how ontological imaginings following an episode of wonder will necessarily remain on the virtuous path, revealing a vision that does not descend into a mishmash of, as Hepburn would say, "agreeable sensory stimuli or reverie."[82] In defense of Fuller, one can say that since he makes no claims that the revelations of an experience of wonder have authority beyond the individual experiencing it, his account still stands. Furthermore, that during wonderment one ventures upon ontological imagining does not necessarily mean that one automatically renders them true, and even if one does, Fuller does not state that whatever is experienced carries a truth-value that extends beyond the individual. In this sense, Fuller keeps the experience within the dimension of the personal; however, if we search for the kind of truth that transcends personal metaphysical imaginings brought about by an episode of wonder, which we might add still can be deluded or simply a case of ontological "Imagineering," that is, the activity of deliberate engineered imaginings, further metaphysical argumentation and theory as a minimum requirement must be presented. In any case Hepburn's careful deliberations help us stay "intellectually housebroken" and reminds us to be wary of over-interpreting experiences of wonder and having the works of the imagination lead us astray. Truth is elusive and the absolute fragile.

ROGER SCRUTON AND IMAGINATION

Scruton gives his account of imagination in his 1974 book *Art and Imagination*, which is geared toward the formulation of "a theory of aesthetic judgment and appreciation in terms of an empiricist philosophy of mind."[83] *Art and Imagination* is divided into three parts of which the second deals specifically with the topic of imagination. We shall focus primarily on this particular section in Scruton's work and not deal with the first part of his book, which engages with aesthetic description and evaluation, nor the third part of his work that deals with how the imagination can be brought to bear on art.

To Scruton imagination is a species of thought,[84] in the sense that it equals unasserted thought and qualifies as that "which goes beyond what is believed."[85] This is to say that "in imagination one is engaging in speculation, and one is not typically aiming at a definite assertion as to how things are. In imagination, therefore, one goes beyond what is strictly given."[86] Furthermore, Scruton thinks that imagination is a rational activity because:

> The man who imagines is trying to produce an account of something, and is, therefore, trying to relate his thoughts to their subject-matter: he is constructing a narrative, and to do this it is not sufficient merely to go beyond what he is already "given." It is necessary that he should attempt to bring what he says or thinks into relation with the subject: his thoughts must be entertained because of their "appropriateness."[87]

In Scruton's view imagination has two strands, one of them being predicative, the other adverbial.[88] To explain the predicative strand, allow me to bring my daughter, who is fascinated by Superman, onto the scene. Now, my daughter can imagine she is Superman and she can see herself as Superman. She can also form an image of Superman and she can imagine what it would be like if she was Superman. All this predicates an activity or mental act of my daughter. The adverbial strand is different from the predicative because it need not be a mental act. In this regard we may say that my daughter can also be doing something with her imagination or imaginatively, using her "imagination in the performance of some task (whether it be fulfilling a practical aim, or acquiring some particular piece of knowledge)."[89] Scruton elaborates by stating that imagination is like thinking. "Thinking is a mental activity; doing something thoughtfully is often not."[90]

For Scruton, imagination supplies a rubric under which a variety of phenomena can be grouped.[91] These phenomena, to use Scruton's own words are:

> Forming an image ("picturing"); imagining in its various forms (imagining that . . . imagining what it would be like if . . . , imagining what it is like to . . . , some of these constructions are propositional, some not; some relate to knowledge that . . . some to knowledge by acquaintance); doing something with imagination, (imagination as adverbial rather than predicative); using imagination to see something; seeing an aspect[92]

The interesting thing here is concerned with what forming an image or picturing means and Scruton's idea of using the imagination to see something including an aspect of something.

Scruton holds that forming an image or picturing can be grouped under imagination because, like imagination, it is subjected to the will understood as when we receive the request to "imagine or form an image of something"[93] can, as it were, immediately conjure up an image of something or put before our mind's eye a particular picture.[94]

Now consider using the imagination to see something or seeing an aspect. This is an important part of Scruton's view of imagination and it refers to the idea that "it takes imagination to see from the circumstances that one's friend is unhappy or hurt."[95] In this light imagination involves perception but also perceptiveness and, as Scruton points out, it might very well be that it was precisely the inability to flesh out these two aspects of imagination that led Coleridge to conclude that "imagination is the prime source of truth."[96] By highlighting the complex phenomena of "seeing an aspect" under the umbrella of imagination, Scruton offers a very nuanced picture of imagination which complicates matters and consequently challenges the Romantic position. Scruton writes that one aspect "is given by propositional constructions of the form: 'It takes imagination to see that X is sad.'"[97] The other aspect presents itself via the metaphorical sense of "see" as in "it takes imagination to see the sadness in X's face."[98] In this sense the second aspect relates to the formation of a hypothesis and whereas only the first aspect may be labeled as cognitive, understood as a kind of judgment, the second aspect does not qualify as such because what one "'sees' one 'sees' without, in any straightforward sense, believing it to be there."[99]

Scruton elaborates on this somewhat cryptic notion by stating that:

> It is not seeing that X's face is the face of a sad man (for example), or that the music is the kind of music that would be produced by a sad person (for example), or that living on Hill Farm tends to make people sad (for example), that constitutes this kind of seeing, although making

these judgements may help to put us in a position to "see" the sadness that is there.

We cannot explain this sense of "see" as "see imaginatively," and hence relate the element of imagination to the adverbial sense. For seeing, in the normal sense, is not the kind of thing that can be done imaginatively. It is not a voluntary activity, and is not within the control of thought. To add imagination to seeing is to change it from seeing to "seeing."[100]

In the last part of this citation, Scruton refers to the notion of seeing an aspect and to expand on this Scruton states that "'seeing an aspect' cannot be analyzed in terms of 'seeing that' because it does not reduce to a set of beliefs about its object, nor even a set of perceptual beliefs."[101] In this sense there is a problem with what category "seeing as" belongs to because it is a matter of perception. To elaborate, Scruton brings to attention the ambiguous figure of the "duck-rabbit," which we encountered earlier in connection with my daughter's experience of wonder. We recall that the "duck-rabbit" is an image in which both a duck and a rabbit can be identified, which we of course may find amusing but the picture holds a deeper secret. When I showed the "duck-rabbit" to my daughter for the first time she immediately identified the duck but only later, with a certain amount of puzzlement (perhaps even wonder), recognized the rabbit. Her puzzlement is entirely justified because the "duck-rabbit" brings out the perhaps unsettling truth that although we might see the picture differently the picture does not change. What is it that changes then we might ask? Well, we change. Our perception changes once we, like my daughter, realize that the image holds more than the depiction of a duck. We realize that the duck, like the rabbit, are merely aspects of the image.

Scruton ends his discussion on "seeing as" by stating that "'seeing as' is like an 'unasserted' visual experience: it is the embodiment of a thought which, if 'asserted,' would amount to a genuine perception, just as imagination if 'asserted,' amounts to genuine belief."[102] This last point is important to Scruton because a part of his project in *Art and Imagination* is to show that "'the unasserted' nature of 'seeing as' dictates the structure of aesthetic experience."[103] In this sense it is crucial to realize that for Scruton an important part of "seeing as," when it comes to truly understanding aesthetic descriptions, is that they cannot be taken literally.[104] The unasserted visual experience gives us an idea of something that might be the case rather than something that is the case. If I was asked to describe my depiction of the ancient Greek poet and musician Orpheus, it is quite possible that some people would disagree with me and find my efforts fanciful and encourage me to imagine him differently. In other words, aspect-seeing is subject to change and is not a guaranteed fancy-free enterprise, but is nevertheless an enjoyable part of appreciating something aesthetically.[105]

To continue our exploration of Scruton's idea of imagination let us now consider what is "absent" or what is "not present" in "unasserted thought" and is, perhaps, comparable to what makes room for, or gives rise to, what is "newly present" in wonder.[106] To illustrate this we might recall de Pasquale's experience of wonder, which involved seeing his cousin Richie's face, his own face, and a multitude of other faces in the bathroom mirror in conjunction with the stark realization of a seemingly inescapable human mortality. To say that the faces he saw and his realization of human mortality were literally there in the mirror is an overstatement. It will be far more believable to say that they were aspects absent in a literal sense but very much there for de Pasquale as products of his imagination, understood as unasserted thought and what made the world newly present to him or, in other words, wonderful for him.[107]

The same can be said about Sam Keen's experience of wonder, following being handed the mysterious knife by a complete stranger in the ordinary city of Maryville, Tennessee. A sense of gratitude, expectancy, and how the extraordinary may be found in the ordinary haunted Keen for weeks after the handover, but to say that these facets were a part of the actual handover, of the knife is an overstatement. It will be better to say that they were absent in a literal sense but present in the form of aspects, courtesy of Keen's imagination understood as unasserted thought and thus made him see the world anew.

To give a third example, when I was thirty-five years old I lost a good friend of similar age to cancer. Her death troubled me (and still does) because at the time she had recently married, become a mother, and had at long last found the peace and happiness she had sought most of her adult life. For years following her death, I kept seeing her face whenever I found myself in a crowd of people. Her face would appear momentarily but long enough for me to realize that she was there. The first couple of times I saw her, I was, to say the least, surprised and entertained a sense of suspension because I was then as much as now not accustomed to see dead people walking. In each case I made an effort to approach my friend but before I could reach proximity suitable for conversation she would fade away and become someone else. At subsequent sightings (and this, in particular, when seeing her had become a part of my quotidian life), I merely acknowledged her presence and went about my business and in these cases she would usually vanish at a distance of five to eight meters as quickly as she came about. How is one to think about such events? My prevailing theory is that due to my fading eyesight I unfortunately have developed a problem with distinguishing or identifying faces from a distance and it is particularly difficult for me to distinguish between faces in a fast moving crowd because my eyes cannot adapt to the fast changing environment. In conjunction with the "trauma" or "thauma" of my friend's death, which might have left me more troubled than I realized at the time, "seeing" her in the crowd was merely a projection of what in a fashion occupied my mind. My friend was not there in the crowd in a literal sense but very much present as a fabric of my imagination. In this sense I did not perceive the external world directly, but what I saw was influenced by the thing that perceives, which in this case was myself.

Was this an experience of wonder? I think yes, because experiences such as these hint to us something important about human perception, which takes us beyond the notion that we experience the world in the raw or, to put it differently, that we enjoy a one to one relationship with the world around us. Experiences such as these are suggestive of a Kantian conception: human beings are situated in a world of appearances where the things in themselves are unknown to us and are likely to remain so.[108] What we do know or can come to know about is the experiential world or the world of appearances but this entails not only the scrutiny of the objects as they appear to us but also the scrutiny of us as beings of perception. It seems that regardless of whether one is familiar with the philosophy of Kant the notion that we live in a subject-dependent world of appearances, and that things in themselves are obscure to us, is a tremendous source of wonder.

From these examples it is reasonable to propose a link between what is absent in imagination as unasserted thought and that which in wonder is newly present. Let us attempt further to spell out in what sense what is literally absent in ordinary aspect perception is momentarily present in wonder.

One possibility is that it is a matter of what is displaced: that is to say that in ordinary aspect perception what is displaced is the content of the thought understood as the sadness of someone's face or the jolliness of a particular melody, whereas in wonder that which is displaced is not so much the object of wonder but ourselves; or rather that our frame of reference is displaced allowing us at least momentarily to be transfigured or transformed. This resonates with de Pasquale's experience because it can be well said that seeing the faces in the mirror that should not be there, and the subsequent realization of his mortality displaced him or diminished his sense of self, which indicates transfiguration. The same is afoot in Keen's example where we can say that he is displaced by his newfound gratitude, wondering expectancy, and view of the extraordinary in the ordinary. We can also say that it takes place in the third example involving me seeing my departed friend in various crowds. Here it can be argued that I was displaced by the sudden realization that I might just unconsciously be coloring what I see by projecting the memory of my friend's face onto faces I could not distinguish in the crowds due to my fading eyesight.

To further articulate the connection between what is absent in imagination as unasserted thought, and that which in wonder makes the world newly present, it might be conjectured that in wonder what is ordinarily unasserted is at least momentarily asserted. This makes sense because for something to be asserted it is demanded that it be real to us—that it become known. The first time I "saw" my friend in the crowd I believed, at least for a moment, that she was there in a real sense despite the fact that I knew she could not be.

Let us now focus on Scruton's notion of "seeing as" as a mixture between the sensory and the intellectual, how such experiences are subject to judgment of appropriateness and how this relates to wonder.

To begin we might ponder whether wonder was an appropriate state of mind for de Pasquale, Keen and myself to be in following the particulars of our individual cases. If we first look at the case of de Pasquale, it is tempting to subscribe his wonderment solely to him seeing a multitude of faces in the mirror, because it is what immediately strikes us as extraordinary about his experience. However, as much as this is extraordinary it alone does not justify his wonderment, but rather the fact that the extraordinariness of seeing the faces in the mirror in conjunction with his realization of mortality "displaces" him.

Keen's example follows a similar pattern. It is entirely appropriate for him in his situation to wonder but not merely because a stranger handed him a mysterious knife. His wonder is appropriate because the handover of the knife in conjunction with his new found sense of gratitude; wondering expectancy and acknowledgment that something extraordinary happened in the otherwise ordinary world of Maryville "displaced" him.

The same can be said about my own case involving me seeing the face of my deceased friend in the crowd. One could think it entirely appropriate for me to be in a state of wonder following the first sighting, and this not merely because I saw the face of my departed friend in the crowd. My wonder was appropriate because in conjunction with seeing my friend's face I seriously questioned the reality of what I perceived, which brought about the unsettling and displacing realization that I am living in a world of appearances, where, to put it bluntly, the world for me is in part fabricated by me. Now the kind of displacement at work here does not entail a complete loss of the sense of coherence, nor does it compel us to accept a solipsistic stance signaling that nothing exists outside our own minds. What is proposed is merely an altered state of mind that for some time leaves us unhinged in the sense that we are experiencing a disruption in our ordinary perception, or perhaps an expansion of it where we become aware of not only a hitherto unknown possibility, which includes there being more to reality than we think but indeed that this "more" might just at least in part be created by ourselves.

Where does this leave us? It leave us with a preliminary acceptance criterion for wonderment stating that for someone's wonder to be appropriate, or to wonder appropriately, involves that one has something to wonder at which is extraordinary, vivid and significant and that others can understand why a given object is wonderful. This is not to say that we are necessarily assessing whether what is claimed to be wonderful is truly wonderful. What is required is merely that we can accept that a particular object or situation may give rise to wonderment. To better understand this it might be prudent to give an example of a situation where it is inappropriate to wonder or, to put it differently, where a person claims something is wonderful but where we cannot accept or at least will have severe difficulty in accepting that the object in question can give rise to wonder. Such a situation may be found in the Coen brothers' 2009 film *A Serious Man*, where the heavily troubled protagonist, Larry Gopnik, is being advised by a junior rabbi, who without taking the time to become familiar with the many particulars of the protagonist's troubles, including that his wife wants a divorce, suggests that Gopnik's salvation lies in a renewed sense of wonder. The scene plays out as follows:

> Junior rabbi: "Can I share something with you? Because I, too, have had the feeling of losing track of Hashem, which is the problem here. I too, have forgotten how to see him in the world, and when that happens you think, 'Well, if I can't see him he isn't there. He's gone.' But that's not the case. You just need to remember how to see him. Am I right? I mean. . . . The parking lot here. Not much to see. But if you imagine yourself a visitor, somebody who isn't familiar with these autos and such, somebody still with the capacity for wonder. Someone with a fresh perspective. That's what it is, Larry. Because with the right perspective, you can see Hashem, you know, reaching into the world. He is in the world, not just in shul. It sounds to me like you're looking at the world, looking at your wife, through tired eyes. It sounds like she's become a sort of thing. . . . A problem. A thing."
>
> Gopnik: "She is seeing Sy Ableman."
>
> Junior rabbi: "Oh."
>
> Gopnik: "They're planning. . . . That's why they want the get."
>
> Junior rabbi: "Oh. I'm sorry."
>
> Gopnik: "It was his idea."
>
> Junior rabbi: "Well, they do need a get to remarry in the faith. But . . . This is life. You have to see these things as expressions of God's will. You don't have to like it, of course."
>
> Gopnik: "The boss isn't always right, but he's always the boss."

Junior rabbi: "That's right! Things aren't so bad. Look at the parking lot, Larry. Just look at that parking lot."[109]

The scene is hilarious, absurd, and important to our endeavor because as much as the rabbi can see the wonder in the parking lot, it is impossible for the protagonist, and indeed the audience, to accept that it even in some vague sense can give rise to wonderment. This is so because the parking lot is so utterly austere and bleak that one will probably need the mind of the rabbi in order to find it wonder-filled. We might even say that the latter is not enough because nothing in the scene indicates that the rabbi himself finds it full of wonder. For all we know he could be making it all up in his desperate attempt to sound wise and knowledgeable.

Supposedly one could venture that the wonder of the rabbi is justified because he is referring to religious wonderment, which emerges through acknowledging the existence of God and recognizing his handiwork in everything around us, even in the most mundane of things such as a forlorn parking lot. Naturally this complicates matters but it does not completely thwart the voiced criticism. The reason for that is that there is a logical problem with thinking of everything (even though it is attributed to God) as wonderful because if everything is wonderful we might as well say that nothing is wonderful. Now, by emphasizing there being "objects of wonder" and "objects bereft of wonder," I am in effect stating that wonder may not entirely reside in the eye of the beholder. This is a highly problematic position because we are, as it were, addressing whether a particular object (the thing in itself) is a wonder (noun) or not. As much as one can disagree with the rabbi that the bleak and austere parking lot is wonderful we cannot bypass that it might be so to him, meaning that we cannot ignore the workings of the individual subject when it comes to experiences of wonder. In the interest of advancing our understanding of wonder I propose a compromise involving what we could call the "density" of wonder, meaning that some objects like, for example, the comet Hale-Bopp, which was visible from the northern hemisphere in 1997, are "more densely packed" with wonder; understood as such, objects are more likely to induce wonder in comparison to the rabbi's parking lot. The reason for this is that objects like Hale-Bopp are rare and extraordinary celestial travelers that when observed and when reflected upon quickly lift us out of our immediate context and engage our imagination on a metaphysical level, reminding us about the vastness of space and the tiny and fragile part we occupy. In this sense we are moving away from the either/or attitude toward wonder and toward an approach involving a more/less attitude in order to accommodate the idea that there are some objects like Hale-Bopp, which we can more easily accept as wonderful, while others seem like truisms or objects whose wonderfulness is entirely idiosyncratic to the wonderer.

A different aspect of Scruton's philosophy involves what we might call "continuity between intense experiences and subsequent living." This is centered on questioning whether an aesthetic experience can be more than just a thought. Scruton believes this is sometimes the case because, as he puts it, "what I feel in the presence of works of art may find its ultimate expression in my behavior towards my fellows. My 'imagined' feelings can show their effect in the expressions of their 'real' counterparts."[110] In this respect Scruton speaks of a test of sincerity that can determine whether our aesthetic experiences are at odds with ourselves. To illustrate his point he mentions that if a person claims that her feelings of tenderness have been awoken by the portrait of a child, but proves herself incapable of feeling tenderness toward a real child, then her aesthetic experience is at odds with herself and consequently not sincere.

Now would it be reasonable to put forth a similar test of sincerity when it comes to claims or descriptions of wonderful things or objects? It seems so because if something is truly wonderful it is likely to produce in the wonderer a particular state of mind involving perhaps a kind of subdued or subtle reverence, gratitude, or openness which do not only exist in the mind of the wonderer as a fleeting thought but are also carried out in a person's behavior or actions, and may even help shape the person's life over time. The way wonder works is thus similar to Scruton's idea of aesthetic experience and to illustrate how, let us again focus on de Pasquale's wonderment, which comes across as sincere because his experience produced a deep reverence for human mortality that would later shape his philosophical outlook and how he lives his life. Likewise, Keen's wonderment looks sincere because for weeks following his being handed the mysterious knife he experienced gratitude to the stranger and what he calls wondering expectancy. As with de Pasquale, Keen's life has turned out to be a wonder-filled one, and although it probably would be an overstatement to say that it was the wonderful happening in Maryville that led to a lifetime of wonderment for Keen as a philosopher, we can definitely say his subsequent philosophical openness meets an important test for the sincerity of his wondering.

In light of Scruton's approach to imagination, let us now concentrate on the possibility of "cultivating a habit of wonder." Cultivating such a habit is a notion that is somewhat supported by at least two philosophers of wonder, namely Verhoeven and Opdal. Verhoeven thinks that one might have a "talent" for wonder, which hints to us a certain disposition or capability that may or may not be advanced or developed further. The same goes for Opdal, who suggests that children's wonderment might turn into philosophical reflection over time, indicating not only the possibility of an evolution of an individual's relationship with wonder, including perhaps an increased sophistication of what is wondered at but possibly also the habitual return to the wonderful.

How is one to cultivate a habit of wonder? One way might be to educate the imagination.[111] We can cultivate a habit of wonder because we can train our imagination to such an extent that we become accustomed to looking for the richest possible account of something. This is to say that we cultivate an outlook that is generous enough to present us with a variety of aspects or perspectives of which some may exhibit what we might call the "unasserted extraordinariness" of a particular object, phenomenon, or event, which on occasions leaps out as asserted and wonderful. To put it differently, it is possible that we can train ourselves to have an eye for the ordinary as a conveyer of the extraordinary, which springs to mind as asserted and newly present during an experience of wonder.

"Experiencing things for their own sake" is another element of Scruton's philosophy that we might explore in connection with wonder. In his account of the imagination Scruton emphasizes that aesthetic enjoyment is the enjoyment of an object for its own sake.[112] If the activity of the imagination plays a part in wonder it might help explain why wonder often comes across as a joyful experience, but will it make sense to say that when we feel joy during an episode of wonder we feel it toward the object of wonder for its own sake? I would argue against this because although one might take pleasure in the object of wonder, a part of the enjoyment we feel can also be linked to the very "displacement" or "diminishing of self," as I have termed it, which the wonderful object facilitates. What makes wonder joyful is, in other words, not only the object of wonder but is also connected to what it does to us. This takes us back to the idea of wonder having an emotional component or feeling dimension because it can be argued that during wonderment we experience emotional upheaval, mostly in the form of joy, and that this has something to do with the displacement or the diminishing of the self we feel during wonder. If this is the case, it helps us grasp how wonder can be cognitively advantageous.

Moving on we might also say that a part of the enjoyment of wonder lies in the reverence, openness, and gratitude, which one might experience in connection with wonder as we saw in the three examples used earlier in this section. In addition, we might find pleasure in the awareness of ignorance that comes with wonderment and indeed joy in the invitation to undertake further inquiries and bring new discoveries to light, which the wonderful object gives us. To exemplify this we might return to Shakespeare's character Horatio who experienced both fear and wonder during his paranormal encounter with the ghost of the dead king, but also the drive for inquiry and to discover the reason why the apparition walked the night. The same can be said about Robert Boyle and his wonder at the luminous meat brought to him from the larder by one of his servants. A part of his joy was no doubt the appearance of the meat itself given its unusual qualities, but another source of his enjoyment was his own displacement/diminishing of self and the invitation to inquiry that the wonderful meat brought forth.

We began our journey into the realm of imagination by looking at a range of literature of wonder, where imagination is involved in order to further clarify the rationale for investigating imagination in connection with wonder. Subsequently, a general introduction to imagination was given followed by three different approaches to imagination represented by Mary Warnock, Ronald Hepburn, and Roger Scruton. Warnock's Romantic approach revealed that imagination is what animates our perception and makes us able to go beyond what is directly in front of us. Additionally, Warnock brought to light that imagination is connected to creativity and that educating the imagination is important because using the imagination draws not only on the intellect but also on our emotions and feelings, and plays a role in how we can liberate ourselves from the wanton life and become director of our own life. Warnock's contribution to the philosophy of imagination enabled us to expand our understanding of wonder by first highlighting the animating or life-giving aspect of the wonderful experience. In this regard it was brought forward that the imagination is active in wonderment, where we seek a satisfying cognitive schema of what we experience but fail to obtain, such that the object of concern is never fully beheld or understood. Furthermore, it was highlighted that the intensity of the wonderful experience could be explained by the notion that in wonder we realize that despite the work of the imagination a completely satisfying picture of the object of wonder simply does not arrive. By addressing Warnock's notion of the universality of imagination in relation to wonder it became clear that since imagination plays a part in wonder, wonder carries a certain universality as well. In this respect we entertained the idea that it is the work of imagination in wonder that helps turn childish wonder into philosophical reflection, and that attaining an education that is "wonder full" could deepen one's sense of wonder. By addressing wonder as a conveyer of the universal we also found that because of the labor of imagination in wonder, wonder can give rise to the idea that the object of wonder has a general significance beyond itself—that it is universally important, and in this respect we looked to the notion that we are mortal creatures and that we live in a world that is grand and beautiful.

By paying attention to Hepburn's notion of metaphysical imagination as "layered," we found that the first layer of wonder enables us to gather data and appreciate something as wonderful; the second layer enables us to see the object of wonder as significant, and the third layer allows for individual interpretations of the object of wonder, conveying how the world fundamentally is structured. In connection with Hepburn's approach we also addressed the notion of imagination as conveyer of truth and the idea that because imagination is at work in wonderment, wonder is a conveyer of truth. Here it was brought to light that while it is conceivable that there is a revelatory or noetic quality to wonder, caution must be exercised when it comes to ascribing a truth-value to the wonderful experience, because metaphysical imagination has the ability to bring about equally cogent but incompatible views of how the world fundamentally is put together. The notion of commensurability was likewise addressed in connection with Hepburn's approach and we found it quite compatible with Fuller's idea that wonder activates our imagination and encourages us to seek deeper patterns in the universe.

Via Scruton's approach to imagination we became aware that imagination is important to aesthetic appreciation and can be viewed as unasserted thought, which goes beyond what is believed or that which is strictly given. Imagination is a rational activity that has two strands, one of them being predicative, the other adverbial, and it equips us with a rubric under which a variety of phenomena can be grouped. Important to our endeavor is one particular phenomenon named "aspect seeing," which allows us, for example, to see the sadness in someone's face. The notion of aspect seeing is significant because we are in effect putting forth a hypothesis based on what we see without in any straightforward sense, believing whatever it is that we see to be there. Seeing an aspect of something or "seeing as" is akin to an unasserted visual experience, meaning that when it comes to appreciating something aesthetically it should not be taken literally.

Scruton's approach to imagination also helped us advance the understanding of imagination's role in wonderment, as it enabled us to craft a link between what is absent in imagination as unasserted thought and what in wonder is newly present. In wonder we experience the world as newly present and we do this because we are displaced, understood in the sense that our frame of reference is displaced allowing us for perhaps merely a moment to assert what is normally unasserted and thus experience ourselves as transfigured. Scruton's approach also allowed us to consider what it takes for us to wonder appropriately and in this respect a preliminary acceptance criterion for wonderment was proposed, stating that for someone to wonder appropriately she has to wonder at what is extraordinary, vivid, and significant, and that her wonderment, as it were, can be accepted by others. Scruton's approach to imagination likewise gave rise to thoughts about the continuity between intense experiences and subsequent living in relation to wonder, and it was brought forth that if someone is experiencing wonder in a true sense she experiences being in a state of mind that embraces perhaps a kind of subtle reverence, gratitude, or openness that influence her behavior and may continue to do so over time. Additionally, in connection with Scruton's approach, we touched on the notion of cultivating a habit of wonder via educating the imagination, and it was ventured that by training our imagination we can become accustomed to always seeking out the richest possible account of something, and have an eye for the ordinary as conveyer of the extraordinary. In connection with Scruton's approach, we also examined if the joy we feel during an episode of wonder can be exclusively linked to the object of wonder. The answer was not necessarily so, because although it is possible to find joy in the object of wonder a part of the joy might also consist of (1) being displaced or experiencing a diminishing of self; (2) the reverence, openness, and gratitude one might experience, and (3) the awareness of ignorance about the object of wonder and the invitation to undertake further inquiries.

Lastly it can be said that the three accounts of imagination presented provide a rich view of imagination, and from the analysis it is evident that imagination plays a significant role in the experience of wonder. To take this further and in particular with regards to what the activity of imagination in wonder does to us, we shall now explore the implications of the role of imagination in wonder.

NOTES

1. Robert C. Fuller, *Wonder—from Emotion to Spirituality* (Chapel Hill, NC: The University of North Carolina Press, 2006), 2.
2. Ibid., 158.
3. Philo Hove, "The Face of Wonder" in *Journal of Curriculum Studies*, 28(4), 1996, 437.
4. Sophia Vasalou, "Introduction" in *Practices of Wonder Cross-Disciplinary Perspectives*, ed. Sophia Vasalou (Eugene, OR: Pickwick Publications, 2012), 4.
5. Philip Fisher, *Wonder, the Rainbow and the Aesthetics of Rare Experiences* (Cambridge: Harvard University Press, 2003), 55.
6. Jerome Miller, *In the Throe of Wonder—Intimations of the Sacred in a Post-modern World* (New York: State University of New York Press, 1992), 40.
7. Eva T. H. Brann, *The World of the Imagination* (Lanham, MD: Rowman & Littlefield Publishers Inc., 1991), 18, 20.
8. Ernan McMullen, "Enlarging Imagination" in *Tijdschrift voor Filosofie, 58ste Jaarg* (2), 1996, 231.
9. Brann, *World of the Imagination*, 18.
10. Ibid.
11. See Mary Warnock, *Imagination* (London: Faber and Faber Limited, 1976), 1 and Colin McGinn, *Mindsight* (Cambridge: Harvard University Press, 2006), 2.
12. Brann, *World of the Imagination*, 9–15.
13. David Hume, *A Treatise of Human Nature* (New York: Penguin, 1985), 56.
14. Mary Warnock, *Imagination and Time* (Hoboken, NJ: Blackwell, 1994), 126.
15. See Ron Norman's paper *Cultivating Imagination in Adult Education* presented at the Proceedings of the 41st Annual Adult Education Research (AERC), 2000, 1.
16. Brann, *World of Imagination*, 333.
17. McGinn, *Mindsight*, 4.
18. Paul L. Harris, *The Work of the Imagination* (Hoboken, NJ: Blackwell, 2000), 8.
19. Warnock, *Imagination*, 35.
20. Gustave Dore, *The Dore Illustrations for Dante's Divine Comedy* (New York: Dover Publications, Inc., 1976).

21. McMullen, *Enlargining Imagination*, 253.
22. Aaron Hughes, "Imagining the Divine: Ghazali on Imagination, Dreams, and Dreaming" in *Journal of the American Academy of Religion, 70*(1), 2002, 33.
23. Sociologist Gerad Delanty's idea of 'Cosmopolitan Imagination' from "The Cosmopolitan Imagination" in *Revista CIDOB d'Afers internacionals*(82/83), 2008; Ethicists David F. Caldwell and Dennis Mobjerg's notion of "Moral Imagination" from "An Exploratory Investigation of the Effect of Ethical Culture in Activating Moral Imagination" in *Journal of Business Ethics, 73*(2), 2007 and political philosopher Jason Frank's "Political Imagination" from "Publius; and Political Imagination" in *Political Theory, 37*(1) all qualify as additional examples of the trend of affixing imagination with another word.
24. Robert Muchembled, *A History of the Devil*, trans. J. Birrell (Cambridge, UK: Polity Press, 2003), 2.
25. Muchembled, *History of the Devil* 14.
26. Dante Alighieri, *The Divine Comedy*, trans. A. Mandelbaum (Everyman's Library, 1995), XXXIV.
27. Taylor Hackford, *The Devil's Advocate* (Warner Bros. Pictures, 1997).
28. Andrew Harrison, "Imagination by Mary Warnock" in *Mind, New Series, 87*(347), 1978, 453. Warnock, *Imagination,* 201.
29. Warnock, *Imagination*, op. cit., 196.
30. Ibid., 201.
31. Ibid., 202.
32. In philosopher Patricia W. Kitcher's introduction to Werner S. Pluhar's translation of Kant's *Critique of Pure Reason*, she writes that the purpose of transcendental philosophy is to examine "the necessary conditions for knowledge with a view to showing that some of those necessary conditions are a priori, universal and necessary features of our knowledge that derives from the mind's own ways of dealing with the data of the senses." See Immanuel Kant, *Critique of Pure Reason*, trans. W. S. Pluhar (Indianapolis/Cambridge: Hackett Publishing Company, Inc.), 1996, xxxxi. The idea is that in our endeavor to gain knowledge of things we make use of categories such space and time, which are not to be found in the world of experience but are very much a priori forms of perception. In this sense a vital part of transcendental philosophy is about realizing that "our knowledge of spatial properties of the objects we perceive do not derive from sensory data, but from our minds" own way of interpreting sensory data. Ibid., xxxviii, xxxix.
33. Ibid., A38/B55.
34. Warnock, *Imagination*, 66.
35. Ibid., 73.
36. Ibid., 78.
37. Ibid.
38. Ibid.
39. Ibid., 81.
40. Ibid.
41. Ibid., 81–82.
42. Ibid., 82.
43. Samuel Taylor Coleridge, *Biographia Literaria*, ed. T. Riikonen and D. Widger (Project Gutenberg, 2004), XIII.
44. Warnock, *Imagination*, 91.
45. Ibid.
46. Ibid.
47. Ibid., 92.
48. Ibid., 202.
49. Ibid., 202–3.
50. Mary Warnock, *The Uses of Philosophy* (Hoboken, NJ: Blackwell, 1992), 153.
51. Ibid., 154.
52. Mary Warnock, *Imagination and Time* (Hoboken, NJ: Blackwell, 1994), 189.

53. Paul Martin Opdal "Curiosity, Wonder and Education seen as Perspective Development" in *Studies in Philosophy and Education*, 20, 2001, 332.
54. Warnock, *Imagination*, 82.
55. It is possible to link wonder with fear. Quinn describes wonder as a species of fear or the most rational form of fear, i.e., the fear of ignorance. See Dennis Quinn, *Iris Exiled: A Synoptic History of Wonder* (Lanham, MD: University Press of America, 2002), 17–18. Fear is also linked to wonder in Fleischman's work and in particular "Dark Wonder," a notion that emerges out of his analysis of Herman Melville's *Moby Dick* highlighting "the ability to accept destruction as the counter player of creation." See Paul R. Fleischman, *Wonder* (Amherst, MA: Small Batch Books, 2013), 368. Wonder and fear are also brought together in the scene from Shakespeare's Hamlet that I mentioned earlier where Horatio first sees the ghost.
56. Ronald W. Hepburn, "Landscape and the Metaphysical Imagination" in *Environmental Values*, 5(3), 1996, 191.
57. Ibid.
58. Ibid., 192.
59. Ibid., 191.
60. Ibid.
61. Ibid.
62. Ibid., 192.
63. Ibid.
64. Ibid.
65. It is possible to question Hepburn's use of the word "theorizing" here because we might ask what does it take to theorize metaphysically? Does one need the mind of a brilliant metaphysician in order to do it or is it an activity that the average person can indulge in? Hepburn is silent on the matter and so we might say that if metaphysical theorizing is for everyone it might be suggested that we read Hepburn's "theorizing" as "conjecturing," which is a looser term.
66. Ibid., 195.
67. Ibid.
68. Ibid.
69. See https://noetic.org/about/what-are-noetic-sciences.
70. William James, *The Varieties of Religious Experience* (New York: Penguin, 1985), 380–81.
71. Samuel Rogers, *Autobiography of Eldar Samuel Rogers*, ed. E. J. I. Rogers (Cincinnati: Cincinnati Standard Publishing Company, 1880), 134.
72. Hepburn, *Landscape and the Metaphysical Imagination*, 195.
73. Ibid.
74. Ibid.
75. Fuller, *Wonder*, 2.
76. Ibid.
77. John Milton, *Paradise Lost*, 2 ed. (Harlow, UK: Longman, 1998), VIII, 461.
78. Brann, op. cit.,*World of the Imagination*, 22.
79. Samuel Taylor Coleridge, *Biographia Literaria*, ed. T. Riikonen and D. Widger (Project Gutenberg, 2004), XIII.
80. Barbette Deutch, *Poetry Handbook: A Dictionary of Terms* (New York: Grosset and Dunlap, 1957).
81. Michel de Montaigne, *Essays of Michel de Montaigne*, trans. C. Cotton and ed. W. C. Hazlitt (Project Gutenberg, 2012), 336–37.
82. Hepburn, *Landscape and the Metaphysical Imagination*, 192.
83. Roger Scruton, *Art and Imagination* (New York: Harper & Row Publishing, 1974), 1.
84. Ibid., 113.
85. Ibid., 97.
86. Ibid., 98.
87. Ibid.

88. Ibid., 93.
89. Ibid.
90. Ibid.
91. Ibid., 91.
92. Ibid., 92.
93. Ibid., 95.
94. Ibid., 94.
95. Ibid., 107.
96. Ibid.
97. Ibid.
98. Ibid.
99. Ibid.
100. Ibid., 107–8.
101. Ibid., 109.
102. Ibid., 120.
103. Ibid.
104. Ibid., 122.
105. Ibid., 143.
106. For the notion that in wonder the world is newly present see H. Martyn Evans "Wonder and the Clinical Encounter" in *Theoretical Medicine and Bioethics, 33*(2), 2012, 123–36.
107. This is not to say that all instances of unasserted thought, or of changed aspect perception, are instances of wonder—nor that unasserted thought or aspect perception constitutes wonder. The important part is to acknowledge that the role of the imagination may be parallel in both.
108. Kant *Critique of Pure Reason* , A38/B55.
109. Ethan Coen and Joel Coen, *A Serious Man* (Focus Features, 2009). The scene contains three Jewish words, which are important to understand in order to fully comprehend what is going on. "Hashem" refers to God. "shul" means synagogue and "**get**" refers to a ritual divorce or divorce papers.
110. Scruton, *Art and Imagination*, 131.
111. Both Scruton and Warnock support the possibility of educating the imagination. Scruton suggests that our taste or ability to appreciate something aesthetically (which involves the use of the imagination) can be advanced by education. See Scruton, *Art and Imagination*, 142–43. Warnock is likewise for educating the imagination and she suggests that one way of achieving such education is to allow the use of creativity. See Warnock, *Imagination*, 10, 207.
112. See Scruton, *Art and Imagination*, 143. Warnock supports the idea that making use of the imagination is joyful. This is so because to her imagination equals shaping, which is essentially connected with joy. See Warnock, *Imagination*, 78.

FOUR
Implications of the Role of Imagination in Wonder

Let us turn our attention to the implications of the role of imagination in wonder and first of all take a closer look at how the wonder-filled experience engages our imagination to the extent that it may alter our perception and enrich our perspective.

Guiseppe Arcimboldo's 1591 Mannerist oil portrait *Rudolf II as Vertumnus* is important because it is extraordinary in the sense that fruits and vegetables from various seasons make up the depiction of Rudolf II. The portrait illustrates that he is one with Vertumnus the Roman god of the seasons and so reigns forever having within him "the eternal spring of the mythical Golden Age."[1] The painting is wonder inducing because despite the allure of the minutely detailed fruits and vegetables their arrangement portrays Rudolf II with a striking resemblance (figure 4.1).

The painting likewise evokes wonder because of its ingenuity. One cannot but marvel at the almost unfathomable finesse it takes for an artist to bring a painting like this to life. Just to come up with the motif is profound and this speaks in turn of one of the key features about Mannerist art. When beholding a Mannerist painting like *Rudolf II as Vertumnus* one is likely to wonder not only at the painting itself but also at the extraordinarily imaginative powers of the painter who painted it.

Upon beholding the extraordinary painting one might easily begin imagining the characteristics of Rudolf II, including what he thought was the true nature of our human condition and in what sense his outlook on the world differed from ours. At the time of its creation the painting would have been controversial, representing the antithesis to centuries of Christian thinking where wonder and meaning in life were to be sought by obtaining knowledge of God and how to live a Christian life. In other words, the painting speaks of rebirth and the patterns of thought we

Figure 4.1. Guiseppe Arcimboldo, *Rudolf II as Vertumnus* (1591) Courtesy of Skokloster Castle, Skokloster, Sweden.

today would attribute to the Renaissance mind. It speaks of a world newly born and of a perspective on the human condition filled with possibilities and the promise of transmutation.

In support of these claims one might, for example, link the painting with the humanist ideas of Pico della Mirandola, who as we recall from the first chapter, gave utterance to the notion that human beings are wonderful in the sense that we lack conditioning, meaning that we are not compelled to act like wild animals but are able to rise above such acts and become something else entirely.

To the wondering contemporary viewer the fruits and vegetables motif may also conjure up imaginings of human beings as creatures "grown out of the planet" who depend on its continuing survival and "well-being." To continue this line of thought we might say that the portrait depicts a certain "earthliness" in connection with human life, which may to some provoke imaginings of an alternative way of life, quite different from the one lived in, for example, polluted megacities of concrete, glass, and steel. It may inspire an outlook different from that of the humanist Pico della Mirandola who we recall argued that human beings are free because our nature is not set in stone. It may inspire us to ponder if our happiness is linked to what we might call twenty-first-century romanticism where themes such as ecological sustainability, green energy, and veganism, together with a close connection to the land, are important.

Arcimboldo's painting provokes an attitude of wonder because when viewed with a certain attitude it allows us, at least momentarily, to transcend the default cognitive schematic of our place in the order of things, experience the flight of the imagination, and enjoy an enrichment of perception and perspective.

Let us move away from Renaissance paintings to the image of the Earth seen from space. To get some idea of the importance of this image certain excerpts from the short 2012 documentary *Overview* may initially help us. The film is directed by Guy Reid, produced by Planetary Collective and besides being a stand-alone project it functions as a prelude to the film *Planetary* and features an array of commentators from different backgrounds who share their views on the understanding and implications of seeing planet Earth from space.

The first excerpts worthy of our attention involve statements belonging in order of appearance to author Frank White, Apollo astronaut Edgar Mitchell, and philosopher David Loy:

> In 1968 Apollo 8 went to the moon. They didn't land but they did circle the moon and I was watching it on television and at a certain point one of the astronauts casually said "we're gonna turn the camera around and show you the earth" and he did and that was the first time I have ever seen the planet hanging in space like that and it was profound.
> —Frank White

> The beauty of seeing Earth as a planet as opposed to being down here among it is a wonderful experience that instructs to get into what we call the Big Picture Effect or the Overview Effect.
> —Edgar Mitchell

> I think that for me like for many other people it was quite a shock. I don't think that any of us had any expectations about how it would

give us such a different perspective. I think the focus had been we are going to the stars. We are going to other planets and suddenly we look back at ourselves and it seems to imply a new kind of self-awareness.

—David Loy

These excerpts provide a rough sketch of what we are dealing with. White makes it clear that for him seeing the image of the Earth hanging in space for the first time was a profound experience. Mitchell who actually went into space and saw the Earth from space elaborates by calling the experience beautiful and wonderful and brings to our attention the effect known as the Overview Effect.[2] Loy reflects on the implications of seeing Earth from space for the first time and explains that for him it was a shocking event that changed our perspective and generated a new kind of self-awareness. Loy continues:

Within the Western tradition I think it is quite new and quite shocking because there has been much more the sense of separation. But if you look at other non-Western cultures especially in Asia the emphasis on those has always been on realization that the self and the world is not separate from each other but that they are really interconnected, that the individual self and the species as a whole is a manifestation of the larger whole.

—David Loy

As for Mitchell's experience, it seems evident that in wonder the imagination is ignited paving the way for an enriched perception of things. It is clear that as his experience unfolds he is not able fully to comprehend it, indicating that his imagination fails to provide him with a satisfying cognitive schema of the object of wonder before him, which, in this case, is the Earth seen from space. Memories of his experience continue to haunt him and eventually lead him to consult his local university and ask their help in clarifying it. Additionally, we might say that his experience gave rise to a perceptual change, which via the Buddhist concept of Savikalpa Samadhi,[3] he was later able to express in more detail as experiencing the world with ecstasy and a sense of total unity and oneness.

The self-awareness or enhanced perception the image of the planet hanging in space produced, directed Mitchell toward the ontological because it conjured up ideas or images of our "true nature" as beings, not separated from the planet but beings that are interconnected and that we, as a species, have a part to play in the way the planet unfolds.

Upon considering the excerpts from *Overview* and the offered interpretations, we are in a position to say that just like Arcimboldo's painting of *Rudolf II as Vertumnus*, the image of Earth situated in the void may induce wonder, prompt our imagination, and help us perceive our place in the order of things in a way perhaps radically different from what we are used to.

The emphasis on sight is also important when we change the focus to two particular scientific artifacts, namely the microscope and the telescope that, just like the X-ray, is capable of helping us to see the world anew.

The microscope is an instrument that makes it possible to see objects that are too small for the naked human eye to capture. It was constructed toward the end of the sixteenth century, and although there are controversies about its original inventor it is clear that spectacle-maker Zacharias Janssen and astronomer Galileo Galilei were involved in its development. Around the time of its invention it was a radical instrument and for some a source of endless wonder as it provided an opportunity to gaze into a "new world."[4] Others were inspired by its magnifying properties to renew their faith in God as it helped "manifest the infinite power of God in the most lowly and familiar places."[5] The seventeenth-century microscopist Louis Joblot captures the wonders of the microscope aptly in his *Observations d'historie naturelle faites avec le microscope*:

> The whole of nature turned out to be new [. . .] the microscope helped us discover on the face of the earth a small world that was entirely new, and gave us the opportunity to see in every single thing an infinity of beings no less wonderful than any we have hitherto known.[6]

Through the microscope Joblot experiences the world anew in the sense that beings whose existence he hitherto had been completely unaware of suddenly sprung to life before his "augmented eyes." It is not hard to imagine that such an experience must have been wonder-filled and to capture some of its essence we might consider Philippe Crassous's dramatic 2010 capture of a hydrothermal worm via a scanning electron microscope.[7] Hydrothermal worms are deep-sea creatures about the size of bacteria, and are mainly found close to hydrothermal vents in the ocean and they look absolutely monstrous. Crassous's dramatic depiction not only sends a clear message about how far microscopy has evolved in terms of revealing details of objects too miniscule for us to sense unaided but also provide us with an idea of the kind of wonder people must have experienced upon observing microscopic beings for the first time. Additionally, one might point out that Crassous's worm also functions as a tribute to the marvelous "supposed macroscopic" monstrosities associated with the imaginings of the medieval and Renaissance period and which we still wonder at today.[8]

The very realization that there is something beyond our normal scope of vision—something that we without the aid of a microscope would totally miss out on—encourages wonderment. It ignites the imagination and enriches our perception of the order of things for it raises many questions about how this hidden microscopic world is intertwined with our everyday lives. One could argue that the development of microbiology and its well-known importance to contemporary medicine and healthcare takes the punch out of this argument. One could also press the point that since the invention of the microscope the microscopic world has been researched so extensively that it hardly qualifies as terra incognita anymore, which consequently brings about a certain diffusion of at least some peoples' sense of wonder in relation to it. However, it is fair to say that the extent to which we can explore the world of the microscopic depends on the advancement of technology and our capability of producing images of ever-smaller things. Thus, to say that the microscopic world has lost its wonder is an overstatement, because we are far from being able to explore everything and even if it was possible to have fully explored the world of miniscule things it would still be wonder-filled to creatures like us, precisely because we do not have access to it without the aid of technology.

Likewise, perhaps the telescope is an artifact that can facilitate an experience of wonder because it allows us to see objects too remote for our normal sight to detect. The sixteenth-century German/Dutch spectacle-maker Hans Lippershey is credited for inventing it,[9] but it was the improvements to the instrument by Galileo and his application of it to the field of astronomy that with our present purpose in mind makes it important. To elaborate on this point consider ambassador to Venice under James I, Sir Henry Wotton's letter of March 13, 1610, to the Earl of Salisbury concerning the works of Galileo:

> I send herewith unto His Majesty the strangest piece of news (as I may justly call it) that he hath ever yet received from any part of the world; which is the annexed book of the Mathematical Professor at Padua, who by the help of an optical instrument [. . .] hath discovered four new planets rolling about the Sphere of Jupiter [. . .] so upon the whole subject he hath first overthrown all former astronomy . . . and next all astrology. By the next ship your Lordships shall receive from me one of the above instruments, as it is bettered by this man.[10]

Like the microscope, the telescope allows us to see parts of the world that is normally hidden to us and upon discovering such parts the idea of how the world looks and is ordered is at risk of being overthrown or transfigured. What Wotton speaks of in the letter to the Earl of Salisbury is a testimony to this effect. Galileo's telescopic observations involved Jupiter's four major moons—Io, Europa, Ganymede and Callisto—and their existence cast the geocentric model of the world and the practice of astrology into doubt because neither of these could account for the existence of these moons. This was a monumental discovery and similar to the wonder the educated people of Europe must have experienced when they learned that Christopher Columbus had found a vast continent to the west and so had to change the map of the known world, the people around Galileo must have marveled at his telescopic observations and their implications. Wotton, for one, certainly did as he sent the strange tidings to the Earl of Salisbury and rightly so because Galileo's observations indeed marked the beginning of a paradigm shift and the end of an era where the universe was thought orderly.

Having one's idea of how the world is structured overthrown is a colossal event. It must have encouraged imaginings of an alternative architecture of the universe and perhaps even depictions of what other secrets the telescope in time would reveal as features of our world. As the observations of Galileo were impossible to ignore and since they contradicted the geocentric worldview and that of astrology it led the intellectual to an altogether different place, or with a different perception of the order of things.

Artifacts such as the microscope and the telescope serve as a testimony of human ingenuity and the fact that we, among many things, are artifact-making creatures. The fact that we can invent wonders that enriched our limited senses, enabling us to gaze further and bring to our attention an unseen order of things that would otherwise be beyond us, speaks of our inherently wonderful nature.

WONDER, IMAGINATION, AND THE DEVELOPMENT OF MORAL SCOPE AND SENSITIVITY

Some experiences of wonder ignite the imagination in such a way they give rise to a new kind of perception that develops moral sensitivity or encourages an increase in moral scope.

Robert Nozick's Experience Machine is a wonderful thought experiment that qualifies in this particular regard because it provokes us to give thought to what we really care about and what kind of life is worthwhile living. It has the purpose of establishing a case against hedonism and aims to draw out what the participant in the experiment really treasures in life. Nozick writes:

> Suppose there were an experience machine that would give you any experience you desired. Superduper neuropsychologists could stimulate your brain so that you would think and feel you were writing a great novel, or making a friend, or reading an interesting book. All the time you would be floating in a tank, with electrodes attached to your brain. Should you plug into this machine for life, pre-programming your life's experiences? If you are worried about missing out on desirable experiences, we can suppose that business enterprises have researched thoroughly the lives of many others. You can pick and choose from their large library or smorgasbord of such experiences, selecting your life's experiences for, say, the next two years. After two years have passed, you will have ten minutes or ten hours out of the tank, to select the experiences of your *next* two years. Of course, while in the tank you won't know that you're there; you'll think it's all actually happening. Others can also plug in to have the experiences they want, so there's no need to stay unplugged to serve them (Ignore problems

such as who will service the machines if everyone plugs in). Would you plug in? What else can matter to us, other than how our lives feel from the inside? Nor should you refrain because of the few moments of distress between the moment you've decided and the moment you're plugged. What's a few moments of distress compared to a lifetime of bliss (if that's what you choose), and why feel any distress at all if your decision *is* the best one?[11]

The experiment is relevant to our current exploration of wonder and imagination for a number of reasons. First of all it is about imagined state of affairs twice over in the sense that we are not merely asked to imagine such a thing as the experience machine but also to imagine what we would choose if we were given the opportunity to enter it. This gives rise to wonderment because as much as the thought experiment can be criticized as science fiction or detached from reality, the question of what we would choose in a situation where we had the option of plugging into the machine is a serious one and a potential answer would reveal what we really care about, and may potentially serve as a starting point for further ethical inquiries. In this regard, the experiment prompts a sense of wonder and engages our imagination because most of us would begin to understand that what really matters to us digs beyond immediate pleasures and the experience of how we live our lives. Such matters are only a part of what we truly care about because "we want to do certain things, and not just have the experience of doing them."[12]

Nozick also points out that we do not want to enter the machine because we care about what kind of persons we are. We have an interest in living authentic lives where our experiences are reflected in the character we represent, but if we plug ourselves into the machine the very relationship between our experiences and our character fades away, making the act of attaching ourselves to the experience machine a sort of suicide.[13] This may sound excessive but according to Nozick if a person has been plugged into the machine for a long time it becomes impossible to determine the character of such a person, which to an extent reflects a person who no longer exists. Because the person in the tank is being fed artificial experiences of her own choice we cannot determine if she is good-hearted, caring, courageous, intelligent, patient, and so on. At best she is but a thing in a tank or an indeterminate blob to use Nozick's words.[14] One may ask but what if the person in the tank could be experiencing wonder? Would that not make the choice to plug into the machine attractive? Not necessarily, because it prompts difficult questions such as whether the experience of wonder is an end in itself or important in itself, not forgetting if wonder is attractive merely because it is pleasurable and if wonder would be attractive if it was accompanied by an emotional upheaval closer to fear rather than joy.

Moving on, the thought experiment can also give rise to a wondering reflection about reality; to what extent contact with a deeper reality matters to us; and it may prompt us to reflect upon what the world is, what and who we are and to what end we have ordered our lives. In Nozick's view the experience machine deprives us from being in touch with a deeper reality because of its artificiality. One could argue that a deeper reality in theory could be simulated but such a simulation would be a man-made one, meaning that the thing in the tank, regardless of how we look at it, is cut off from any contact with the deeper reality beyond the constructed one being fed to it.[15] In this regard Nozick's thought experiment prompts wonder because it requires us to imagine a certain state of affairs or, to put it differently, it draws us into these serious and deeper issues and thus it might give rise to what we could call a new perspective or perception on human life, and spark moral questions concerning how we should live and to what end we organize our lives. In this sense the wonder we might experience from engaging with Nozick's experiment resonates well with Fuller's outlook on wonder, as it encourages us to live a life "attuned to the widest possible world of personal fulfillment"[16] or human flourishing because it questions the stewardship of pleasure. From this vantage point we are able to say that the experience of wonder that arises from engaging with Nozick's thought experiment can be a source of ethics and give way for an increase in moral scope and sensitivity.

Robert Nozick is not the only political philosopher who makes wonder-provoking thought experiments that activate the imagination and help us gain moral sensitivity and scope. Political philosopher John Rawls's thought experiment, the "veil of ignorance," which stems from his opus, *A Theory of Justice*, also qualifies as it teases out our wonder-driven capacity for imagination, ushers us to think beyond the actual, and play with hypothetical possibilities which undergirds the epistemic capacity for moral reflection.

In *A Theory of Justice*, Rawls argues that if we were to build an ideal just society it is vital first of all to establish an original position, that is a position that nullifies the biases of the "builders." Human beings, unfortunately, have a tendency to exploit one another or to make unjust rules and regulations that somehow favor a particular kind of people or a particular way of life. In order to eliminate such biases Rawls suggests that before we begin designing this ideal just society we must put ourselves behind a "veil of ignorance." Rawls writes:

> It is assumed then, that the parties do not know certain kinds of particular facts. First of all, no one knows his place in society, his class position or social status; nor does he know his fortune in the distribution of natural assets and abilities, his intelligence and strength, and the like. Nor again, does anyone know his conception of the good, the particulars of his rational plan for life, or even the special features of his psychology such as his aversion to risk or liability to optimism or pessi-

> mism. More than this, I assume that the parties do not know the particular circumstances of their own society. That is, they do not know its economic or political situation, or the level of civilization and culture it has been able to achieve. The persons in the original position have no information as to which generation they belong [. . .] As far as possible, then, the only particular facts which the parties know is that their society is subject to circumstances of justice and whatever that implies. It is taken for granted, however that they know the general facts about human society. They understand political affairs and the principles of economic theory; know the basis of social organization and the laws of human psychology. Indeed, the parties are presumed to know whatever general facts affect the choice of the principles of justice.[17]

The genius of the experiment is that the participant is forced to imagine the outcomes of the rules and regulations she puts forth and the kind of society it ultimately will fabricate, while knowing that she has to participate in the society she is "designing" in some unknown form and to labor toward a society that is not in her favor would be counterintuitive. In this sense the experiment will make the homophobe ponder whether it is just to restrict the rights of citizens in the ideal society based on sexual orientation now that she may end up being a homosexual living in that very society herself. Likewise, the experiment is bound to make the racist person consider whether her ideas about assigning special privileges to people of a certain race in the ideal society are just because she does not know which race she, as a coming citizen of the ideal society, will belong to. In addition, we can say that the experiment encourages the misogynist to reconsider his position on women and how his views are to be incorporated into the ideal society because he may have to live in that society as a woman.

Now Rawls's thought experiment is a powerful tool that may help us explore what we think is just; however, it is also an experiment that may prompt an attitude of wonder, not so much because it promotes certain liberal political values, but because the participant quickly becomes aware of any biases or unjust personal preferences she harbors in relation to the imagined just society. To suddenly face such an awareness is displacing and leads to a diminishing of self, because although we can say that through the experiment the participant might gain a new understanding of herself, this particular understanding or enlargement of her world also encompasses an awareness of ignorance about herself including perhaps how she has come to harbor the particular biases or personal preferences she happens to have in the first place, and why it is that they have remained hidden until now. Such awareness intensifies the cognitive focus because the participant turned wonderer will now, via the use of the imagination, seek both to fully grasp her newly present situation and do away with her ignorance. However, because full understanding does not arrive a sense of being displaced or having one's self diminished emerges leaving the wonderer in a state of emotional upheaval in a world newly present. In this light it is clear that participating in Rawls's thought experiment is an exercise that is likely to induce wonder, but can we say that the experience of wonder emerging from engaging in Rawls's thought experiment also facilitates an increase in moral scope or sensitivity? Yes and no I would say. Yes, because the increased self-awareness including the awareness of ignorance can be seen as a bulwark against overconfidence or absolute surety, which fuels many an unjust moral conviction, and it leaves one open to wonder both in an epistemic and moral sense. No, because it is quite possible that because the thought experiment is destabilizing, some people would simply refuse to wonder and deploy psychological defense mechanisms in order to preserve emotional stability. Furthermore, one might say that the particular openness to wonder that the experiment might install depends very much on the individual's ability to use her imagination, and because some people have a poor use of this particular ability or simply do not have a talent for it, we cannot say for sure that wonder-provoking thought experiments such as the veil of ignorance will result in an increase in moral scope or sensitivity. At best we can say that it is a possible effect of the wonder experienced through engaging with it.

Moving on, let us now look to the term "speciesism," coined in 1970 by psychologist Richard D. Ryder and brought to the attention of a wider audience by philosopher Peter Singer. According to Singer speciesists "give greater weight to the interests of members of their own species when there is a clash between their interests and the interests of those of other species."[18] To contextualize this we might highlight that many human beings are consumers of animal-based food, clothing, and commodities made from animals such as wallets and bracelets. We could also say that human beings have an affinity for using animals for entertainment and that the existence of institutions such as zoos, aquariums, or circuses, where animals are often kept under questionable conditions, is a testimony to this effect. Furthermore, it can be pointed out that human beings, without much consideration, at least in some parts of the world, use animals for research and that countless animals have in the past suffered and perished due to scientific experimentation aiming at producing knowledge, human medicine, or cosmetics.

Now realizing what speciesism means and that one qualifies as a speciesist by endorsing animal suffering through consumer habits can, for some, call up at least momentarily an experience of wonder because they may never have thought of themselves as contributors to animal suffering. It might turn everything upside down and especially if a person prior to being presented the concept, entertained unconscious ideas that ruled out the possibility of nonhuman animals having moral status. Fuller's idea that wonder exercises our ontological imagination comes into play here, because for some the realization that one is a speciesist can be displacing or diminish the self to the extent that it provokes a reexamination of one's outlook on the position of human beings in the world, including perhaps the viability of traditional Western ideas concerning the position of human beings in the "hierarchy of things." What we are talking about here is the kind of ideas that have helped shape the Western approach to animals, such as Aristotle's idea that "plants exist for the sake of animals and the other animals for the good of man";[19] the part of the Bible where it says: "And God said, Let us make man in our image, after our likeness: and let them have dominion over the fish of the sea, and over the fowl of the air, and over the cattle, and over all the earth, and over every creeping thing that creepeth upon the earth";[20] Aquinas's idea that "it matters not how man behave to animals, because God has subjected all things to man's power"[21] and Kant's notion dictating that "so far as animals are concerned, we have no direct duties. Animals are not self-conscious, and are there merely as means to an end. That end is man."[22] Understanding that one is a speciesist is a process that is likely to fuel wonder and ignite our imagination, but will it necessarily bring about an increase in moral scope and sensitivity? No, because although some might begin to actively minimize the use of animal-based products or completely convert to a vegetarian or vegan lifestyle, it is far from certain that everyone will be motivated to such action from dealing with the concept of speciesism. Some people advocate a different and perhaps to them absolute creed or system of belief that is never questioned and which does not recognize the moral importance of nonhuman animals. In other words, they are simply not compelled to change or even to play with the thought that giving nonhuman animals moral status is a sign of moral advancement. Additionally, we may speak of the refusal to wonder and the idea that for some people the power of habit is simply too great, meaning that once you have established a particular way of life you are more or less set in your ways and to change is far from easy because it brings discomfort, which most people shun.

Taken this into consideration I think it fair to say that becoming aware that one qualifies as a speciesist invites wonder and the intense use of the imagination, but it need not increase moral scope and sensitivity. An increase in such is in this respect not a key component or constituent of wonder but at best a possible effect or result of it. Now, despite this formulation, some might still think that I have spoken too warmly about Nozick's experience machine, Rawl's veil of ignorance, and the concept of speciesism advocated by Ryder and Singer, and how we through our engagement with them may experience wonder, the flight of the imagination, and that this in some cases may result in an increase in moral scope and sensitivity. It can be argued that my argument merely speaks to the already morally inclined, but such an objection seems to take for granted that the amoral person exists, a position which is worthwhile examining.

In fact, it is quite possible that the amoral person is a modern myth because giving up living the ethical or moral life equals giving up finding robust reasons for action, that is, reasons that transcend purely selfish and egoistical attitudes or unexamined emotions and feelings. Of course one could argue that this deprivation of reasoning is indeed the modus operandi for many people, but such an attitude does not entitle us to say that such people are amoral. It merely suggests the sidetracking of moral reasoning and the prevalence of immoral behavior. To be immoral does not mean that one is beyond morals but merely indicates that a person behaves inconsiderately with no or little care for self and others. Thus we are still able to say that for some the wonder that will emerge from engaging with, for example, the concept of speciesism can give rise to an increase in moral scope and sensitivity.

It can also be speculated that what appears as immunity or indifference to an increase in moral scope and sensitivity as a possible effect of wonder signals a refusal to wonder. It could very well be that a person recognizes the emerging wonder but treats it as a threat to her integrity, and for the sake of preserving her stable way of life dissociates herself from possible effects of the examples or plainly denies their importance. However, such behavior does not mean that her hostility to wonder is permanent or entitles her to amoral status. Given that human beings are always situated in a limbo between actuality and potentiality, meaning that they inherently harbor the potential for change, we can not completely rule out that a person entertaining a refusal to wonder will not at some future point recognize the value of it and experience the possible effects of wonder. To put it differently, we could speculate that realizing that one is a speciesist and what it implies may need some time in order to "sink in." The point is that an increase in moral scope and sensitivity following an experience of wonder needs not take place in the moment of wonder but can happen over time. Taking this into consideration the existence of the amoral person, immune to the possible transfiguring effects of wonder, is a doubtful matter and that one with the passing of time may experience an increase in moral scope and sensitivity as a result of wonder.

WONDROUS AFTERGLOWS AND DEEP WONDER

Let us return to Keen's wonder-filled encounter with a stranger in Maryville, Tennessee, who gave him a mysterious gift in the form of a knife. We know that he, during the weeks after this strange meeting, experienced what he refers to as a pervasive sense of gratitude to the stranger who handed him the knife together with a rather mysterious "wondering expectancy" brought about by the realization that this wonderful happening took place in the ordinary world of Maryville. In connection with

Keen's encounter I suggested that what he experienced during the weeks following the handover of the knife could be termed a "wondrous afterglow," but I refrained from disclosing any further detail as to what this term covers.

A wondrous afterglow is first and foremost a possible effect of wonder, which is to say that it, strictly speaking, is not a part of what we can call the core components of wonder. It is a state of mind that can spring from wonder which persists over time[23] thus qualifying as a sort of "lingering wonder," involving in some instances (like in Keen's) a pervasive sense of gratitude and a wondering expectancy.

Now given that gratitude is an emotion[24] and that a "wondering expectancy" involves in some vague sense a feeling that something positive is going to happen, we might, in conjunction with the fact that Keen's experience lasted for weeks, ponder if a wondrous afterglow in any sense is an emotion. This is quite plausible because there is judging from Keen's recollection a strong feeling component to the experience; however, because of the endurance of it and the difficulty of describing what it actually consists of, perhaps it is best to think of a wondrous afterglow as a mood. In support of this stands Ben-Ze'ev, who we recall informs us that as opposed to an emotion, which can last for seconds to days but typically lasts for a few minutes to a few hours, a mood has general or diffuse intentional objects and may persist for hours, over days, to weeks and months.[25]

An additional key feature of the wondrous afterglow could be that it ignites the imagination and opens up the mind to a different and perhaps more embracing view. Keen's pervasive sense of gratitude to the stranger who handed him the knife suggests so because to harbor a sense of gratitude is not necessarily as straightforward as it might seem. Keen's later work on the emotion of gratitude supports that because he states that when we experience gratitude "we perceive existence as an unconditional gift, a blessing, a beatitude bestowed on us that we have neither earned nor deserved."[26] In this light Keen's gratitude to the stranger means something more than being thankful to someone for receiving a gift in an ordinary sense. It bears witness to a person who by having a knife presented to him as a gift from a complete stranger for some time has opened up to a world beyond the physical. Or to put it differently, it suggests that through his experience Keen became open to a metaphysical and ontological dimension or, to paraphrase Keen, the appreciation of "being within the eternal mystery of Being."[27]

To cast further light on the notion of a wondrous afterglow let us turn to the idea of differentiated wonder which I touched on toward the end of chapter 1, with reference to Hove's idea that a deep level of wonder may reveal certain fundamentals about the human condition including that we are vulnerable creatures. Hove's deep leveled wonder hints at the ethical dimension of human life and this is a notion that resonates with the contrast suggested by philosopher Ian Kidd between deep and shallow wonder, pointing to the former as driven by an ethical imperative and the latter as guided "merely" by an intellectual one.[28] For Kidd, shallow wonder corresponds to the kind of wonderment that scientists and unweavers of the rainbow such as Dawkins defend, and he argues that although such wonderment can be powerful it merely inspires further scientific work. To harbor a deep sense of wonder is for Kidd to engage with the metaphysical and ethical. It is to walk a path that ultimately leads to wisdom.

To elaborate on Kidd's distinction, we might say of the shallow wonderer that she does not get pushed out of her "comfort zone" in the sense that whatever puzzlement the experience of wonder brings to life the shallow wonderer will dismiss it as broken knowledge and attempt to rectify it within her current scientific perspective. The experience of wonder does not bring about (or at least is not recognized by the wonderer as) a framework-shattering cognitive shift that boosts the imagination and enables recognition of the metaphysical and the ethical, and so the shallow wonderer remains in a sense untouched or untransformed.

Of course this is not to say that a scientist cannot be a deep wonderer or that a person qua being a scientist, forever will be bereft of deep wonderment. It is quite possible to be committed to scientific work and the accumulation of knowledge and at the same time see the importance of the metaphysical; the ethical and besides minding one's scientific interest be on a quest for wisdom. However, I would argue that deep wonder demands the intense use of the imagination because to have before the mind's eye a clear cut picture of the domain of science, the area of metaphysics and the realm of ethics is not easy to exclude as they are, to an extent, interwoven.

In the attempt to push Kidd's idea further we might speculate if there is a connection between Kidd's notion of "shallow" and "deep" wonder and Scruton's idea of imagination as "seeing" and "seeing as." According to Kidd, "Shallow" wonder gives rise to an epistemic imperative understood as we attempt to gain knowledge about a particular matter. "Deep wonder" is an entirely different thing because during an experience of "deep wonder" an ethical imperative emerges which encourages us to act and live differently. Now Scruton's idea of imagination as "seeing as" fits very well with Kidd's "deep wonder" and thus we might say that in "deep wonder" we go further beyond the obvious or the strictly given, while not departing from the appropriate. In this sense, it is imagination as "seeing as" or that which allows us to detect the sadness in someone's face that propels us into the ethical dimension. To elaborate, it is imagination, as "seeing as" that allows us to recognize and embrace, for example, the vulnerability, mortality, sameness, needs, importance or value of the other. To exemplify, we might argue that philosopher Jeremy Bentham displayed a remarkable sense of "deep wonder" when he wrote the famous footnote in *An Introduction to the Principles of Morals and Legislation* reading:

> The day may come when the rest of the animal creation may acquire those rights which never could have been witholden from them but by the hand of tyranny. The French have already discovered that the blackness of the skin is no reason why a human being should be abandoned without redress to the caprice of a tormentor. It may one day come to be recognized that the number of the legs, the villosity of the skin, or the termination of the os sacrum are reasons equally insufficient for abandoning a sensitive being to the same fate. What else is it that should trace the insuperable line? Is it the faculty of reason, or perhaps the faculty of discourse? But a full-grown horse or dog is beyond comparison a more rational, as well as a more conversable animal, than an infant of a day, or a week or even a month, old. But suppose they were otherwise, what would it avail? The question is not, Can they reason? nor Can they talk? but, Can they suffer. [29]

For a man of his time and position to recognize the value of people whose skin-color varies from his, and to extend this value to nonhuman animals by highlighting the importance of their possible capability of suffering definitely speaks toward it, because it can rightly be said that Bentham in his outlook ventures beyond the norms or what is strictly given by the culture he is situated in. In this sense it might be suggested that his philosophical outlook is rooted in "deep wonderment" where the appropriate usage of the imagination as "seeing as" has allowed him the recognition of the vulnerability, mortality, sameness, needs, importance, value and so forth of creatures capable of suffering. That is, he puts forth an aspect of such creatures unfamiliar to or ignored by many of his contemporaries and indeed many people today. In addition, we might say that reading the *Introduction to the Principles of Morals and Legislation* today can be a highly edifying experience because it easily provokes a deep sense of wonder that sets ablaze our imagination as "seeing as," enabling us to recognize the importance of, for example, the suffering of animals and so in effect elevates us onto, ethically speaking, higher grounds.

In this light wonder comes across as an enduring matter and so here we find a possible connection between deep wonder and the idea of a wondrous afterglow; however, the two concepts are not necessarily identical. Deep wonder is enduring, involves an ethical imperative and ignites the imagination, but even though the experience is likely to hold an emotional component it is quite possible that this component undergoes modification. I say this because all of the major ethical philosophical traditions, including virtue ethics, deontology, and utilitarianism represent the exercise of emotional control and finding reasons for action. With this in mind we have an incitement to view deep wonder as an attitude, a disposition or simply the outcome of philosophical reflection. A wondrous afterglow looks different in the sense that it is enduring, involves the metaphysical, but need not involve the ethical. The imagination is clearly active during the experience and there is a strong emotional component to it, which lasts over time, giving us the incitement to classify the whole experience as a mood.

The intense use of the imagination stands as an important communality between deep wonder and a wondrous afterglow, for without it the finer points of the individual experiences are unlikely to be perceived. To give a few examples, it will be hard to experience deep wonder in connection with Nozick's experience machine without an intense use of the imagination because it is the imagination that reveals to us the problems of plugging into the machine. It is the same intense use of the imagination that reveals injustice in connection with Rawls's thought experiment, the veil of ignorance. Furthermore, we might say that it is the intense use of the imagination that, in connection with the concept of speciesism, enables us to abstract ourselves from the habits and customary beliefs that otherwise promote the practice of speciesism. Concerning imagination and a wondrous afterglow we can say that it is courtesy of the imagination that Keen is able to experience gratitude and a wondering expectancy because unless the imagination was active, he would not be able to put before his mind's eye, even in a vague sense, who he was grateful to and what he was grateful for, not to forget what he was expecting, in all his wonder.

Does this enable us to say that it is the intense activity of the imagination that makes these experiences happen? Not quite, because it can be argued that although the intense use of the imagination is important, the gradual deepening of wonder or the longevity of the wondrous afterglow as a mood is also influenced by the degree of dislocation, reorientation or displacement, and awareness, of ignorance we experience in such states of mind.

By engaging with Arcimboldo's *Rudolf II as Vertumnus*; seeing Earth from space; the microscope and the telescope, it has been brought forth that an experience of wonder may alter our perception and enrich our perspective in such a way that we might question our very nature and place in the universe.

With reference to Nozick's experience machine, Rawls's veil of ignorance, and the concept of speciesism promoted by Singer, it has also been argued that an experience of wonder may ignite the imagination to such a degree that a new kind of perception that develops moral sensitivity or encourages an increase in moral scope emerges.

Additionally, we have explored the relationship between a wondrous afterglow and deep wonder and found that, although there are overlaps between the experiences, differences can be detected. Deep wonder comes with an ethical imperative and seems to be an attitude, disposition, or the outcome of philosophical reflection, whereas a wondrous afterglow need not involve the ethical and appears to be a mood.

The time has come to situate wonder in a wider context and explore wonder through a neo-Aristotelian lens involving the relatively recent ethical term "human flourishing" and the idea of virtue. This, together with what has been uncovered about wonder so far, will make clear how cultivating a balanced sense of wonder contributes strongly to our flourishing as human beings.

NOTES

1. Lorraine Daston and Katharine Park, *Wonders and the Order of Nature* (New York: Zone Books, 1998), 211.

2. The Overview Effect is a term coined by Frank White in 1987 involving a cognitive shift induced by a change in physical perspective. One of the most important changes to the mind experiencing the Overview Effect is that "everything is interconnected and interrelated, each part of a subsystem of a larger whole system" See Frank White, *The Overview Effect, Space Exploration and Human Evolution* (Boston: Houghton Mifflin Company, 1987), 4.

3. In the Buddhist tradition Samadhi refers to a state of deep concentration developed though meditation practice (Lopez, 2004, p. 554). Savikalpa is a complex word that includes the word "sa" meaning "with" and "vikalpa" meaning "conceptuality." I am grateful to the late Matthew Neale for pointing this out to me in one of our many heart-warming conversations.

4. See Claude-Olivier Doron, "The Microscopic Glance: Spiritual Exercises, tThe Microscope, and the Practice of Wonder in Early Modern Science" in *Practices of Wonder Cross-Disciplinary Perspectives*, ed. S. Vasalou (Eugene, OR: Pickwick Publications, 2012), 180, 192.

5. Ibid., 192.

6. Ibid.

7. Images of the creature can be found in Dean Praetorius's article "Hydrothermal Worm Viewed under an Electron Microscope" featured in the *Huffington Post* July 18, 2011:   https://www.huffingtonpost.com/2011/07/18/hydrothermal-worm-electron-microscope_n_901833.html?guccounter=1

8. For insights into such marvels and imaginings see: Ambrose Pare, *On Monsters and Marvels*, trans. J. L. Pallister (Chicago: The University of Chicago Press, 1982). Katharine Park and Lorraine J. Daston, "Unnatural Conceptions: The Study of Monsters in Sixteenth- and Seventeenth-Century France and England" in *Past & Present, 92*, 1981; and Norman R. Smith, "Portentous Births and the Monstrous Imagination in Renaissance Culture" in ed. T. S. Jones and D. A. Sprunger, *Marvels, Monsters, and Miracles: Studies in the Medieval and Early Modern Imaginations*, (Kalamazoo, MI: Medieval Institute, 2002).

9. H. C. King, *The History of the Telescope* (London: Charles Griffin and Company Limited, 1955), 30.

10. Sir Henry Wotton, *The Life and Letters of Sir Henry Wotton* Vol. 1, ed. L. P. Smith (Oxford: Oxford at the Clarendon Press, 1907), 486–87.

11. Robert Nozick, *Anarchy, State and Utopia* (New York: Basic Books, 1974), 42–43.

12. Ibid., 43.

13. Ibid.

14. Ibid.

15. Ibid.

16. Robert C. Fuller,*Wonder—from Emotion to Spirituality* (Chapel Hill, NC: The University of North Carolina Press, 2006), 158.

17. John Rawls, *A Theory of Justice* (Oxford: Oxford University Press, 2000), 118–19.
18. Peter Singer, *Practical Ethics* (Cambridge: Cambridge University Press, 1993), 58.
19. Aristotle, *Politics*, trans. H. Rackham (Cambridge: Harvard University Press, 1967), I. III. 7.
20. Genesis 1:26.
21. Thomas Aquinas, *Summa Theologica*, Vol. 1 (Oxford: Oxford University Press, 1947), questions 64.1 and 65.3.
22. Immanuel Kant, *Lectures on Ethics*, trans. L. Infield (New York; Harper and Row, 1963), 239–40.
23. Paul R. Fleishman's view of wonder supports the idea that wonder can persist over time. He speaks about wonder being the "experience that endure in your psyche, that hitch a ride and won't let go." See Paul R. Fleishman, *Wonder*, (Amherst, MA: Small Batch Books, 2013), 112.
24. Robert C. Solomon, *True to Our Feelings* (Oxford: Oxford University Press, 2007), 257–58.
25. Aaron Ben-Ze'ev, "The Thing Called Emotion" in *The Oxford Handbook of Philosophy of Emotion*, ed. Peter Goldie (Oxford: Oxford University Press, 2010), 55.
26. Sam Keen, *In the Absence of God: Dwelling in the Presence of the Sacred* (New York: Harmony Books, 2010), 91.
27. Ibid.
28. Ian Kidd introduced his notion of deep and shallow wonder in a talk given at the Centre for Medical Humanities second symposium on Wonder: "Wonder and Co."—varieties of intensified experience, Kenworthy Hall, St. Mary's College, Durham, on March 19, 2014.
29. Jeremy Bentham, *An Introduction to the Principles of Morals and Legislation* (Oxford: Oxford University Press, 1879), 311.

FIVE
Wonder, Human Flourishing, and Virtue

To show how wonder can contribute to human flourishing and how it can do so in a strong sense, it is important to understand what flourishing means. Different disciplines have contributed to the literature on flourishing and to ensure a reasonable understanding of the concept one could focus on classical hedonism: a "theory of value in which pleasure is the sole good and pain the sole evil."[1] Alternatively, one could turn to psychologist Martin Seligman and adopt an approach to happiness and flourishing which emphasizes a high degree of personalization.[2] Likewise, one could approach flourishing from an economical angle and focus on the satisfaction of basic economic needs as the foundation of happiness.[3] Another path to understanding flourishing could be obtained by paying direct attention to quality of life measures and how health care is using such to determine what well-being consists of.[4] Nevertheless, we shall concern ourselves with a picture of flourishing based on the works of three contemporary neo-Aristotelian philosophers who not only have important things to say about human flourishing but are all indirectly advocates of wonder.

DOUGLAS RASMUSSEN AND HUMAN FLOURISHING

Philosopher Douglas Rasmussen's paints his neo-Aristotelian approach to human flourishing in his article "Human Flourishing and the Appeal to Human Nature."[5] This article is important because while it appeals to human nature it also recognizes human individuality. As Rasmussen puts it "the fundamental intuition behind this project has been not only that it is the flourishing of individual human beings that ultimately matters but the individuality of flourishing as well."[6] Rasmussen offers a contemporary outlook on human flourishing involving some central features of Aristotle's philosophy. Among these central features we find the concept of Eudaimonia, which has been traditionally and inaccurately translated into "happiness" and thus communicating the idea that it refers to a subjective good rather than an objective one, which it was for the ancient Greeks.[7] Because of this, Eudaimonia is often misperceived as only a subjective good and not an objective one. In addition Rasmussen stipulates that human flourishing is a technical and complex notion and that its exact meaning is somewhat obscured by a variety of different theories concerning the human good. Furthermore, Rasmussen informs us that human flourishing is a relatively new term in ethics and is a crucial part of the neo-Aristotelian ethicist's endeavor to establish an alternative to consequentialist and deontological ethics.[8]

More specifically, Rasmussen's neo-Aristotelian approach to human flourishing involves a view of the human good that is (1) objective, (2) inclusive, (3) individualized, (4) agent-relative, (5) self-directed, and (6) social. In addition, Rasmussen emphasizes that practical wisdom and human nature is significant to human flourishing.[9] In what is to come we shall briefly deal with each of these components in turn.

1. To Rasmussen human flourishing is an objective good and is to be considered an activity, an actuality and an end or function. In this sense human flourishing is a way of life that involves particular activities and is desired for its own sake. Human flourishing is "that-for-the-sake-of-which human conduct is done and though flourishing is dependent on human agency for its success its status as ultimate end is not agent dependent."[10]

2. Despite being the ultimate end of human conduct, human flourishing in Rasmussen's view is an inclusive end that does not reduce the value of anything else to that of mere means. Human flourishing is to be viewed as the most final end understood as an end that is never sought for the sake of anything else as it includes all final ends. In this light human flourishing includes and incorporates basic goods such as knowledge, health, friendship, creative achievement, beauty, and pleasure; and such virtues as integrity, temperance, courage, and justice. This is grounded in the idea that the goods and virtues mentioned are all final and valuable in their own rights, but at the same time they qualify as partial realizations or expressions of the most final end, which is human flourishing. In this sense it is quite possible to categorize, for example, the act of staying healthy both as something that one does for its own sake and something that one does for the sake of flourishing. Rasmussen argues that this is possible because flourishing is not the result of the efforts of a lifetime nor is it to be seen as a future enjoyment, but is equivalent to that of a life that is worthwhile throughout.[11]

3. Rasmussen views human flourishing as individualized and diverse. "No two cases of human flourishing are the same and they are not interchangeable."[12] Unlike the daily-recommended intake of vitamins and minerals, the generic goods and virtues of human flourishing cannot be determined according to a natural backdrop and applied in the same manner across different human lives. My wife's flourishing, for example, is not completely the same as mine, meaning that if we have to determine what makes a human being flourish a certain degree of personalization is called for. In Rasmussen's view it is only when an individual's particular talents, potentialities, and circumstances are jointly engaged that the good and virtues mentioned earlier become real, or as he puts it, achieve determinacy.[13]

4. In Rasmussen's perspective human flourishing is also agent-relative and this is to be understood in the sense that it is always the good for some person or other. In addition it is important to realize that one does not flourish automatically and that a person is not merely a placeholder for flourishing. The value of human flourishing is found in and exhausted by those activities of a person that constitute that person's flourishing.[14] What this means is that there is an intimate relationship between flourishing and a person's life. Rasmussen explains that the status of human flourishing as ultimate end or value comes from within and is obtained only in relationship to a person's life. In this sense human flourishing does not refer to some value we can point to but is something that involves a reference to the individual for whom it is good. At first glance agent-relativity may seem confusing because how can human flourishing uphold its objective image and at the same time claim this intimate relationship with the individual? The two notions seem to be poles apart and incommensurable. Rasmussen defends his position by pointing out that unlike the kind of utilitarianism advocated by philosophers such as Henry Sidgwick and John Stuart Mill, his conception of human flourishing does not rely on the ambition of establishing an ethical system that is impersonal and agent-neutral. According to Rasmussen, such ethical theorizing is unsound. As he puts it:

> There is no great divide in the nature of things between the facts that can and cannot be ethically relevant. Particular and contingent facts can be ethically important. Of course, some may be more important than others in achieving human flourishing, but this cannot be determined from one's armchair alone. Certainly, there is for this neo-Aristotelian view, no basis for holding that individual, social and cultural differences among people are ethically irrelevant. They are to the contrary, highly significant.[15]

The important point here is that just because something is considered a value to an individual's personal project and no one else's it is by no means morally irrelevant. In fact, Rasmussen emphasizes the opposite is the case and he argues that such values deserve attention simply because of their relation to the individual. Consider the climber Alex Honnold, who, without the use of rope, scales cliffs such as the northwest face of Half Dome in Yosemite National Park (US). Most people would probably find his climbing activity unnecessarily risky or even immoral, but for Alex Honnold free solo climbing is valuable and so according to Rasmussen morally relevant when we judge his character because we are talking about the flourishing of Alex Honnold and not, for example, mine.

Rasmussen also mentions a more subtle confusion with agent-relativity and this involves the problem of whether something can be of value in its own right and at the same time be agent-relative. According to Rasmussen this objection makes the mistake of confusing instrumental value with agent-relative value and points out that though it is conceivable that all values may be related to some individual this does not mean that their value rests in their being means or instruments. To further support his case Rasmussen reminds us that human flourishing is inclusive and his approach to the concept involves that the constituent goods and virtues are valuable in their own right, but at the same time essentially related to individual human beings and the lives they live. In this sense there can be no talk about incompatibility concerning something being valuable in its own right and agent-relative because the value of goods and virtues is not a matter of their being means or instruments of flourishing but as Rasmussen writes, "their being expressions or realizations of it."[16] Furthermore, the notions that human flourishing is the ultimate value and that it can be perceived as agent-relative are quite compatible. This is because the goal is the flourishing of each individual and its value is found in the activities that "comprise the fulfillment of individual human beings."[17] In this sense it is important to understand that human flourishing is not something that competes with the good of individual humans but essentially makes up the very flourishing of their lives. Thus the good of individuals is their individual flourishing, and individual flourishing and human flourishing, are essentially the same.

Confusion may also appear in relation to agent-relativity because it can be mistaken for egoism. Rasmussen explains that because human flourishing is agent-relative it does not imply that human flourishing cannot incorporate concern or worry for others, or that acting for the welfare of another could not be the primary motivator for one's behavior.[18] In this sense it is possible that acting for the good of another could prove to be as Rasmussen writes, only-good-for-you and not necessarily anyone else. Parents going out of their way to nurture their children or friends helping one another exemplify how flourishing can be agent-relative and involve concern for others. According to Rasmussen, it is even plausible to perceive agent-relativity as compatible with concerns for others in situations that are not viewed as situations of flourishing. To illustrate what Rasmussen has in mind here, we might point out that fire fighters may risk their lives in the attempt to save a person trapped in a burning house, or a university professor may sacrifice her valuable spare time in order to aid a particularly troubled student. If human flourishing were a completely egocentric enterprise it would be hard to imagine a flourishing fire fighter and indeed a university professor sacrificing themselves and their time in the way described above. Based on these examples it seems clear that agent-relativity and egoism are two distinct things.

5. According to Rasmussen human flourishing is also a self-directed activity meaning that self-direction is necessary "to the very character of human flourishing."[19] In other words, there would be no point to human flourishing if self-direction was not a part of it. In addition Rasmussen insists that "self-direction is the central necessary constituent or ingredient of human flourishing—that feature of human flourishing without which no other feature could be a constituent."[20] The idea here is that one does not flourish automatically and that regardless of one's achievements in life, self-direction is crucial to all acts of flourishing. To flourish as a human being is something that one does and one has to make an effort to "discover the goods and virtues of human flourishing as well as to achieve and implement them."[21]

6. By nature human beings are social animals. Our maturation requires a life with others and unlike, for example, mushrooms, we do not reach maturity all by ourselves. A human being is a being with other-orientated potentialities and our flourishing depends as it were on their actualization.[22] In this sense it is important to note that having concerns for others or to entertain social concern is crucial because human flourishing is achieved with and among others. Rasmussen's point is that we are not abstract individuals but beings tied to society and community and that as "much of what is crucial to our self-conception and fundamental values is dependent on our upbringing and environment."[23] In this respect one might wonder if it is at all possible for a hermit to flourish or if this is simply ruled out per definition. Rasmussen does not say anything specific about this but he does offer a few clues to his position on the issue. Rasmussen is a neo-Aristotelian and he mentions the Aristotelian notion that "only a beast or a god would live outside the polis."[24] Furthermore, he points out that our sociality is crucial for our self-understanding and that well-being and "concern for political frameworks is not ethically optional for the individual."[25] Thus it seems fair to say that Rasmussen would argue that living the life of a hermit would greatly compromise a person's flourishing.

Rasmussen's six neo-Aristotelian points about human flourishing are insightful and offer an entry-point to human flourishing with a view of the human good that is objective, self-directed, socially achieved, and yet remaining exceedingly personal. As Rasmussen writes: "the good-for-me is not, and cannot be, the good-for-you, but this is not to say that any choice must be one's own and must involve considerations that are unique to oneself."[26]

Rasmussen emphasizes that in addition to acknowledging the above-mentioned six components it is important to recognize the role of practical wisdom and the appeal to human nature in human flourishing. In Rasmussen's view, practical wisdom refers to the excellent or virtuous use of practical reason; practical reason meaning the intellectual faculty exercised in relation to guiding conduct.[27] To appreciate the importance of practical wisdom in Rasmussen's approach to human flourishing it is vital to remember that he advocates the existence of a plurality of goods. Given these circumstances, practical wisdom is a necessity and is presented as the ability of the individual to work out what is desirable and choice-worthy with regards to the flourishing life among a myriad of different valuable goods. Rasmussen emphasizes the significance of practical wisdom even further as he states that no single good or virtue qualifies as a super good or a super virtue, having the ability to reduce all other goods to being merely of instrumental value.[28] Goods, such as health, creative achievement, friendship, beauty, pleasure, and knowledge, and virtues, such as integrity, courage, temperance, and justice, all seem necessary for human flourishing and are, in Rasmussen's view, to be considered valuable in themselves as opposed to having the status of mere means. Furthermore, Rasmussen mentions that each is but one of the components of flourishing and because human flourishing is individualized each one must be achieved, maintained, and enjoyed in a way that allows them to be "integrated with everything else that makes up the flourishing life of the individual whose flourishing we are talking about."[29] For Rasmussen human flourishing is clearly linked to the individual, and goods and virtues are achieved via considering one's set of "circumstances, talents, endowments, interests, beliefs, and histories that descriptively characterize the individual [including that] individual's community and culture."[30] Now this particular view casts light over Rasmussen's account of human nature and its involvement in human flourishing. He admits that an examination of human nature may reveal what he refers to as basic or generic goods and virtues. However, such an examination does not bring forth "what the weighting or balancing of these goods and virtues should be for the individual."[31] In this respect what constitutes human flourishing for any individual is not revealed in full from an examination of human nature. Human nature is nevertheless still very important to the neo-Aristotelian conception of human flourishing because the appeal to nature signals that "human flourishing is the end (telos) or function (ergon) of human life."[32] According to Rasmussen it also combats a serious critique of the role of nature in human flourishing labeled the "naturalistic fallacy," stating that it is a mistake to "deduce a statement of what ought to be from a statement of what is the case, or deducing a statement about a value from a statement about fact."[33] Rasmussen explains that if human flourishing is to be understood as the natural end for human life and if we were to accept that the human good consists in that very end, then it is not the case that all facts are valueless. According to Rasmussen, "this means that for human beings their good is based on and understood in terms of facts pertaining to their nature."[34] Furthermore, it reveals that "for the class of beings that have natural ends or functions, goodness is ontological in the sense that it is a potentiality that is actualized."[35] What Rasmussen stipulates here is quite controversial because it means that "it is not always a fallacy to go from a fact to a value, because some facts are inherently value-laden"[36] as it were.

While Rasmussen's account provides a good entry point to human flourishing and therefore is relevant to our inquiry into wonder there are potential problems associated with his view.

The first concern is related to Rasmussen's idea that a full examination of human nature may reveal only what is basically and generically good for human beings in terms of their flourishing. Essentially I think Rasmussen is right about this but it is important to note that it is hard, if not impossible, to know when one has reached a full or just sufficient understanding of human nature. Thus it is essential that one should continue to examine human nature as it could potentially reveal important and yet unrecognized features of our shared human nature, and may give us a more detailed account of what we should care about in relation to the kinds of creatures we are and how we flourish in the widest possible understanding.

The second concern about Rasmussen's account of human flourishing, concerns his idea that individual flourishing is achieved via considering one's set of circumstances, talents, endowments, interests, beliefs, and histories that descriptively characterize the individual, including that individual's community and culture. Rasmussen's view seems agreeable but could perhaps benefit from further specification. To illustrate this one might, for example, focus on the problem concerning the task of finding out one's talents and endowments, which can be hard to determine with certainty. Consider, for example, the case of de Pasquale mentioned in the first chapter. In his article "A Wonder Full Life," he reports that as a nine year old he was put into a class for the mentally retarded because his test score on the average IQ test was as he puts it "just a hair above what an orangutan would have scored."[37] Had he not questioned "authority" at the time it is quite possible that he would have been discouraged from further education, never would have pursued a career in philosophy and consequently later on never have written about his "Wonder Full Life" in the inspiring way that he does. This example illustrates potential problems with these sorts of tests and how they are used as guides in people's lives. Regardless of the quality of a particular test and the quality of its application, it can be ventured that the results it delivers must always be met with a critical eye. The danger is that the result is taken to be a fact understood as something absolute and unchangeable over time and so can be used with certainty to determine the future for a person. Wonder is called for because it can be argued that such a test aims to flesh out the very nature of a person, which is problematic because the person who is tested is situated in a spot between actuality and potentiality. Who is to say for sure how a person can develop and to what extent past and current challenges cannot be overcome and extend a person's flourishing? This points to the idea that if one does not wonder at attempts claiming certainty about one's talents or endowments it could potentially have a colossal negative influence on one's flourishing.

A similar point about criticality can be made about Rasmussen's emphasis on community and culture in his approach to human flourishing, which brings me to my third and final concern in relation to Rasmussen's account of human flourishing.

To recapitulate Rasmussen thinks that goods and virtues are achieved via considering one's set of circumstances, talents, endowments, interests, beliefs, and histories that descriptively characterize the individual, including that individual's community and culture.[38] In this regard it is necessary to depict in greater detail in what sense communities and, in particular, culture influence one's flourishing. For example, most people would agree that having good health is valuable to human flourishing, but how health is understood and how it is positioned among the various other goods in terms of importance may differ from culture to culture. To give an example, consider the ancient state of Sparta, which, owing to its militaristic focus, viewed health and fitness of the citizens to be of utmost importance. This entailed that children were examined for their health and fitness and those that were considered "puny and deformed" were thrown into a chasm to die whereto we can say that the Spartans were effectively practicing a form of eugenics.[39] Furthermore, the primary obligation for a Spartan citizen was to be a good soldier whose worth exceeded that of several men belonging to other cities.[40] It is quite possible that given this particular culture his view of health differs significantly from that of the average person today. This example clearly illustrates the importance and role of culture in depicting what makes a "good" good, and its influence on human flourishing. As the anthropologist Adam Kuper points out in his book *Culture: The Anthropologist's Account*: "Cultural identity can never provide an adequate guide for living. We have multiple identities, and even if we have a primary one we may not want to conform to it."[41] What Kuper in effect is stating is that when one is concerned with how human beings may flourish, it is important to adopt a critical attitude to culture including the culture one is situated in.

Rasmussen provides great insight into the notion of human flourishing. However, it is strange that he says nothing about wonder and the individual's capacity for wonder, because when it comes to the kind of individual flourishing he advocates there is indeed much for the individual to wonder about, including what human nature consists of and in what sense such a nature demands attention in relation to the formulation of what makes a particular individual flourish. Furthermore, wonderment is called for with regards to Rasmussen's approach because his emphasis on individual flourishing pays little attention to the possible generic goods that may be determined from an investigation of human nature. In order to make advances in this area let us now turn to the philosophy of Alasdair MacIntyre.

ALASDAIR MACINTYRE AND HUMAN FLOURISHING

In his book *Dependent Rational Animals*, philosopher Alasdair MacIntyre presents an approach to human flourishing grounded in the idea that we are vulnerable dependent rational animals with the ability to become independent practical reasoners. MacIntyre's contribution to the debate about human flourishing is important to our present investigation about wonder because he furthers the inquiry into human nature and what we have in common rather than where we differ. *Dependent Rational Animals* is in MacIntyre's own words a work of correction and signals a departure from his earlier approach to moral philosophy.[42] One significant departure involves the attempt to integrate what he calls Aristotle's metaphysical biology[43] in his approach to ethics, which is a notion he repudiated in his earlier book *After Virtue*. What this means is that instead of attempting to give an account of virtue that situates virtue within social practices, the lives of individuals, and the lives of communities (which was the focus in *After Virtue*), *Dependent Rational Animals* centers on the notion that human beings are biological entities and that to suppose an ethics independent of biology is wrong.[44] In addition, it is important, as MacIntyre also explains, not to see his book as an attempt to once and for all settle the debate on human flourishing. The debate is ongoing and MacIntyre's book contains, as he admits, a good deal of unfinished philosophical business.[45] For our purposes here I will present a selection of important points put forth by MacIntyre that can contribute to our understanding of human flourishing and wonder. More specifically the focus will be on (1) animality and human nature, (2) vulnerability and dependence, and (3) the importance of becoming an independent practical reasoner and how the development of virtues makes this possible. Finally a few comments and a short criticism of Macintyre, including suggestions of how we might take his work further, will be extended.

MacIntyre's focus on animality and human nature is important to his understanding of human flourishing. He argues that human beings often forget that we are but animals among animals and that our nature is primarily, if not exclusively, bodily.[46] Since the early sixteenth century, the term "animal" has been used to label a class whose members include spiders, bees, chimpanzees, dolphins, and humans, but not plants, inanimate beings, angels, and God. However, it has also been utilized in naming a class consisting only of nonhuman animals.[47] In MacIntyre's view the latter usage of the word has become dominant in Western society and in its wake a particular habit of mind has emerged that distracts us from recognizing just how much we share and have in common with certain other animal species. This shared "territory" is important to MacIntyre's overall vision of flourishing, which is in principle not only applicable to human beings. He argues that just like human beings some animals such as dolphins have intentions and reasons for action, and that these highly intelligent animals are able to pursue goods such as learning how to interact with other dolphins (and sometimes human beings) in ways that contribute toward their flourishing.[48] Concerning the term "flourishing" MacIntyre explains further that he is committed to give, in some form, a naturalistic account of what is good for a particular species. However, he does this in the spirit of caution as he does not think the meaning of "good" can be produced solely from a list identifying natural characteristics.[49] Furthermore, MacIntyre does not support the notion that "good is a property that supervenes upon some set of natural characteristics [which] is to give a name to the problem of how to understand the relationship between goodness and such characteristics, not to solve it."[50] In this sense he seems skeptical toward an account of the good following an investigation of nature, but at the same time he seems critical toward purely subjective accounts of the good and those accounts associated with a particular cultural outlook. MacIntyre acknowledges that this is a significant philosophical problem to which he has no solution and where philosophy still has work to do.

Nevertheless, MacIntyre enriches our understanding of the human condition and what makes us flourish by further investigating our human nature and makes us aware of our animal nature and that we are vulnerable and dependent creatures. In order to begin to appreciate the importance of vulnerability and dependency in MacIntyre's account of human flourishing let us consider the following entry from his opening chapter:

> We human beings are vulnerable to many kinds of afflictions and most of us are at some time afflicted by serious ills. How we cope is only in small part up to us. It is most often to others that we owe our survival, let alone our flourishing, as we encounter bodily illness and injury, inadequate nutrition, mental defect and disturbance, and human aggression and neglect.[51]

It seems quite clear from the quotation that MacIntyre thinks human beings are both vulnerable and dependent. Furthermore, he believes that it is often to others we owe our survival and flourishing. In addition, the quotation offers a list of "encounters" highlighting what we may refer to as the bodily, the mental, and the social dimension of human vulnerability. The bodily dimension highlights, not surprisingly, that we are bodily beings and MacIntyre clearly points to this by stating that we encounter bodily illness and injury during our lives. Recognizing that we are bodily creatures is important for our flourishing because bodily illness and injury may cause everything from momentary inconvenience to permanent disability and untimely death.

By stating that human beings may encounter mental defect and disturbance MacIntyre also points to a vulnerable mental dimension of human existence. Recognizing that we are mental creatures and that this part is vulnerable is significant for our flourishing. To illustrate just how we are vulnerable in a mental sense one might point to the symptoms people experience in relation to workplace stress. Stress at work can cause everything from irritability, aggressiveness, isolation, and insomnia to raised blood pressure, stomach disorders, anxiety, and low self-esteem.[52] To experience symptoms such as these clearly indicates a vulnerable mental dimension, which could compromise our flourishing.

Continuing to draw on the social dimension of human life, MacIntyre also refers to human aggression and neglect as factors that expose our vulnerability. We flourish among other people but it is not always that other people provide the support we need in order to flourish. A child born into an abusive family where she faces inadequate nutrition and violence would testify to this effect. This example shows how human beings as social creatures are vulnerable and how neglect from fellow human beings may influence our flourishing negatively.

Let us now consider a third point in MacIntyre's philosophy, which is concerned with the importance of becoming an independent practical reasoner and how the development of virtues makes this possible.

Human beings share their practical lives and in order to flourish as the kinds of beings we are we pursue goods. MacIntyre explains that what is "good" is what we ascribe to what benefits humans as the kind of creatures they are, and what benefits human beings in virtue of their particular roles within particular contexts of practice.[53] However, as there are many different kinds of goods we are forced to make choices, which (for better or worse) arises from the human capacity for evaluating reasons for action.[54] According to MacIntyre what helps bring about good choice-making is our capacity for independent practical reasoning. However, to excel in this respect is an achievement that rests upon the development of particular characteristics.[55] These characteristics include first of all that one learns to detach oneself from immediate desires. Furthermore, it is important to be able to imagine alternative realistic futures, and lastly to have the ability to "recognize and to make true practical judgments concerning a variety of kinds of good."[56] In addition, MacIntyre claims that acquiring these characteristics is possible only for those who have acquired an assortment of intellectual and moral virtues as they allow a person to make up her own mind on the choices she faces.

To better appreciate why MacIntyre thinks the development of virtues is important in becoming an independent practical reasoner let us briefly focus on what he labels the virtue of temperateness. In MacIntyre's view this particular virtue is important to flourishing and centers on avoiding extreme behavior and finding the temperate spot or middle ground between, for example, extreme self-indulgence and unappreciative and insensitive puritanism. Temperateness makes a person consider her particular circumstances because it does not demand the same of an athlete in training as it does for a recuperating patient in need of rebuilding her strength.[57] There is more to be said about virtue but for now it is important to stress that there is a moral dimension inherent to the kind of flourishing advocated here, and it shows itself by paying attention to human vulnerability, dependence, and how our ability to function as independent practical reasoners rises from the development of virtues.

MacIntyre's philosophy is concerned with the political, because how we organize ourselves influences our flourishing. What is especially noteworthy about his account of human flourishing in this respect is its criticality toward the influence of institutions. In particular, MacIntyre is concerned with the role of institutionalized networks of giving and receiving, and how structures of unequal distribution of power are involved in victimization and exploitation, and how such are capable of masking and protecting the distributions in question.[58] Furthermore, MacIntyre argues that if we are not aware of these structures the quality of our practical judgment and reasoning are at risk. He writes:

> The virtues which we need in order to achieve both our own goods and the goods of others through participation in such networks only function as genuine virtues when their exercise is informed by an awareness of how power is distributed and of the corruptions to which its use is liable.[59]

Thus, MacIntyre's focus on genuine virtues in relation to networks, the notion of power and corruption adds yet another layer of complexity to our human condition. In addition, MacIntyre explains that it is characteristic of our human condition that we, over time, find ourselves holding positions within some set of institutionalized relationship. These relationships may cover everything from being a member of a family or household, going to school, undertaking an apprenticeship, or becoming involved with a local community or larger societies. This is complicated further by the notion that some of these relationships promote human flourishing and others do not. Macintyre explains that some relationships are constitutive in the sense that without them it would be impossible to attain or be sustained in attaining goods.[60] Friendship, for example, qualifies as such. However, different kinds of relationships exist that merely voice established hierarchies of power and the uses of power, which as dominating and depriving instruments, often obstruct our movements toward goods.[61] MacIntyre is concerned with dominating and abusive relationships and it can be well said that he desires for human kind to establish a social order or an "ecosystem" of human relationships that promote the development of people capable of living flourishing lives, understood as people who can reason independently and practically.[62] In other words, in order to be an independent practical reasoner one must be able to give to others an intelligible account of one's reasoning. In this respect MacIntyre adds that the intelligible account required need not be theoretical and one does not need to match the reasoning powers of a logician to be an independent practical reasoner.[63] MacIntyre explains further that independent practical reasoners are concerned with means and not ends. Now does this mean that the logician is concerned with ends while practical reasoners are engaged in deliberations on means only? Not quite, because according to Macintyre the independent practical reasoner can deliberate about ends; however, when she does she deliberates on a practical level, meaning that she treats ends as means to still further ends. In this respect, practical reasoning helps one decide what action is to be taken to achieve a given goal. In addition, MacIntyre explains that we are only able to pose questions and answers in this regard because of the extent to which we agree about goods and about the good.[64] In this light MacIntyre's view of practical reasoning consists of reasoning together with others and generally within an established set of social relationships. From this perspective the good of the individual is pursued alongside the good of those who makes up the established set of social relationships. A practical and adequate understanding of what makes us flourish encompasses the whole set of social relationships in which we have come to live out our lives. This brings us to an important passage in MacIntyre's book, which reads:

> If I am to flourish to the full extent that is possible for a human being, then my whole life has to be of a certain kind, one in which I not only engage in and achieve some measure of success in the activities of an independent practical reasoner, but also receive and have a reasonable expectation of receiving the attended care needed when I am very young, old and ill, or injured. So each of us achieves our good only if and insofar as others make our good their good by helping us through periods of disability to become ourselves the kind of human being—through acquisition and exercise of the virtues—who makes the good of others her or his good, and this not because we have calculated that, only if we help others, will they help us, in some trading of advantage for advantage.[65]

Macintyre highlights that for a human being to flourish to the fullest it is important to recognize the importance of achieving a certain level of success when it comes to the activity of independent practical reasoning. Furthermore, our flourishing is dependent on being a part of a social order that, through the exercise of virtues, comes to value care that supports flourishing and is able to provide such care to its members should they need it. A society functioning in this way has successfully fused the common good with the good of the individual without relying on a business model of mutual reciprocity. On this note let us end the presentation of MacIntyre and continue to comment and criticize his approach to human flourishing insofar as it is relevant to wonder.

Despite the advancements that MacIntyre offers, his approach does not represent a complete account of human flourishing and there is room for improvement. One area that might require more attention concerns the problem of giving an account of the good. MacIntyre is committed to give some form of a naturalistic account of what is good but at the same time he does not think that such an account can be purely naturalistic. In addition, he seems to be skeptical about individual accounts and accounts that are produced from within a particular culture or society. His skepticism is grounded in the idea that relationships can be disruptive of our flourishing. This is an important point but unfortunately MacIntyre also brings the inquiry into the human good to a stalemate as he offers no solutions as to how we can further our understanding of it. This is problematic and I will explore this problem more fully later where I shall engage with an altogether different approach to human flourishing. Meanwhile, let us consider MacIntyre's commitment to the idea that our individual good is achieved insofar as others make their good our good. At first glance this may sound quite reasonable because if we have radically different conceptions of the good, forming the relationships necessary for our flourishing seems difficult. However, one may attempt to criticize this by pointing out that MacIntyre's philosophy resembles in its outlook on morality too much that of small-scale communities found in Greece at the time of Aristotle. It is one thing to establish a moral community equipped with a shared understanding of virtue and human flourishing within a small-scale polis counting thousands of people, and quite another to have the same aspirations for a complex, modern multi-cultural city-state, counting millions of subjects. In such societies, social institutions, as anthropologist George Silberbauer explains, are highly elaborated, specialized, and although integrated as components of the whole socio-cultural system, they are relatively separated from and impervious to one another.[66] This complicates matters to such a degree that it makes it unlikely that such relatively separated institutions would begin speaking the same moral language and make a common conception of human flourishing central to their operations. In this light one could criticize MacIntyre for being utopian in his outlook. To strengthen this point, consider, for example, the existence of multinational profit-orientated corporations with little or no care for human flourishing. Is it realistic to think that such corporations will change their attitudes toward profit and human capital in favor of approaches to those that incorporate the notion of human flourishing? This seems hard to imagine because, after all, business is an economic pursuit and ethics is not the point of gravity in business operations.[67] To counter the accusations of MacIntyre's outlook being utopian, in this case one might argue that it is possible that a company or firm can be supportive of human flourishing and at the same time make profit. Imagine if a group of human flourishing supporters successfully campaigned against purely profit-orientated firms and start a trend among the population of a large-scale society that made citizens boycott purely profit-orientated businesses. It is perfectly possible that upon realizing the loss of customers, and consequently profit, the purely profit-orientated businesses would quickly begin changing their outlooks and policies in favor of human flourishing. One could argue that ethically speaking the changes would come about for the wrong reasons but it does not refute the possibility that having a successful profit-orientated business can coincide with advocating human flourishing. In this sense MacIntyre's "utopia" could be realized, but it demands that the people of society whom the businesses view as customers value the idea of human flourishing, take action and begin challenging the relationships they are a part of that do not support human flourishing.

MacIntyre's approach to human flourishing is important and advances the conception of human flourishing provided by Rasmussen. The reason for this rests mainly on the notion that MacIntyre readdresses human nature and focuses on what we have in common rather than where we differ. Additionally, by exposing the complexity of being a social creature without abandoning our biological anchoring, MacIntyre takes us beyond Rasmussen's "individual flourishing" and situates us in a larger context where the relationships we are engaged in are crucial for our flourishing. Furthermore, we must acknowledge that not all of these, be they family relationships or relationships with powerful large-scale institutions such as private corporations, religious communities, or political movements, necessarily support our flourishing. In this sense MacIntyre encourages us to evaluate how we organize ourselves in society and to think about to what end our relationships aspire.

Overall, MacIntyre's contribution to the human flourishing debate is estimable, because it is a fine example of bridge building where a serious attempt is made to correlate a "naturalistic view" of human beings and a "culturalistic view" of human beings in order to point out what is important when we talk about human flourishing. With this said, let us push on and focus on the philosophy of Martha Nussbaum, which can be seen as a tool that may help us assess to what extent particular social practices or ways of life contribute to human flourishing.

MARTHA NUSSBAUM AND HUMAN FLOURISHING

Philosopher Martha Nussbaum's contribution to the understanding of flourishing known as the "Human Development approach" and also as the "Capability Approach" or "Capabilities Approach" has evolved into a theoretical paradigm.[68] Provisionally the approach can be used as a means to comparative quality-of-life assessment and to theorizing about basic social justice that holds central the question of what each person is able to do and to be. The approach takes each person to be an end and is not merely concerned with the well-being of people but also what opportunities are available to each person.[69] In this regard the approach offers an alternative to traditional quality of life models, which promotes the notion that the quality of life of a nation only improves when the Gross Domestic Product per capita increases.[70]

Since the 1990's, the Capabilities Approach has enjoyed increased popularity and has had an impact on international agencies concerned with welfare, such as the World Bank and United Nations Development Programme. Most nations now produce their own capability-studies of the well-being of people in different regions and groups in their own societies.[71] Testifying also to this increased popularity are the numerous articles and books on the topic and the launch of the Human Development and Capability Association in 2004.[72] The association has an annual meeting, publishes a journal labeled the *Journal of Human Development and Capabilities* and sponsors a wide range of seminars and activities all over the world. Economist Amartya Sen introduced the notion of capabilities as an approach to welfare economics[73] and he and Nussbaum are founding presidents.

As a philosopher, Nussbaum can be termed a universalist that from an Aristotelian perspective argues for ethical progression, human development, and the improvement of the position of especially women around the world who are burdened by unreasonable local traditions that prevent them from flourishing. Furthermore, it can be ventured that her work on human flourishing is distinct from that of Rasmussen and MacIntyre in the sense that it is designed to work in praxis. This means that Nussbaum's approach can be used as a tool of measurement that can help us determine whether a particular practice or view is commendable from a point of flourishing.

To depict what Nussbaum thinks is important with regards to flourishing we shall, in the following, focus on the "thick, vague conception of the good" and what she calls the basic list of human functional capabilities formulated in her article "Aristotelian Social Democracy."[74] In order to appreciate Nussbaum's position it is vital to understand some key elements of Aristotle's philosophy. In the *Nichomachean Ethics*, Aristotle states that human beings have a capability for reason[75] and in *The Politics*, Aristotle states, "in general all men really seek what is good, not what was customary with their forefathers."[76] It can be argued that we use our rationality to seek out what is good for us as human beings in the sense that we use a conception of the good to justify our actions and our ways of life. A conception of the good provides a measure for actions and viewpoints, however, conceptions of the good vary among human beings and there are different opinions about what the *right* conception of the good is. In order to solve this problem philosophers have sought to justify their conception of the good by referring to abstract formulas, which would leave no room for doubt or arbitrary subjective influences. Such abstract formulas are found embedded in utilitarianism and Kantianism, but they have so far proven problematic, and in part responsible for the popular turning to relativism. However, it is important to note that the relativistic stance does not refute Aristotle's claim that human beings look for the good and not for the way of their ancestors. Nor does it reject the possibility that a broad objective account of the human good can be established. It is on that background that Martha Nussbaum advocates this particular idea and puts forth what she calls "the thick vague conception of the good."[77] Nussbaum writes:

> The Aristotelian uses a conception of the good that is not "thin," like Rawls's "thin theory"—that is, confined to the enumeration of all-purpose means to good living, but "thick"—dealing, that is, with human ends across all areas of human life. The conception is, however, vague and this in a good sense. It admits, that is, of many concrete specifications; and yet it draws, as Aristotle puts it, an "outline sketch" of the good life.[78]

In other words, Nussbaum's approach refrains from drawing on any singular conception of what it is to be a human being and at the same time her approach, as philosopher John M. Alexander has expressed, it "could be compatible with different moral, religious and philosophical doctrines."[79] Nussbaum explains that her approach is:

> Both internal to human history and strongly evaluative and its aim is to be as universal as possible, to set down the basis for our recognition of members of very different traditions as human across religious and metaphysical gulfs. . . . The account is the outcome of a process of self-interpretation and self-clarification that makes use of the story-telling imagination far more than the scientific intellect. The basic idea of the thick vague theory is that we tell ourselves stories of the general outline or structure of the life of a human being. We ask and answer the question, what is it to live as a being situated, so to speak, between the beasts and the gods, with certain abilities that set us off from the rest of the world of nature, and yet with certain limits that come from our membership in the world of nature? The idea is that we share a vague conception, having a number of distinct parts, of what it is to be situated in the world as human, and of what transitions either "up" or "down" so to speak, would turn us into beings no longer human—thus

(since on the whole we conceive of species identity as at least necessary for personal identity) into creatures different from ourselves.[80]

Nussbaum presents two stages of the "thick vague conception of the good." The first stage is a first approximation to what appears to be a part of any human being's life and is important because it brings forth a general outline of what it is to be human. The approximation counts the following entries:

Mortality

All human beings face death and learn as they progress through life that they are mortal creatures. However, awareness of one's mortality does not entail one liking it. Apart from certain circumstances in which death will be desirable given the available alternatives it is true that humans beings, in general, wish to live and have an aversion toward death. To a certain extent mortality is what defines and sets the framework for humans. Should we encounter an immortal anthropomorphic being (as Nussbaum calls it), "its way of life would be so different from our own that we had to categorize it differently."[81] The same would happen if we encountered "a mortal being that showed no tendency to avoid death or to seek to continue its life."[82] We would view it as a disturbed being or simply a being that was radically different from ourselves.

The Human Body

Nussbaum states that all human beings are bodily creatures and that the body itself sets limits on what can be experienced. Nussbaum writes:

> The fact that any given human being might have lived anywhere and belonged to any culture is a great part of what grounds our mutual recognition; this fact has a great deal to do with the general humanness of the body, its great distinctness from other bodies.[83]

Nussbaum continues by pointing out some common features about our embodiment:

1. *Hunger and thirst.* Despite small variations in the diets being situated in a particular culture all human beings are equally dependent on food and drink in order to live. Furthermore, all human beings have appetites that are indices of need. Nussbaum remarks that appetitive experience might be shaped by culture and may not correspond directly to what the body really needs. However, "we discover enormous similarities and overlap. Moreover human beings in general do not wish to be hungry and thirsty (though they might choose to fast for some reason)."[84]
2. *Need for shelter.* The naked human body is fragile and without protection from the elements, unlike so many of our fellow animals

whose furry or scaly exterior provides protection. It is a fact that the naked human being would not survive for long in an environment without refuge from "excessive heat of the sun, from rain, from wind, from snow and frost."[85]

3. *Sexual desire.* Even though sexual desire comes short of eating and drinking it is a feature in practically every human being's life. To be asexual would be a sign of a being that was far from human since "sexual desire is and has all along been a very strong basis for the recognition of others different from ourselves as human beings."[86]

4. *Mobility.* Human beings are partly constituted by our ability to move from place to place and this not merely with the help of the vast body of transportation we have invented but also with the aid of "our very own bodies."[87] Not to be able to move or being prevented from moving is a source of discontent and "an anthropomorphic being who without disability, chose never to move from birth to death would be hard to view as human; and a life altogether cut off from mobility seems a life less than fully human."[88]

Capacity for Pleasure and Pain

In general, human beings have the capacity to experience pleasure and pain. Even though such experiences might vary across cultural borders and the experience itself may vary from individual to individual, the capacity can be viewed as a universal human trademark. Furthermore, Nussbaum argues that the aversion to pain is a part of being human. Conclusively she states that "a society whose members altogether lacked that aversion would surely be considered to be outside the bounds of humanness."[89]

Cognitive Capacities: Perceiving, Imagining, Thinking

All human beings have sense-perception, the ability to imagine and the ability to think and making distinctions. Furthermore, Nussbaum writes with a reference to Aristotle that we have the ability to reach out for understanding. In relation to this, if a group of people existed who were totally deprived of sense-perception, imagination, or reasoning and thinking "we are not in any of these cases imagining a [group] of human beings, no matter what they look like."[90]

Early Infant Development

All human beings begin their life as helplessly dependent and vulnerable babies. A being in such a state experiences closeness and distance from those its very life depends on.[91] Nussbaum mentions that "this common structure to early life gives rise to a great deal of overlapping experience that is of great importance for the formation of emotions and desires, and that is a major source of our ability to see ourselves in the emotional experiences of those whose lives are otherwise very different from our own."[92] She furthermore argues that should we encounter a group of apparent humans and discover that they never had been babies or did not know of the experience of dependency, need, and affection, one can argue that "their form of life was sufficiently different from our own that they could not be considered part of the same kin."[93]

Practical Reason

All human beings participate or at least try to participate in managing their own lives. They form or acquire a conception of the good and (more or less) lay out a strategy in terms of how they should live. This involves being able "to choose, evaluate and to function accordingly."[94] Bearing in mind the diversity of human life, this has of course many concrete forms and "is related in complex ways to other capabilities, emotional, imaginative, and intellectual."[95]

Affiliation with Other Human Beings

Nussbaum writes: "Aristotle claimed that human beings recognize and feel a sense of affiliation and concern for other human beings."[96] In this relation she points out that we find a close nexus between the conceptual and the empirical. It is a fact that "we recognize other human beings but at the same time our concept of human beings is shaped (in an open ended way) by what we find ourselves able to recognize."[97] Furthermore, Nussbaum points out that "we value the form of life that is constituted by these recognitions and affiliations—we live to and with others, and regard a life not lived in affiliation with others to be a life not worth living."[98] Aristotle claims that we define ourselves in terms of a minimum of two kinds of affiliations, namely "intimate family relations and social or civic relations"[99] and Nussbaum agrees with this point.

Relatedness to Other Species and to Nature

Human beings represent one species among many other different species including plants placing us in a complex interlocking ordered universe.[100] This ordering both supports us and limits us in many ways but what is important to recognize is the fact that we are dependent on this particular order, and many human beings find that we owe it respect and concern. Nussbaum argues a creature "who treated animals exactly like stones and could not be brought to recognize some problem with that would probably be regarded as too strange to be human."[101] The same thing would happen to a creature, which "did not care in any way for the wonder and beauty of the natural world."[102] In relation to this, Nussbaum makes an ominous comment in her text. She adds that perhaps we are in the process of witnessing a part of our kind "become other than what a human being has usually been taken to be; perhaps we shall someday be called upon either to change our conception of humanness or to acknowledge a fundamental gulf in forms of life among humans."[103] Nussbaum does not offer any details concerning whom she has in mind but if the transhumanist movement[104] should ever succeed in, for example, "liberating" a human being from her "biological constraints" or otherwise change her human condition I suppose this being would qualify.

Humor and Play

Human beings, regardless of their culture and place of living, have a tendency to make room for recreation and laughter. Human beings are recognized as the animal who laughs and Nussbaum states furthermore that "laughter and play are frequently among the deepest and also the first modes of our mutual recognition."[105] Children play and laugh in Africa as well as in Norway and is not a feature connected to a specific culture or race. Should one encounter a child unable to laugh and play then surely it would be a sign of a deep disturbance. Should this situation be permanent then "the consequence may be that we will prove unable to consider the child capable of leading a fully human life."[106] An entire society deprived of this ability would seem strange and frightening to us. Nussbaum argues: "We certainly do not want a life that leaves this element out; and on the whole we want more of it than circumstances permit us to have."[107]

Separateness

Nussbaum informs us that however much we live for and toward others, we are, each of us, "one in number, proceeding on a separate path through the world from birth to death."[108] Each person dies alone and this is so because we are separate beings. "If a person walks across the room, no other follows automatically. When we count the number of human beings in a room, we have no difficulty figuring out where one begins and the other ends."[109] Nussbaum argues that this is a highly relevant point since individuality is absent or unrecognized in certain societies or cultures. In relation to this Nussbaum also reminds us that "even the most intense forms of human interaction, for example, sexual experience, are experiences of responsiveness, and not of fusion."[110] This demonstrates that whatever viewpoint one has with regard to lovers or offspring they are all separated and individual creatures.

Strong Separateness

Nussbaum writes that human life has its own context and surroundings because of its separateness. Objects, places, a history, particular friendships, locations, and sexual ties are linked to the individual and according to Nussbaum this is how a person, to some extent, is able to identify herself. Nussbaum acknowledges that societies (or cultures) vary in the degree of strong separateness they advocate. However, Nussbaum finds a disregard for strong separateness significantly problematic. She argues:

> There is no life, short of a life of total imprisonment, and perhaps not even that life, that really does fail to say the words "mine" and "not-mine" in some idiosyncratic and non-shared way. What I touch, use, love, respond to, I touch, use, love, respond to from my own separate point of view. The items I call "mine" are not exactly the same as those called that way by any other person.[111]

In Nussbaum's view human beings see one another as beings that wish to have some separateness of context or a private zone to move about in. Furthermore, she claims that they wish to have some special items to use and hold and cherish.

This concludes Nussbaum's first approximation about what seemingly is a part of any human life and from this vantage point she moves on to the second stage of her approach, resulting in a list of basic human functional capabilities. The following slightly abridged list is from Nussbaum's book *Creating Capabilities*[112]:

1. *Life.* Being able to live to the end of a human life of normal length; not dying prematurely, or before one's life is so reduced as to be not worth living.
2. *Bodily health.* Being able to have good health, including reproductive health; to be adequately nourished; to have adequate shelter.
3. *Bodily integrity.* Being able to move freely from place to place; to be secure against violent assault, including sexual assault and domestic violence; having opportunities for sexual satisfaction and for choice in matters of reproduction.
4. *Senses, imagination, and thought.* Being able to use the senses, to imagine, think, and reason—and to do these things in a "truly human" way, a way informed and cultivated by an adequate education, including, but by no means limited to, literacy and basic mathematical and scientific training. Being able to use imagination and thought in connection with experiencing and producing works and events of one's own choice, religious, literacy, musical, and so forth. Being able to use one's mind in ways protected by guarantees of freedom of expression with respect to both political and

artistic speech, and freedom of religious exercise. Being able to have pleasurable experiences and to avoid nonbeneficial pain.
5. *Emotions.* Being able to have attachments to things and people outside ourselves; to love those who love and care for us, to grieve at their absence; in general, to love, to grieve, to experience longing, gratitude, and justified anger. Not having one's emotional development blighted by fear and anxiety.
6. *Practical reason.* Being able to form a conception of the good and to engage in critical reflection about the planning of one's life.
7. *Affiliation.* (A) Being able to live with and toward others, to recognize and show concern for other human beings, to engage in various forms of social interaction; to be able to imagine the situation of another. (B) Having the social bases of self-respect and non-humiliation; being able to be treated as a dignified being whose worth is equal to that of others. This entails provisions of nondiscrimination on the basis of race, sex, sexual orientation, ethnicity, caste, religion, and national origin.
8. *Other species.* Being able to live with concern for and in relation to animals, plants, and the world of nature.
9. *Play.* Being able to laugh, to play, to enjoy recreational activities.
10. *Control over one's environment.* (A) *Political*—being able to participate effectively in political choices that govern one's life; having the right of political participation, protection of free speech and association. (B) *Material*—being able to hold property and having property rights on an equal basis with others; having the freedom from unwarranted search and seizure. In work, being able to work as a human being, exercising practical reason and entering into meaningful relationships of mutual recognition with other workers.[113]

To fully appreciate Nussbaum's work it is important to understand what she means by capability and functioning. In Nussbaum's term, capabilities refer to a person's abilities (internal capabilities), but also to "the freedoms or opportunities created by a combination of personal abilities and the political, social, and economic environment (combined capabilities).[114] Functionings are different from capabilities and she describes them as active realizations of one or more capabilities. In other words, functionings give capabilities their end, which is a notion much esteemed by Nussbaum, because a society might successfully promote internal capabilities but "cut off the avenues through which people actually have the opportunity to function in accordance with those capabilities."[115]

To appreciate Nussbaum's approach to human flourishing it is also important to note that she is pluralist about value, which is to say she is for diversity of value but not relativistic about value.[116] What this means is that she does not want all of us to be the same but at the same time she insists that there are certain kinds of lives that, if measured against the list of basic human functional capabilities, simply do not flourish as much as others. Furthermore, Nussbaum is concerned with what she calls entrenched social injustice and inequality, which is to say that she is concerned with the lives of people who, because of a particular cultural or political environment, are at risk of being socialized or otherwise forced into a particular way of life that works against their flourishing. [117] Thus it becomes clear that Nussbaum's work is very much concerned with social justice. It insists that for a life to be worthy of human dignity it demands "at a bare minimum, an ample threshold level of the ten Central Capabilities,"[118] which is to say that in order for an individual to flourish she must have at least a degree of the ten capabilities present in her life.

One may seek to criticize Nussbaum's approach by venturing that it is merely a human rights approach in new clothing. This is an understandable criticism because both the human rights approach and Nussbaum's position accept that by virtue of being human people have particular entitlements and that it is worthwhile respecting such entitlements. Nevertheless, there are differences between the two approaches and one significant difference is that Nussbaum's approach acknowledges that nonhuman animals also have entitlements, meaning that her approach is more encompassing than the human rights approach.[119] To further point out differences consider the wording of point C of article 29 of the convention of the rights of the child. It reads:

> The development of respect for the child's parents, his or her own cultural identity, language and values, for the national values of the country in which the child is living, the country from which he or she may originate, and for civilizations different from his or her own.[120]

While the human rights approach on the issue of education emphasizes the importance of cultural identity and values, Nussbaum's approach provides a platform from where such can be criticized.[121] This is important because it is not a given that all parents, cultures, and national values, and so forth, promote human flourishing and if they do not we must ask ourselves why they should be respected.

Another potential problem with Nussbaum's contribution to our understanding of human flourishing lies in the commentary she has made to the basic list of human functional capabilities. She holds that in order for a person to flourish in a minimal sense that person has to have an ample threshold level of the capabilities but the phrase "ample threshold" is ambiguous. This could be problematic because unless Nussbaum's list of capabilities clearly communicates what it takes for an individual to flourish it loses its potency as a tool for promoting it.

One might also object to Nussbaum's approach by claiming that it is paternalistic and effectively robs people of the freedom to make their own choices about what is good for them. Nussbaum's response to this objection is that the argument from paternalism is important and if one advocates the capability approach one should be mindful about paternalism. However in defense of her position she states:

> A commitment to respecting people's choices hardly seems incompatible with the endorsement of universal values. Indeed, it appears to endorse explicitly at least one universal value, the value of having the opportunity to think and choose for oneself. Thinking about paternalism gives a strong reason to respect the variety of ways citizens actually choose to lead their lives in a pluralistic society, and therefore to prefer a form of universalism that is compatible with freedom and choice of most significant sorts. But religious toleration, associative freedom, and the other major liberties are themselves universal values. They require a universalist account for their recognition and their protection against those who don't want other people to make choices for themselves.[122]

Nussbaum's defense points out something important about her approach and the pluralistic society she advocates, which is that a pluralistic society depends on the recognition that we wish to make choices for ourselves and that we do not want other people to make choices for us, which spells out a universal value important to all who embrace pluralism.

Further criticism of Nussbaum's approach has been brought forward by philosopher Philip McReynolds, who thinks that it is problematic that Nussbaum focuses on what he calls public choices in order to help individuals achieve their own individual goods without offering any strategy for how to actually achieve those goods. McReynolds elaborates by saying that once we have established capabilities, individuals are left to their own devices in terms of evaluating their own specific ends and projects which consists in more or less arbitrary acts of will. Furthermore, he thinks that Nussbaum's approach signals a sort of libertarianism without morals and that this is a problem.[123] In defense of Nussbaum one might point out that her approach is simply not designed to solve individual moral dilemmas but it helps us realize our common humanity and how we may flourish as human beings. One could of course see this as a shortcoming and that there is more work to be done in terms of Nussbaum's approach. Alternatively, one might point out that even though Nussbaum does not offer Kantian principles or utilitarian algorithms, she still thinks that ethical truth is important. In fact, she thinks that some ways of life are better than others and that some ways can be rightly criticized and categorized as stupid, pernicious, and false.[124] This is grounded in Nussbaum's acknowledgment of Aristotle's work and the importance of practical reason and virtues in human flourishing.[125] It may be that such a position does not offer the kind of rationale that McReynolds claims to be missing in respect to making the correct choices, but given that no such rationale exists it is in matters such as these as Nussbaum writes "better to be vaguely right than precisely wrong."[126]

Having begun by looking at Rasmussen's view of flourishing, we were introduced to six important features of human flourishing informing us that human flourishing is objective, inclusive, individualized, agent-relative, self-directed, and social, and emphasizes practical wisdom, virtue, and an appeal to human nature in its formulation. MacIntyre added to our understanding of human flourishing given his attention to animality, vulnerability, and dependency, and advanced our understanding of human flourishing by pointing out the complexity of being a social creature and the significance of being involved in relationships that are supportive of human flourishing. Furthermore, MacIntyre emphasizes the importance of becoming an independent practical reasoner and how virtues make this possible. He also presented us with some difficulties about human flourishing including the problem of gaining a clear view of what human flourishing is. According to MacIntyre it is important to be skeptical about appeals to nature, the subjective or culture with respect to portraying human flourishing. Macintyre's skepticism is apt but unfortunately it leads to what I labeled a stalemate and the challenge of how to further our understanding of human flourishing. Lastly we looked at Nussbaum's approach to human flourishing, which involves the formulation of a "thick vague conception of the good" and a "basic list of human functional capabilities." Nussbaum's approach is refreshing and although it does not dismiss the problem of the "MacIntyrian stalemate," it represents a remarkably sturdy and open way of addressing human flourishing. It is sturdy in the sense that it is hard to challenge any of the entries on the list of capabilities, and it is open in the sense that the list in question is changeable and can be improved. From the examination of the three contemporary views of human flourishing, a picture has emerged that can sufficiently aid us in determining whether cultivating a balanced sense of wonder can be a strong contributor to living a flourishing human life. Flourishing is something that no one upon reflection would choose to live without. It is an activity that demands our attention and invites wonder because each dimension of flourishing, that is, the individual (Rasmussen), the social (MacIntyre), and the political (Nussbaum) is partly clouded. In other words, wonder is called for in relation to the continuing exploration of these dimensions. The next step is to examine what elements in our lives contribute to human flourishing, and to determine if wonder can also be a source of human flourishing.

SOURCES OF HUMAN FLOURISHING

Broadly speaking for something to count as a source of flourishing it must in some way or another contribute to our flourishing as human beings and to illustrate this we shall in the following look at four examples: literacy, friendship, humor, and physical exercise.

Literacy can be considered a source of human flourishing because the ability to read and write is empowering. United Nations Educational Scientific and Cultural Organization (UNESCO) informs that literacy is the foundation of lifelong learning. It empowers people and provides them the opportunity to participate fully in society and to improve their livelihoods. Literacy is the driving force behind sustainable development in the sense that makes greater participation possible in the labor market and simply expands life opportunities because it improves child and family health, nutrition, and reduces poverty.[127]

Furthermore, one might argue that being able to read and write enables one to engage, understand, and perhaps challenge biased interpretations or readings of particular laws, political manifestos, or religious scriptures which threaten to or perhaps already effectively dampen the flourishing of particular groups or individuals.

Friendship is also a source of flourishing which representatives of the positive psychology movement, such as psychologists William Compton and Edward Hoffman point out. They argue that there is mounting evidence from psychology and medicine stating that our attitudes toward friendship are important and influence individual wellness, vitality, and longevity.[128] Founder of the positive psychology movement, psychologist Martin Seligman is of a similar attitude as he thinks friendship to be a strong asset to health.[129] However, as contemporary philosopher Mark Vernon argues in his book *The Philosophy of Friendship*, the term "friendship" is complex and ambiguous[130] and thus we must exercise caution in our appraisal. Aristotle recognizes three kinds of friendship based on utility, pleasure, and virtue in the *Nicomachean Ethics*, and argues that friendship is one of the most indispensable requirements of life for no one would choose to live without friends, even if they had all other goods ready at their disposal.[131] Yet he acknowledges that what constitutes friendship is a matter of controversy and "there is much difference of opinion as to the nature of friendship."[132] A detailed discussion on what constitutes friendship is beyond the scope of our current endeavor, but for our present purposes it will also suffice to point out that viewing friendship as a source of flourishing from a neo-Aristotelian angle is definitely a possibility. Given that we are social creatures (which Rasmussen, Macintyre, and Nussbaum advocate), there is a point in seeing friendship regardless of the different ways we may conceive it as "overlapping expressions of the same family of shared human needs and desires,"[133] which is to say that when we look to our friends we might discover something about ourselves. This is an important point and to elaborate let us turn to philosopher Mette Lebech and her engagement with the ancient Greek notion that "a friend is another self."[134] Lebech explains that to view a friend as another self is to flag that one is able to see the other as an interpretation, or perhaps an explanation, of the "first self" in the same way a mirror image does for the original self.[135] Naturally such interpretations and explanations can be deceiving just like the mirrors in a fun house may distort our shape and the way we look, but if we seek to understand ourselves through our friends we will find communalities that we might not find if we, for example, were to seek understanding of ourselves in the image of a computer or a wolf. This does not mean that we cannot in some aspects resemble computers or wolves or that there are overlaps, but what is important here is the idea that from looking to our human friends we can discover that we are creatures of a particular kind, which is important for our flourishing. From this position it seems quite clear that friendship can be a source of flourishing because besides promoting individual wellness, vitality, longevity, health, and friendship clearly helps us understand ourselves.

Humor or to have a sense of humor is likewise a source of human flourishing seen from a neo-Aristotelian perspective. Compton and Hoffman write that, in general, having a good sense of humor is beneficial and can help people "recover from illness, cope with life stresses and anxiety about death, enhance immune system functioning, reduce the psychological experience of pain, and increase the chances of successful infertility treatments."[136] It has also been argued that should one require the service of healthcare workers humor continues to be important. The American nursing pioneer Virginia Henderson points out that "laughter and humor between patients and health-care workers can be as good as, or better than, a medication. It can create a warm 'climate,' promote good interpersonal relationships, and relieve feelings of frustration, anxiety or hostility."[137] Furthermore, psychologists William Viney and Bret King inform us that Hippocrates, the father of Greek medicine, is known for prescribing laughter to his patients as early as the fourth century BC.[138] In this light, humor seems to be a source of flourishing as it clearly has positive effects on our general health and sense of well-being. Additionally, having a sense of humor can help us discover what goods are important to us in relation to our flourishing because as anthropologist Mary Douglas points out "a joke is a play upon form, that affords an opportunity for realizing that an accepted pattern has no necessity."[139] A humorous speech can also be a play upon form and help us realize that an accepted pattern has no necessity. Consider an excerpt from the eulogy delivered by British comedian John Cleese at the memorial service of fellow Monty Python Graham Chapman:

Graham Chapman, co-author of the "Parrot Sketch," is no more.

He has ceased to be, bereft of life, he rests in peace, he has kicked the bucket, hopped the twig, bit the dust, snuffed it, breathed his last, and gone to meet the Great Head of Light Entertainment in the sky, and I guess that we're all thinking how sad it is that a man of such talent, of such capability for kindness, of such unusual intelligence should now so suddenly be spirited away at the age of only forty-eight, before he'd achieved many of the things of which he was capable, and before he'd had enough fun.

Well, I feel that I should say, "Nonsense. Good riddance to him, the freeloading bastard! I hope he fries."

And the reason I feel I should say this is, he would never forgive me if I didn't, if I threw away this glorious opportunity to shock you all on his behalf. Anything for him but mindless good taste. I could hear him whispering in my ear last night as I was writing this: "Alright, Cleese, you're very proud of being the very first person to ever say 'shit' on British television. If this service is really for me, just for starters, I want you to become the first person ever at a British memorial service to say 'fuck!'" [140]

The eulogy is a play upon form as it breaks away from the formality that most people in Britain presumably would expect from a memorial speech. As the recordings of this now famous speech show Cleese manages to bring laughter to his fellow mourners, who probably never expected to be laughing at Chapman's funeral. The humorous eulogy brings a certain catharsis to the mourners and it reminds them that despite Chapman's departure they are still very much alive, that mourning can be carried out in a cheerful way, and that despite the death of a loved one there is a bright side to life. In this light it is clear that having a sense of humor can help a person identify and question habits or particular practices in the society she is a part of, which consequently can have a positive effect on her flourishing. As MacIntyre would say, a significant part of flourishing is finding out how one actually flourishes and sometimes this involves questioning the environment you are in and the way of life you are leading. Achieving this through humor understood as a play upon form can be very effective.

Physical exercise also qualifies as a source of flourishing and particularly because of its positive impact on our health and well-being. It is well documented that exercise reduces blood pressure, improves blood cholesterol levels, and lowers body mass index (BMI). Furthermore, figures show that physical inactivity is the fourth leading risk factor for global mortality and accounts for an estimate of 5.2 million deaths every year. Exercise also benefits mental health, including the improvement of mood; the reduction of symptoms of stress, anger, and depression; and it alleviates anxiety and prevents cognitive decline.[141]

Additionally, physical exercise can also contribute to the development of an ethical outlook and spirituality, and in support of this stands the Japanese martial art of aikido, which we might translate into the way of peace or harmony. Now aikido is characterized by physical and quite technical training through which the student learns how to defend herself against a variety of attacks, but it also has an ethical and spiritual dimension, which the student gains insight into through the physical training. Philosopher Barry Kroll writes that:

> Aikido affords a framework for understanding argument as harmonization rather than confrontation. Two movements, circling away (*tenkan*) and entering in (*irimi*) suggests tactics for arguing with adversaries. The ethical imperative of aikido involves protecting one's adversary from harm, using the least force necessary, and when possible transforming aggression into cooperation.[142]

Important to the practitioner of aikido is the protection of one's adversary, and in this sense the art is about controlling the anger and aggression of the opponent in such a way that she is harmed as little as possible, as much as it is about exercising self-control. Now there are several ways of illustrating in what capacity aikido has a spiritual dimension and one could, for example, examine the rituals and etiquette involved in aikido or the influence of the Omoto religion on the art for guidance.[143] However, we shall concern ourselves with a quotation of the founder of aikido, Morihei Ueshiba, which bears witness to the spiritual dimension of aikido. Ueshiba writes "In Aikido we never initiate an attack. The desire to attack is proof that one lacks confidence to emerge victorious. That is, one has already been defeated in spirit."[144] This attitude or spirit which is incorporated into the physical training of aikido in conjunction with the fact that the art is bereft of competition makes it a spiritual art as much as it is a martial art.

WONDER AS A SOURCE OF FLOURISHING

Quite in tune with the mythological origin of wonder we might view wonder as a courier, understood as a state of mind that can deliver or introduce something of great value into our lives. To understand this better let us first of all take a closer look at how wonder may facilitate other states of mind, including gratitude, reverence, an imaginative attitude, openness, and humility, all of which can contribute to human flourishing. Now these candidates have been chosen not because they are the only possible effects of wonder that may contribute to our flourishing, but because we have already touched on each of them in some form or other in relation to wonder and flourishing. Secondly, I shall argue that to wonder virtuously or in a balanced way contributes to human flourishing in a strong sense.

To understand how wonder may help foster gratitude and how this may be a source of flourishing, let us begin by taking a closer look at what gratitude is. Keen holds that gratitude is "joy's twin" and an emotion that can heal bitterness,[145] and by recalling Nussbaum's work, we find that under point five on her list of basic human capabilities she presents gratitude as a human emotion, that alongside love, grief, longing, and justified anger enables us to have attachments to things and people, which is crucial to our flourishing.

Additionally, we may highlight that positive psychologists, such as Compton and Hoffman, praise the importance of gratitude in connection with flourishing, and state that it, at its core, has the power to bring about "positive connections among people and allow us to express our highest values and potential," and that grateful people have a tendency to be happy, and that gratitude is important for healthy personality functions.[146] Psychologists Robert A. Emmons and Charles M. Sheldon expand on this by stating the following:

> Grateful people may have more psychic manoeuvrability than the ungrateful, enabling them to be less defensive and open to life. [Gratitude is] a source of human strength, and an integral element promoting the civility requisite for the flourishing of families and communities.[147]

Key to Emmons and Sheldon's view of gratitude as a source of flourishing is that it facilitates a certain mental flexibility, which leaves us open to what life has to offer. Additionally, they hold that gratitude promotes the civility or courtesy, which is important to the flourishing of larger groups of people.

In the literature, gratitude is often presented as an emotion that is associated with religion or religious practice. Emmons and Shelton observe that:

> The roots of gratitude can be seen in many of the world's religious traditions. In the great monotheistic religions of the world the concept of gratitude permeates texts, prayers, and teachings. [. . .] Worship with a gratitude to God for his many gifts and mercies have a common theme, and believers are urged to develop this quality. As such gratitude is one of the most common emotions that religions seek to promote and sustain in believers. Thus for many people, gratitude is at the core of spirituality and religious experience.[148]

Although one can appreciate the link between gratitude and the religious dimension, it is important to recognize that feeling gratitude to something greater than oneself can also manifest in a secular context. Emmons and Shelton explain that profound experiences of gratitude can be "associated with reverent wonder toward an acknowledgment of the universe."[149] Thus gratitude links to the ability to wonder and the recognition that the universe and our existence are a tremendous mystery. Keen seems to support this idea as he writes:

> For those with an inclination toward religion, gratitude is expressed as praise to G-d from Whom All Blessings Flow. But there is no need to make a leap of faith to a transcendent creator who is responsible for our existence. Gratitude may lead to worship or it may remain a simple acknowledgment that our existence is an inexplicable gift.[150]

To some this may seem odd or dissatisfying because extending gratitude usually implies that one extends it to some sort of sentient being, be it a fellow human being, a nonhuman animal,[151]

To some this may seem odd or dissatisfying because extending gratitude usually implies that one extends it to some sort of sentient being, be it a fellow human being, a nonhuman animal,[152] or a presumed deity. Likewise, when we think of something as a gift it usually implies that it is given by or to somebody. From this standpoint one might say that feeling gratitude in relation to reverent wonder toward an acknowledgment of the universe, or to feel gratitude associated with an acknowledgment of our existence as an inexplicable gift, is peculiar because in doing so we are expressing gratitude without having a clear idea of who we are grateful to. In defense one can say that although we may not know whom we are grateful to, we can give utterance to what we are grateful for. One could be grateful for being able to fathom that we are a part of a world of fantastic proportion of which we so far have only caught a glimpse, and we can be grateful for our particular existence because, after all, as philosopher Blaise Pascal would say, there is no reason why we should be here and not there or exist in a completely different time.[153] In this sense we can defend the notion of secular gratitude without compromising the gravity of what we are grateful for.

To exemplify in what sense gratitude can spring from an experience of wonder and how it can be a source of flourishing, we might recall that in the introduction wonder and gratitude were brought together in the example involving Keen and his recollection of being handed a mysterious knife at the age of six. The example revealed that for weeks after the event Keen experienced what he describes as a "pervasive sense of gratitude to the stranger" who handed him the knife.[154] To elaborate, it seems that his gratitude in this respect was well placed because the event brought forth in him a sense of wonder or made him wonder in a particular way, which contributed to the developing of an inquisitive mind and fostered attitudes central to his flourishing, including "openness, availability, epistemological humility in the face of the mystery of being, and the ability to admire and be grateful."[155]

It can also be argued that wonder, gratitude, and flourishing were brought together in Robert Gleaves's and Pam Clemmer's 1998 reports to Leonid MAC concerning their experiences of the 1966 Leonid meteor shower mentioned in the second chapter. Both Gleaves and Clemmer indicate in their reports that their individual experiences are of wonder, but it might also be suggested that their reports reveal the gratitude they harbor for having experienced the meteor shower. Now both individuals do not use the word "gratitude" directly in their reports, which naturally speaks against the idea of such an effect. However, if we focus on Clemmer's report, it is reasonable to say that it is indicative of her gratitude because she emphasizes that the sight of the meteor shower was unique, unforgettable, and spectacular, and produced in her the feeling that she had witnessed something that no other person on the planet had seen or would ever behold again. In this light it seems that she indirectly is expressing gratitude for having witnessed the meteor shower.

Likewise, we might say that Gleaves indirectly is expressing gratitude for having experienced the event because he thinks of it as a wonderful birthday gift, and claims that recalling what happened that particular morning in 1966 almost brings tears to his eyes. The fact that Gleaves is almost moved to tears is important because it can be interpreted as a sign of gratitude for having witnessed this singular and most extraordinary meteor shower. In support of this claim stands the phenomenon of wonder-joy-tears which psychologist William Braud describes as tears that are:

> Accompanied by feelings of wonder, joy, gratitude, awe, yearning, poignancy, intensity, love, and compassion. They are an opening up of the heart to the persons or profound circumstances being witnessed. [. . .] These kinds of tears also indicate feelings of profound gratitude for such confrontations. Additionally they can indicate moments of profound insight.[156]

Wonder-joy-tears links wonder and gratitude and if we view Gleaves's report in light of this phenomenon, it can be argued that he is experiencing perhaps a mild case of wonder-joy-tears that almost, but not actually, produces tears. Naturally this is pure speculation but given the magnitude of the event Gleaves is recalling, the fact that he still treasures it as a wonderful seventeenth-year birthday gift so many years after the event, and that he finds it important enough to file a report or testimony to Leonid MAC on the matter speak toward it.

In what sense does Clemmer and Gleaves's wonder-induced gratitude contribute to flourishing? If we focus more specifically on the natural wonder they experienced and ask how one could be grateful for having experienced such an event, it might be suggested that witnessing a rare and beautiful spectacle like a massive meteor shower contributes to a person's flourishing because it makes the world wonder-filled, newly present, and reorientates the spectator toward a larger and far more mysterious world than she perhaps previously realized. This is edifying and can be seen as a good that contributes toward flourishing and thus to feel grateful for such a lesson, courtesy of the universe, seems entirely appropriate. We can also conjecture that to feel grateful for witnessing a massive meteor shower contributes to a person's flourishing in the sense that it can spark wondering interest in space or simply the natural world. Rachel Carson, who focuses on retaining children's inborn sense of wonder by highlighting what the outdoors or nature has to offer, expressed concerns about people having difficulty leaving their well-lit houses and entertaining obliviousness to the beauty of the starry sky overhead, despite the fact that on most nights most people can behold its beauty and "wonder at the meaning of what [they] see."[157] Clemmer and Gleaves probably do not belong to the group of people Carson is concerned about but are likely to belong to a group of grateful stargazing wonderers ready to share their experiences with others. If this were indeed so I would say that they, via the monumental event they witnessed in their youth, have discovered a good that aids them in their flourishing, because to be aware of the magnificence and beauty of the universe is to be aware that we reside in it and are a part of something beyond our comprehension.

Keeping this in mind I think we have established that entertaining a sense of gratitude prompted by an experience of wonder can be a source of flourishing.

Moving on, let us now examine if a sense of wonder may help foster reverence, which in turn can promote human flourishing. To appreciate why this may be the case it is important to understand more about what reverence is, its relation to wonder, and how it contributes to flourishing.

Solomon thinks that reverence is an emotion that "presumes something greater than yourself, something awesome, wondrous, marvelous [yet] something less than worship but considerably more than either affection, respect, or admiration."[158] He furthermore holds that reverence is inherent to spirituality, highlights our limitations, and prompts a sense of responsibility.[159] Where does this leave us? One could venture that Solomon's view of reverence seems to say that reverence is an emotion that qualifies as an effect of wonder or, as it were, is subordinate to it, because without the ability to wonder and to presume there is something greater than oneself, it is unlikely that reverence would even emerge.

Additionally, we can say that because reverence prompts awareness of our limitations and responsibility, it is fair to insist that wonder-induced reverence contributes to human flourishing. To be aware, for example, of human vulnerability and dependence (which we might label as limitations) is to harbor an important understanding of creature-hood,[160] and thus what goods to be mindful about and to look out for as we are living out our lives as the creatures we are. Having a sense of responsibility likewise contributes to human flourishing because to feel responsible for oneself and others ties in with our dependency and vulnerability, and help us form flourishing societies. In a way reverence is a cure against hubris and as Keen has expressed it, acts as a bulwark against "narcissism, nihilism, and anarchy" and helps us put the "civil" in "civilization."[161]

To continue, it might also be argued that wonder can prompt an imaginative attitude, which can be seen as a source of flourishing because in some cases it might enrich a person's perception or moral scope. In support of this it has been argued earlier that engaging with Arcimboldo's *Rudolf II as Vertumnus*; seeing the Earth from space; utilizing artifacts such as the microscope and the telescope; engaging with philosophical thought experiments such as Nozick's experience machine, Rawls's veil of ignorance, and the concept of speciesism may give way to wonder and ignite the imagination in such a way that it enriches perception and presents us with an entirely different perspective, revealing the world anew. Such enrichment might contribute to human flourishing because it makes us appreciate the world and our place therein in a sophisticated and nuanced way, which in turn can empower us to take responsibility for ourselves and our lives, and give serious thought to what generic and individual goods are needed in order for each one of us to flourish as the creatures we are.

The case of de Pasquale stands in support of this effect. His experience of wonder and consequent realization of human mortality encouraged him to take ownership of his life and seriously engage with the ancient question of how one should live. His experience might have fostered a long lasting displacing mood or attitude that eventually led him to the study of philosophy, and later on in his professional career enabled him to give utterance to his own ideas about what is important when it comes to living a good human life. De Pasquale writes:

> I am no different from any other middle-age tenured professor. I enjoy mastering esoteric fields of knowledge, I would love for the college to award me a chair of philosophy, and I could surely use and would love to have a Lincoln Navigator to take my four kids camping. I do not doubt the value of scientific knowledge, worldly success or material pleasure; I only question the importance that people give to these values.[162]

The case of Keen follows a similar pattern. It can be said that Keen's experience of wonder as a child gave rise to a wondrous afterglow that later turned into a particular imaginative attitude that has endured in him to this day. We might suggest that this is what enabled him to question what goods were needed in order for him to flourish, and to discover that they included studying theology and philosophy of religion and, in the late 1960s, giving up his permanent position as professor of theology in exchange for a life in California working as a freelance writer for magazines such as *Psychology Today* and eventually becoming a celebrated author and trapeze artist. This particular imaginative attitude might have helped him formulate his own wonder-provoking ideas on what makes up the good human life, which we may find a glimpse of in the following extract which speaks for itself:

> I think you have to keep asking, "What is unfulfilled in me?" "What haven't I done?" It's the idea of a calling: what is it that appeals to you, that calls to you? Look for the vacuum in your life and move into those areas. It takes some courage, but there comes a point where you have to make that leap.[163]

With this in mind we are able to say that an imaginative attitude, which may spring from an experience of wonder, can be a source of human flourishing.

Can an experience of wonder lead to openness of mind and does this contribute to human flourishing? To answer this question we need to know what is meant by openness, how it links to wonder and in what sense it works toward flourishing.

Openness of mind is to be free from the constraints of dogma. It is the ability and willingness to take new ideas seriously, to examine them before accepting or rejecting them. It is to understand the possible dangers of ideology, fundamentalist beliefs or paradigms, and that one might entertain such consciously or unconsciously.

The literature on wonder suggests that there is a connection between wonder and openness. Fuller writes that "wonder imbues the world with an alluring quality, fostering increased openness and receptivity rather than immediate utilitarian action."[164] This points to the notion that in wonder we are invited to see things from a different perspective and so might become aware of other and hitherto hidden possibilities. To get an additional hold on the link between wonder and openness we recall that the link between the two was mentioned briefly in chapter 1 in connection with "shared wonder," and the climb to the top of Mt Fuji that my wife and I undertook some years ago to watch the sunrise from the summit. As we watched the sun come up we joyfully experienced a particular openness toward the world and readiness for change, together with bafflement about what the world is. Additionally, openness was highlighted in connection with our dealings with Scruton's approach to imagination and the notion of continuity between intense experiences and subsequent living in relation to wonder. In this respect it was suggested that if a person is experiencing wonder in a true sense she experiences being in a state of mind that embraces perhaps a sort of subtle or beginning reverence, gratitude, or openness that consequently may influence her behavior over time. The common denominator is the widening of understanding and the increased sensitivity that wonder-induced openness brings to the table. To explain, one could say that the openness my wife and I experienced on top of Mt Fuji brought forth an expanded understanding of the world and indeed of our very lives as fluid or ever-changing, together with an increased sensitivity to the possibilities that life has to offer.

With this in mind can we say that openness contributes to flourishing? Yes we can, because being closed-minded is surely one of the things we would opt not to be if we were given a choice. Openness enables us to explore different ideas and goods outside what is known to us, and in doing so we may discover goods that we never believed existed, or that some of the goods we already have may not really do us any good in the sense that they do not contribute to our flourishing.

Moving on, is it defensible to say that an experience of wonder makes us humble or produces humility, which contributes to human flourishing? To make the case we must understand what humility is; how it can be an effect of wonder and how humility works toward our flourishing.

Humility is a rather understudied subject and because it is surrounded by controversy it is difficult to address. This becomes apparent if we follow the popular notion of thinking about humility as a virtue.[165] To elaborate, we might say that although Aristotle acknowledges that being virtuous contributes to a person's flourishing he does not view humility as a virtue but equals it with being small-souled,[166] which he defines as a vice in the sense that it is to claim less than one deserves.[167] Instead of seeing humility as a virtue, Aristotle speaks of pride in the sense that it is virtuous to entertain pride as long as it is proper or in accord with one's own excellence. By Aristotle's measure this enables us to say that it is virtuous for a craftsman who excels at his craft to be proud and *mutatis mutandis* vice-full (deficient pride/humble) if he refrained from being proud of his excellent skills.

Aristotle's idea of humility as a vice contrasts the view upheld by most Christian ethicists where the belittling of oneself[168] in the face of God and his work, "loving one's enemies," and the practice of "turning the other cheek"[169] is considered virtuous, while entertaining pride a sin (vice).[170] That pride is considered a sin in Christianity complicates matters because it illuminates the paradox of humility and the difficulty we face in addressing it today. If we accept the Christian view that humility is a virtue it is tempting to ask if it is possible to be proud of being humble. If the answer is *yes*, then it looks like we are not harboring the humility we are proud of; but if we answer *no*, we acknowledge that one cannot be proud of being humble, which is problematic because to do so signals a disregard of a good, praiseworthy quality or feature that one harbors, which is irrational.[171]

The discrepancy between the two outlooks is obvious and brings to our attention a significant challenge in terms of understanding humility as a virtue. However, we need not be discouraged because it is not the objective here to accept and overcome this challenge. A viable way forward that will help us in our present endeavor is to acknowledge the importance of the challenge but to move around it and address humility from a different angle. In this light it might be prudent to think of humility as an emotion that may arise in us due to a particular event or realization. Two questions present themselves in this respect and one of them involves what the emotion of humility signifies, and the other asks us to clarify what we have in mind when we say that the emotion of humility may arise from a particular event or realization. To begin answering the first question it seems to me that if we think of humility as an emotion it fits what we can call the general intuition of what humility consists of in our time. The intuitions in question can be found in the writings of philosopher Henry Sidgwick, who points out that generally we think of humility as that which "prescribes a low opinion of our own merits."[172] If we were to accept this view we must attempt to understand what may give rise to such an emotion because refraining from doing so is to invite Aristotle's criticism and stand accused of being irrational.

The experience of wonder can at least momentarily give rise to the emotion of humility, and to prove this point we might recall Gerald Kuiper's report of his students' reaction to the 1966 Leonid meteor shower from chapter 2. The scientific minded students who had made an effort to record the number of meteors literally gave up their project and as Kuiper writes, simply stood and gazed in wonder once the meteors began falling at a rate of approximately forty per second. If we take this into account it is reasonable to say that courtesy of the meteor shower the students, besides experiencing wonder, also experienced a sense of humility as an effect of wonder, and this not merely because they had to give up their study, but because they in their wonder realized the humbling fact that we are part of something huge, something vast and seemingly endless, which is beyond our comprehension. Would feeling belittled or humbled in the face of a massive meteor shower, or the universe as we know it, invite Aristotle's criticism? I do not think so because unlike Aristotle who operated with the geocentric model of the universe, which puts our planet (and him) at the center of it and in effect allows a sense of pride, our modern conception of the universe is one that mostly installs humility. The reason for this is that for all we know we are but the inhabitants of a small planet orbiting a bright star, which in all likelihood will not shine forever. Where Aristotle may have found pride in being from *somewhere* central we can seemingly only muster humility because we are really from *nowhere* remotely central, given our planet is but one among a myriad of other planets, solar systems, and galaxies. If Aristotle knew what we know about our place in the whole and the clouds of unknowing that surrounds this whole and our very existence, it is not unthinkable that he would have acknowledged that there is a merit to being humble. This leads us to our final question concerning in what sense humility can contribute to flourishing. Compton and Hoffman speak of the positive effect of humility and point out that humility "enhances social relationships [and is] important for living a life of quiet joy, satisfaction, wisdom, and contentment."[173] This rings true because first of all not many seem to favor the arrogant personality. Second, we might say that being humble and entertaining a low opinion of one's own merits can contribute to living a life of joy, satisfaction, wisdom, and contentment because humility may spring from a deep felt realization of the vastness and beauty of the universe, the mystery of our existence, and the wonder that we conceptually are able to grasp that it is so.

Thus we have established, at least preliminarily, that humility, which may spring from an experience of wonder, can contribute to human flourishing.

Moving on, let us now put forward an argument for the conclusion that cultivating virtuous wonder or entertaining a balanced sense of wonder contributes to human flourishing in a strong sense. To make the case we must understand what virtuous wonder or a balanced sense of wonder is, and what is at play when we evoke the word "strong" in connection with flourishing. Starting with the latter one might venture that for something to contribute to human flourishing in a strong sense it must be of particular importance to it or even crucial in the sense that without it a person's flourishing will be compromised. Virtue understood as excellence that has to manifest in all activities[174] qualifies as such and is a crucial and specific part of the neo-Aristotelian conception of flourishing. It is so because virtue is a good that cannot be purchased, found, or in any way be given, and is a quality that one has to develop. Virtue is, as MacIntyre describes it, "not inborn, but a consequence of training."[175] From our dealings with Rasmussen, MacIntyre, and Nussbaum, it is clear that the development of virtues is an important part of human flourishing and especially in relation to what Rasmussen terms practical wisdom, what MacIntyre calls independent practical reasoning, and what Nussbaum refers to as practical reason. In addition, MacIntyre informs us that the development of virtue is crucial for an individual as she otherwise would not be able to detach herself from immediate desires, which helps bring about good choice-making. MacIntyre also helps us to a better understanding of virtue by focusing on the virtue of temperance. In his view this particular virtue centers on avoiding extreme behavior and sees the eye of the storm between self-indulgence and unappreciative and insensitive puritanism. One could argue that when we talk about wonder as a virtue it refers to wonderment located between the Scylla of excess and the Charybdis of deficiency. In other words, to wonder in a virtuous way is to harbor a balanced sense of wonder that transcends an extreme form of wonderment. Virtuous or balanced wonder neither accommodates the immediate wonderments of a fool or a child, nor displays the outright hostility to wonder attributed to the vulgar, crude, and reductive adult. To harbor a balanced sense of wonder involves being able, at least to some degree, to harness or control wonder. It is a product of refinement where one's wonderment turns out to be just right.

This particular line of thinking might to some evoke Aristotelian ideas of virtue and rightly so. For Aristotle virtue is connected to the notion of the mean, which is located between excess and deficiency. Experiencing a sense of wonder while pondering that bachelors are not married is wondering in excess.[176] It is to wonder foolishly or immaturely and such wonder would rest uneasily with any sensible person. To assume that there is an answer to every question and avoiding wonderment by blindly consulting experts or authorities to obtain answers would be to harbor a deficient sense of wonder, which would equally sit ill with any temperate person. In addition, we might say that the person who never wonders because she believes there is nothing to wonder about or because she advocates a strict "*nil admirari*" attitude is equally unbalanced, because it is simply wrong that there is nothing to wonder about. On this account Tallis reminds us that it is a wonder that he exists and the fact that there is an entity called "Raymond Tallis" is entirely unexplained.[177] Along the same lines Keen argues that wonder is elicited "over and over again by the startling realization that there is no reason for the world or anything to exist."[178] To give further weight to the level of difficulty in fostering a balanced sense of wonder, it is worthwhile taking a closer look at a famous passage from Aristotle's *Nicomachean Ethics*. The passage engages with the emotion of anger and aims at making the reader understand that getting angry is easy, but to remain virtuous while being angry one must consider if one is angry toward the right person, to the right amount, at the right time, for the right purpose, and in the right way.[179] For our purposes we might say that it is easy both to wonder and to dismiss wonder altogether, but to reach a balanced sense of wonder where one's wonderment is directed at the right person, object, or situation in the right amount, and in the right time, and for the right purpose, and in the right way is the more difficult task and not within everybody's immediate reach. To illustrate that wonderment, when applied appropriately and in a well-balanced manner can contribute strongly to our flourishing, I shall now present three examples where the first depicts wonder in excess, the second illustrates lack of wonderment, and the third is concerned with a case of virtuous wonder.

One possible way of describing how wonder in excess is not a source of flourishing is to take a look at psychedelic experiences. A psychedelic experience is prompted by the ingestion of what is referred to as hallucinogenic drugs, which could involve, for example, lysergic acid diethylamide (LSD), *N,N*-dimethyltryptamine (DMT), or mescaline. According to Keen, what characterizes the psychedelic experience is that the distinction between objects and moments in time becomes blurred. Things flow together, time slows down, and the static and distinct outlines of the world of experience no longer apply. It involves a breakdown of the boundaries between the senses and consequently making it possible to, for example, see music, hear colors, and see smells. Furthermore, with time suspended it becomes possible to enjoy prolonged voyages "into the taste of bread and wine, or into a phrase of music, or loved face."[180] Keen explains further that this radical change in perception leaves one in a state of pure awareness where the "I" or the "ego" is left behind and that in such a state of mind: "a beautiful object like a rose may be intuited in pure wonder because there is no longer an 'I' looking at myself looking at the rose."[181] In relation to the psychedelic experience, Keen highlights the idea of too much wonder (or wonder in excess) and argues that despite the infinite and wonderful possibilities such an experience offers, it leads to a state of mind that removes us from human agency, individuality, concern, and commitment to social relations such as parents and friends. Furthermore, it seduces us into the illusion that there may be an authentic existence without decisions and the risk of failure, and such an existence Keen argues "belongs to the gods, and the man who seeks it loses the feel of the earth upon which he stands."[182]

Keen's take on the psychedelic experience and his reasons for shunning it are understandable. It is not so much what the psychedelic experience renders us capable of, but more which of our powers it takes away. One could venture that what Keen is bringing forth is the idea that the psychedelic mind capable of enjoying wonders inaccessible to us in our everyday lives is incapable of functioning as an independent practical reasoner, to use MacIntyre's terminology. If we mirror this against Mac Intyre's view of flourishing it would seem that the psychedelic voyager pays a heavy price for her extraordinary perception. Not to be able to act as an independent practical reasoner is highly problematic and to be bereft of this ability would, from a MacIntyrian viewpoint, seriously dampen a person's prospects of flourishing. Keen's point that the psychedelic experience removes the voyager from commitment and concern for others is likewise problematic for flourishing. This becomes clear if we consult Nussbaum's entry number seven about affiliation on her list of capabilities. Here Nussbaum notes that an essential part of flourishing is to be able to live with and toward others and to recognize and show concern for other human beings. Finally, one might point out that since the psychedelic experience uproots a person and induces ego-loss the very idea of flourishing, which finds meaning in the intimate relationship between the agency of a person and the time and place she is situated in, is derailed. It simply does not make sense to talk about "psychedelic flourishing." To be clear I am not stating that the psychedelic experience is worthless or that psychedelics cannot have therapeutic properties and be edifying. All I am stating is that while under the influence of psychedelic substances a voyager's capability of minding her flourishing is compromised to a smaller or lager degree, depending on the level of "intoxication." In this light we have established a sturdy case for the claim that wonder in excess cannot act as a source of flourishing at least in a strong sense.

The next example is concerned with the lack of wonderment and the question of whether this can lead to flourishing. Let us consider the following scene from Samuel Beckett's *Molloy*, where the anti-hero Moran debates Father Ambrose on the idea that if laughter is essentially a human property the question concerning whether Jesus laughed seems important with regards to the doctrine depicting Jesus as the second person of the trinity. The conversation goes as follows:

> Like Job haha, he said. I too said haha. What joy it is to laugh, from time to time, he said. Is it not? I said. It is peculiar to man, he said. So I have noticed, I said. A brief silence ensued . . . Animals never laugh, he said. It takes us to find that funny, I said. What? He said. It takes us to find that funny, I said loudly. He mused. Christ never laughed either, he said, so far as we know. He looked at me. Can you wonder? I said.[183]

Judging from the situation the difference in character between Moran and Father Ambrose is obvious. Moran comes across as the questioning, humorous, and wondering man, and Father Ambrose displays the character of a person who is disciplined, somewhat doctrinal, and lacks wonderment. Now is this lack of wonderment regrettable if we mirror it against our understanding of wonder and human flourishing? One might say yes because, as Fuller remarks, a life that harbors no sense of wonder is not attuned to the widest possible world of personal fulfillment.[184] In addition, one might point out that given Father Ambrose's interest in religion his wonder-deprived situation is lamentable because wonder and religion are quite compatible. According to Fuller, wonder paves the way for spirituality without reducing our basic belief in the existence of something "more" to narrow doctrines or creeds.[185] Poet and playwright D. H. Lawrence would remind Father Ambrose that the sense of wonder is the natural religious sense,[186] and Keen would say that if Father Ambrose could allow more wonder into his life he would discover a renewed sense of the sacred.[187] One could speculate that if Father Ambrose could experience a sense of wonder he would gain a deeper understanding of his religious path (which he must already see as a good or a part of his conception of the good).

Now it is true that besides the reference to Fuller, none of the three philosophers we have engaged with concerning human flourishing directly flag wonder as a source of flourishing. However, wonder in this respect can be looked upon as an add-on and indeed perfectly compatible with the ideas put forward by these philosophers. If we think of Rasmussen's point about flourishing being a self-directed activity, wonderment can help prompt an individual to take charge of her life and aid in the discovery, development, and maintenance of those virtues that could help her attain the goods her life requires. Wonder could easily go hand in hand with MacIntyre's idea of the independent practical reasoner and the search for the goods that makes one flourish. If one harbors deficient wonderment it would seem hard for an independent practical reasoner to locate the goods that would contribute toward her flourishing. With regard to Nussbaum's account, wonder could be added to her list of basic capabilities. For example, her entry number four could not only address senses, imagination, and thought, but also wonder, because a sense of wonder "pushes" and can help us become informed, educated, and aid us in producing works and events of our own choice, be they religious, literary, or musical in nature. Likewise, wonder could be added to entry number six, labeled practical reason. When one wonders about something it sharpens our cognitive focus and awareness of ignorance. Thus it could play a significant role in formulating a conception of the good, fuel critical reflection, and assist in the planning of one's life as it has in the life of de Pasquale. Based on this we have a strong case for claiming that a life lacking in wonder could compromise the flourishing of an individual.

Moving on, let us now focus on virtuous wonder or a balanced sense of wonder, and how it contributes to human flourishing in a strong sense. Recall the example of wonder involving Elder Samuel Rogers's account of the 1833 meteor shower mentioned in the beginning of the first chapter. Rogers informs us that the heavenly display was wonderful and he categorizes it as the grandest and most beautiful scene he ever beheld. We also know that some of his fellow stargazers did not share his view of the spectacle and interpreted the event as foreshadowing the end of the world. Others concluded that the many meteors represented the first of a series of calamities sent by God because he was displeased with them.

Rogers's wonderment contributes to his flourishing because it deals with two basic goods, namely, beauty and knowledge, which according to Rasmussen qualify as valuable in their own right and are partial expressions of human flourishing.

To elaborate, we can say that Rogers owes a part of his flourishing to the event he experienced because it brought him beauty in the form of a spectacular meteor shower, and knowledge in the form of the realization that the world he inhabits occasionally gives away displays of cosmic grandeur and beauty, which one might be lucky enough to witness. If we look to Nussbaum's entry number four on her list of capabilities we can see that making use of one's senses, imagination, and thought is a vital part of her view of flourishing. Rogers makes good use of these precise qualities because he uses his visual sense to appreciate the meteor shower and likewise he makes use of his imagination and capability for thought. We know this because if he did not he would not be able to categorize the event as wonderful, grand, and beautiful and neither would he be able to recall and appreciate it years later when he wrote his autobiography.

In addition, it may be ventured that Rogers is wondering in a virtuous or balanced way and that this contributes to his flourishing in a strong sense. Rogers appropriately recognizes the wonderfulness, grandness, and beauty of the event without drawing unreasonable or hasty conclusions about its significance and meaning. Amid the extraordinary meteor shower, the various dramatic responses from the people around him, his own emotional upheaval in face of the cosmic fireworks, he walks on a knife's edge but remains centered and shows no sign of either lack of wonderment or too much of it. Despite his knowledge of meteor showers he does not dismiss the event as trivial or insignificant, nor does he, despite his belief in God, interpret the event as a sign that the end of days has arrived or that God somehow is displeased with him. He manages to steer between the Scylla of excess and the Charybdis of deficiency and thus he wonders in a virtuous, excellent, or balanced way, which is difficult and thus praiseworthy. To balance wonder is a demanding activity and it does not happen automatically. By balancing his wonderment, Rogers shows his character, training, and ability to reason independently and practically. Upon seeing the spectacular meteor shower he quickly harnesses his metaphysical imagination, and aligns his emotions to fit what is happening consequently balancing his wonder, which subsequently enabled him to quite appropriately describe the meteor shower as wonderful.

Based on this we have a strong case for claiming that a balanced sense of wonder contributes strongly to human flourishing.

To recapitulate we have been engaged with showing how wonder can contribute to human flourishing. To do this we started by engaging with three different approaches to human flourishing represented by Douglas Rasmussen, Alasdair MacIntyre, and Martha Nussbaum. Rasmussen's neo-Aristotelian approach to human flourishing revealed a view of the human good that is (1) objective, (2) inclusive, (3) individualized, (4) agent-relative, (5) self-directed, and (6) social. In addition, Rasmussen highlighted that practical wisdom and human nature are significant to human flourishing. The main criticism of Rasmussen's approach was that there might be more that can be uncovered about human flourishing by investigating human nature, which led to focus on MacIntyre's approach to the subject. MacIntyre's approach to human flourishing advances our understanding of human flourishing by pointing out our animality, vulnerability, and dependency on others. He also emphasizes that it is crucial for one to become an independent practical reasoner in order to live a flourishing life. Furthermore, MacIntyre highlights the importance of paying attention to the complexity of being a social creature. In this regard MacIntyre is particularly attentive to the relationships we engage with and how crucial these are for our flourishing. In this sense it is important to acknowledge that not all relationships may necessarily be supportive of our flourishing. According to MacIntyre this depends on the development of virtues, which enables us to recognize what is good and make good choices. The main criticism of MacIntyre concerns the stalemate situation he brought about by his skepticism of naturalistic, subjective, and cultural accounts of the good. After having dealt with MacIntyre's approach we looked to Nussbaum because she offers a platform that clarified some of the "grey" areas advocated by MacIntyre. This brought to our attention the "thick vague conception of the good" and the open-ended list of basic human functional capabilities that may help promote human development. The main criticism of Nussbaum's approach was that the ample threshold level of the ten capabilities required is ambiguous and weakens the applicational value of the list of capabilities.

After gaining some understanding about what human flourishing involves and what might qualify as a source of flourishing, we turned to investigate if wonder could be viewed as such. The subsequent inquiry into how wonder induced gratitude, reverence, openness, humility, imaginative attitude, and finally virtuous wonder, and confirmed that it is indeed possible that wonder promotes human flourishing. The section on virtuous wonder deserves to be highlighted because it demonstrates the problems with lacking wonder, with wondering in excess, and how wonderment works if practiced in a virtuous way. Additionally, it clarified that a balanced sense of wonder, which is synonymous with virtuous wonder, contributes to human flourishing in a strong sense because striking a balance in one's wonderment does not happen automatically but depends on our engagement.

NOTES

1. L. W. Sumner, *Welfare Happiness and Ethics* (Oxford: Oxford University Press, 1996), 83.
2. Martin Seligman, *Flourish* (London: Nicholas Brealey Publishing, 2011).
3. Richard Layard, *Happiness Lessons from a New Science*, 2nd ed. (New York: Penguin, 2011).
4. Dan Brock, "Quality of Life in Health Care and Medical Ethics" in *The Quality of Life*, ed. M. Nussbaum and A. Sen (Oxford: Oxford University Press, 1993).
5. Douglas Rasmussen, "Human Flourishing and the Appeal to Human Nature" in *Social Philosophy & Policy*, 16, 1999.
6. Ibid., 43.
7. Ibid., 2, 59. See also Alasdair MacIntyre, *Dependent Rational Animals* (London: Duckworth, 1999), 59.
8. Rasmussen, "Human Flourishing," 1–2.
9. Ibid., 3, 14, 30.
10. Ibid., 3.
11. Ibid., 3–5.
12. Ibid., 6.

13. Ibid.
14. Ibid.
15. Ibid., 8.
16. Ibid., 9.
17. Ibid.
18. Ibid., 10.
19. Ibid., 10–11.
20. Ibid., 11.
21. Ibid.
22. Ibid., 12.
23. Ibid., 13.
24. Ibid.
25. Ibid.
26. Ibid., 14.
27. Ibid., 16.
28. Ibid., 14.
29. Ibid.
30. Ibid.
31. Ibid.
32. Ibid., 32.
33. Ibid.
34. Ibid., 33.
35. Ibid.
36. Ibid.
37. See Juan de Pasquale, "A Wonder Full Life" in *Society and Culture Blog* (*Notre Dame Magazine*, 2003).
38. Rasmussen, "Human Flourishing," 14.
39. See Paul Cartledge, *Spartan Reflection* (London: Duckworth, 2001), 84; and Richard J. A. Talbert, *Plutarch on Sparta* (London: Penguin Books, 2005).
40. Peter Connolly, *Greece and Rome at War* (London: Greenhill Books, 2006), 38.
41. Adam Kuper, *Culture: The Anthropologists' Account* (Cambridge: Harvard University Press, 2000), 247.
42. Alasdair MacIntyre, *Dependent Rational Animals*, x.
43. MacIntyre does not offer a definition of what he labels "Aristotle's metaphysical biology" but to understand what he means in greater detail one might examine his view of teleology. Philosopher Christopher Steven Lutz reports that in a lecture presented in Notre Dame in 1995 MacIntyre voiced that his account of teleology presupposes that human beings, despite their differences, share a common identity and what he calls a species-specific notion of flourishing, and a common teleological goal. In addition, and importantly to the notion of metaphysical biology, MacIntyre states that these things cannot be reduced to physical phenomena and presuppose the idea that our nature is in part metaphysical. See Christopher Stephen Lutz, *Tradition in the Ethics of Alasdair MacIntyre: Relativism, Thomism, and Philosophy* (Lanham, MD: Lexington Books, 2009), 134.
44. Ibid.
45. Ibid., xii.
46. Ibid., 8.
47. Ibid., 11.
48. Ibid., 22.
49. Ibid., 78.
50. Ibid., 79.
51. Ibid., 1.
52. See WorkStress, The UK National Work-Stress Network, 2018, http://www.workstress.net/what-stress.
53. MacIntyre op. cit. 65.
54. Ibid., 96.

55. Ibid., 82.
56. Ibid., 96.
57. Ibid., 87–88.
58. Ibid., 102.
59. Ibid.
60. Ibid.
61. Ibid., 102–103.
62. Ibid., 105.
63. Ibid., 106.
64. Ibid., 106–7.
65. Ibid., 108.
66. George Silberbauer, "Ethics in Small-Scale Societies" in *A Companion to Ethics*, ed. Peter Singer (Hoboken, NJ: Blackwell, 2001), 17.
67. Ibid.
68. Martha Nussbaum, *Creating Capabilities* (Cambridge: Harvard University Press, 2011), iv.
69. Ibid., 18.
70. Martha Nussbaum, *Sex and Social Justice* (Oxford: Oxford University Press, 1999), 33; and Nussbaum *Creating Capabilities*op. cit., x.
71. Ibid.
72. The Human Development and Capability Association has a website located at: https://hd-ca.org/
73. Amartya Sen, "Equality of what? Tanner Lecture on Human Values," *Tanner Lectures* (Stanford: Stanford University, 1979), 217.
74. See Martha Nussbaum, "Aristotelian Social Democracy" in *Liberalism and the Good*, ed. R. B. Douglass, G. M. Mara and H. S. Richardson (London: Routledge, 1990).
75. Aristotle, *Nicomachean Ethics* trans. H. Rackham (Cambridge: Harvard University Press, 2003), I. xiii. 10.
76. Aristotle, *Politics*, trans. H. Rackham (Cambridge: Harvard University Press, 1967), II. v. 12.
77. Nussbaum, "Aristotelian Social Democracy," 217.
78. Ibid. Rawls puts forward his "thin theory of the good" in *A Theory of Justice* and it aims to explain the "rational preference for primary goods and to explicate the notion of rationality underlying the choice of principles in the original position." See John Rawls, *A Theory of Justice* (Oxford: Oxford University Press, 2000), 349. Understanding about the original position emerges via engaging in the thought experiment, the veil of ignorance. See chapter 4.
79. John M. Alexander, *Capabilities and Social Justice: The Political Philosophy of Amartya Sen and Martha Nussbaum* (Farnham, UK: Ashgate Publishing, 2008), 66.
80. Nussbaum, "Aristotelian Social Democracy," 217–18.
81. Ibid., 219.
82. Ibid.
83. Ibid., 220.
84. Ibid.
85. Ibid.
86. Ibid., 221.
87. Ibid.
88. Ibid.
89. Ibid.
90. Ibid.
91. One can argue with reference to MacIntyre that this is also experienced later on in any individual's life when, due to old age, the body is weakened, fragile, and no longer able to regenerate sufficiently. Additionally, the very ill and hospitalized human being experiences dependency. In his work on the Danish philosopher K. E. Løgstrup, philosopher Hans Fink points out that Løgstrup goes even further than MacIntyre with regards to our dependence. The idea is that even when we are in the

prime of our lives we are closely interwoven with others. "We are who we are in virtue of our relations to parents, siblings, friends, lovers, colleagues, enemies, children, grandchildren, and strangers of all kinds." See Hans Fink, "The Conception of Ethics in K. E. Løgstrup's *The Ethical Demand*" in *Concern for the Other: Perspectives on the Ethics of K.E. Løgstrup*, ed. S. Andersen and K. V. K. Nierkerk (Notre Dame, IN: University of Notre Dame Press, 2007), 12.

92. Ibid.
93. Ibid., 222.
94. Ibid.
95. Ibid.
96. Ibid.
97. Ibid.
98. Ibid.
99. Ibid.
100. Ibid.
101. Ibid.
102. Ibid.
103. Ibid. 223.
104. For an excellent overview of the history and aim of transhumanism see Nick Bostrom, "A History of Transhumanist Thought" in *Journal of Evolution and Technology*, 14(1), 2005.
105. Nussbaum, *Aristotelian Social Democracy*, 223.
106. Ibid.
107. Ibid.
108. Ibid.
109. Ibid.
110. Ibid.
111. Ibid. 224.
112. For earlier versions of the list see Nussbaum, "Non-relative Virtues," 225 in *The Quality of Life*, ed. Martha Nussbaum and Amartya Sen (Oxford: Oxford University Press, 1993); Martha Nussbaum, *Women and Human Development* (Cambridge, UK: Cambridge University Press, 2001), 77.
113. The full version of Martha Nussbaum list of capabilities can be found in her *Creating Capabilities* (Cambridge: Harvard University Press, 2011), 33–34.
114. Ibid., 20–21.
115. Ibid., 21.
116. Ibid., 18–19.
117. Ibid.
118. Ibid., 32. Nussbaum's list of capabilities has grown more nuanced since it was first published. For example, in her book *Sex and Social Justice* from 1999 she states that "the capabilities approach, as I conceive it, claims that a life that lacks any one of these capabilities, no matter what else it has, will fall short of being a good human life." See Martha Nussbaum, *Sex and Social Justice* (Oxford: Oxford University Press, 1999), 42.
119. Nussbaum, *Creating Capabilities*, 62.
120. United Nations General Assembly, 1989, article 29, retrieved November 14, 2018 from http://www.ohchr.org/en/professionalinterest/pages/crc.aspx.
121. Nussbaum, *Creating Capabilities*, 63.
122. Nussbaum, *Women and Human Development*, 51.
123. Philip McReynolds, "Nussbaum's Capabilities Approach: A Pragmatic Critique" in *The Journal of Speculative Philosophy, New Series*, 16(2), 2002, 148.
124. Nussbaum, "Non-relative Virtues," 261.
125. Ibid., 264.
126. Nussbaum, "Aristotelian Social Democracy," 217.
127. See United Nations Educational, Scientific and Cultural Organization (UNESCO) entry on Literacy at https://en.unesco.org/themes/literacy-all.

128. William C. Compton and Edward Hoffman, *Positive Psychology, The Science of Happiness and Flourishing* (Wadsworth Cengage Learning, 2013), 132.
129. Martin Seligman, *Flourish* (London: Nicholas Brealey Publishing, 2011), 209.
130. Mark Vernon, *The Philosophy of Friendship* (Basingstoke, UK: Palgrave Macmillan, 2005), 2.
131. Aristotle, *Nicomachean Ethics*, (Cambridge: Harvard University Press, 2003), VIII 1.
132. Ibid., VIII. i. 6.
133. Nussbaum, "Non-relative Virtues," 264.
134. Aristotle, *Nicomachean Ethics*, IX. Iv. 5.
135. Mette Lebech, *Venskab Dyder og laster,* Vol. 24 (Philosophia—Tidskrift for filosofi, 1995), 147–48.
136. Compton and Hoffman, *Positive Psychology*, 137.
137. Virginia Henderson and Gladys Nite,*Principles and Practice of Nursing,* 6th edition (New York: MacMillan, 1978), 945.
138. Compton and Hoffman, *positive Psychology*, 136.
139. Mary Douglas, *Meanings: Essays in Anthropology* (London: Routledge, 1975), 96.
140. John Cleese, *Graham Chapman's Memorial Service,* December 1989.
141. C3 Collaborating for Health, *The Benefits of Physical Activity for Health and Wellbeing, 2012,* 4, 6. C3 Collaborating for Health is a non-profit orientated nongovernmental organization based in London, which raises awareness about the negative health effects of tobacco use, physical inactivity, and poor diet. For more information see www.c3health.org.
142. Barry Kroll, "Arguing with Adversaries: Aikido, Rhetoric, and the Art of Peace" in *College Composition and Communication, 59*(3), 2008, 451.
143. The Omoto religion is based on Shinto (Way of the Gods), indigenous to Japan, and was founded by Nao Deguchi and Onisaburo Deguchi in the late nineteenth century. See Richard Fox Young "'Gokyō-dōgen' to 'Bankyō-dōkon': A Study in the Self-Universalization of Ōmoto" in *Japanese Journal of Religious Studies, 15*(4), 1988, 263, 281.
144. Morihei Ueshiba, *The Heart of Aikido: The Philosophy of Takemusu Aiki,* trans. J. Stevens, ed. H. Takahashi (Tokyo: Kodansha International, 2010), 16.
145. Sam Keen, *In the Absence of God: Dwelling in the Presence of the Sacred* (New York: Harmony Books, 2010), 91.
146. Compton and Hoffman, *Positive Psychology,* 236–37.
147. Robert A. Emmons and Charles M. Shelton, "Gratitude and the Science of Positive Psychology" in *Handbook of Positive Psychology,* ed. C. R. Snyder and S. J. Lopez (Oxford: Oxford University Press, 2002), 468.
148. Ibid., 460.
149. Ibid.
150. Keen, *In the Absence of God: Dwelling in the Presence of the Sacred*, 92. In some Jewish circles it is a sign of respect to omit the "o" in God and thus it has become increasingly popular for philosophers of religion and for writers contributing to multifaith forums or websites such as beliefnet.com to write G-d instead of God.
151. Nothing prevents us from feeling or expressing gratitude toward nonhuman animals. Swimmer Adam Walker, for example, felt gratitude to a group of dolphins who saved him from an impending shark attack during his eight-hour swim across the Cook Strait in 2014. See Matthew Young, "'Dolphins saved me from Shark Attack' says champion swimmer" in *The Daily Star*, 2016, retrieved November 19, 2018, https://www.dailystar.co.uk/news/latest-news/486073/Dolphins-saved-shark-attack-champion-swimmer . On the other side it may also be argued that certain non-human animals may feel gratitude toward human beings. Michael Fishback, co-founder of the Great Whale Conservancy (GWC) explains that when he encountered a young humpback whale caught up in local fishing nets and managed to free it, it rewarded him and his crew with many magnificent full-body breeches and tail flips. Fishback took this as "a show of pure joy if not thanks." See Michael Fishback, "Humpback Whale Shows

Amazing Appreciation after being freed From Nets. Retrieved November 19, 2018, from https://www.youtube.com/watch?v=tcXU7G6zhjU.

152. Nothing prevents us from feeling or expressing gratitude toward nonhuman animals. Swimmer Adam Walker, for example, felt gratitude to a group of dolphins who saved him from an impending shark attack during his eight-hour swim across the Cook Strait in 2014. See Matthew Young, "'Dolphins saved me from Shark Attack' says champion swimmer" in *The Daily Star*, 2016, retrieved November 1th, 2018, https://www.dailystar.co.uk/news/latest-news/486073/Dolphins-saved-shark-attack-champion-swimmer . On the other side it may also be argued that certain non-human animals may feel gratitude toward human beings. Michael Fishback, co-founder of the Great Whale Conservancy (GWC) explains that when he encountered a young humpback whale caught up in local fishing nets and managed to free it, it rewarded him and his crew with many magnificent full-body breeches and tail flips. Fishback took this as "a show of pure joy if not thanks." See Michael Fishback, "Humpback Whale Shows Amazing Appreciation after being freed From Nets. Retrieved November 19th, 2018 from https://www.youtube.com/watch?v=tcXU7G6zhjU.

153. Blaise Pascal, *The Pensees*, trans. J. M. Cohen (New York: Penguin Books, 1961), 57.

154. Sam Keen, *An Apology for Wonder* (New York: Harper and Row, 1969), 211.

155. Ibid., 211–12.

156. William Braud, "Experiencing Tears of Wonder-Joy: Seeing with the Heart's Eye" in *The Journal of Transpersonal Psychology*, 33(2), 2001, 99.

157. Rachel Carson, *The Sense of Wonder* (New York: HarperCollins, 1984), 55.

158. Robert C. Solomon, *Spirituality for the Sceptic: Thoughtful Love of Life* (Oxford: Oxford University Press, 2002), 32.

159. Ibid., 39–40.

160. The term creature-hood is taken from Helen Oppenheimer's article "Christian Flourishing" (Oppenheimer, 1969, p. 163).

161. Keen, *In the absence of God: Dwelling in the Presence of the Sacred*, 98.

162. Juan de Pasquale, "A Wonder Full Life" in *Society and Culture Blog 2012* (*Dame Magazine*, 2003).

163. See Scott London, "Renewing Our Sense of Wonder: An Interview with Sam Keen" in *Scott London*, Retrieved November 19, 2018. http://www.scottlondon.com/interviews/keen.html

164. Robert Fuller "Wonder and the Religious Sensibility" in *Journal of Religion*, 2006, 370.

165. See Keen, *In the Absence of God: Dwelling in the Presence of the Sacred*, 126–27; James Kellenberger, "Humility" in *American Philosophical Quarterly*, 47(4), 2010, 321–36 & Norvin Richards, "Is Humility a Virtue" in *American Philosophical Quarterly*, 25(3), 1988, 253–59.

166. To be small-souled contrasts that of being great-souled (megalopsuchos) involving claiming much and deserving much. See Aristotle, *Nicomachean Ethics*, Iii. 3.

167. Aristotle, *Nicomachean Ethics*, IV. Iii.

168. Theologian and mystic Eckhart von Hockheim, better known as Meister Eckhart, goes even further and talks about perfect humility which he believes "proceeds from annihilation of self." See Meister Eckhart "On Detachment" in *Meister Eckhart: The Essential Sermons, Commentaries, Treatises, and Defence*, trans. E. Colledge and B. McGinn (New York: Paulist Press, 1981), 286. This contrasts with the view of Aristotle to whom Meister Eckhart's perfect humility would be a sign of being small-souled. According to Aristotle a person who is small-souled is a man who claims less than he deserves when his deserts are great. See Aristotle, *Nicomachean Ethics*, op. cit., IV. Iii. 7.

169. Alasdair Mactintyre, *A Short History of Ethics* (London: Routledge, 1998), 78.

170. That pride is a sin is obvious to the Christian when she reads the Bible and in particular the Proverbs. Here we find entries such as "when pride cometh, then cometh shame," Proverbs:11. 2. and "Pride goeth before destruction, and an haunting spirit before a fall" Proverbs 16:18. Additionally, we can say that Dante's Purgatory,

where the prideful is punished by carrying the weight of heavy stones, speaks toward pride being a sin in Christianity. See Dante Alighieri, *The Devine Comedy* (Everyman's Library, 1995), Purg., Canto X, 259.

171. Kellenberger, "Humility," 338.

172. Henry Sidgwick, *The Methods of Ethics* (Chicago: University of Chicago Press, 1874), 334–35.

173. Compton and Hoffman, *Positive Psychology*, 241.

174. MacIntyre, *A Short History of Ethics*, 63.

175. Ibid., 64.

176. I owe this point to R. W. Hepburn. See Ronald W. Hepburn, "The Inagural Address: Wonder" in *Proceedings of the Aristotelian Society, Supplementary Volume, 54*, 1980, 6.

177. Raymond Tallis, *In Defence of Wonder and Other Philosophical Reflections* (Durham, UK: Acumen, 2012), 1.

178. Keen, *In the Absence of God: Dwelling in the Presence of the Sacred*, 85.

179. Aristotle, *Nicomachean Ethics*, II. Ix. 2.

180. Keen, *Apology for Wonder*, 185.

181. Ibid., 186.

182. Ibid., 190.

183. Samuel Beckett, "Molloy" in *The Beckett Trilogy* (London: Picador Books, 1979), 93.

184. Robert C. Fuller, *Wonder: From Emotion to Spirituality* (Chapel Hill, NC: The University of North Carolina Press, 2006), 158. Fulfillment can be seen as synonymous with flourishing. See Daniel M. Heybron, *The Pursuit of Unhappiness* (Oxford: Oxford University Press, 2008,) 193.

185. Fuller, *Wonder: From Emotion to Spirituality*, 2.

186. D. H. Lawrence, *The Later D. H. Lawrence* (New York: Alfred A. Knopf, 1959), 382.

187. Keen, *In the Absence of God: Dwelling in the Presence of the Sacred*, 85.

Conclusion

Wondering about Wonder

In this book I have defended the idea that cultivating a balanced sense of wonder is a strong contributor to living a flourishing human life. It represents a detailed study of wonder and contributes to the rehabilitation of wonder as a subject worthy of philosophical attention despite its low prestige. In the very beginning we established that wonder is a difficult subject to study and nail down, primarily, because as a phenomenon, it is about as intangible and airy as anything can be. Thus in chapter 1: "The Lure of Wonder," an attempt was made to sketch a picture of wonder by first of all presenting and interpreting a selection of different experiences of wonder gathered from literature and real life experiences. This anchored the phenomenon of wonder in human experience and suggested that wonder is a state of mind comprised of seven constituents. (see figure C.1below)

The experience of wonder is sudden, extraordinary, and personal. It intensifies the cognitive focus and the work of the imagination because the object or source of wonder remains elusive or unknown and thus

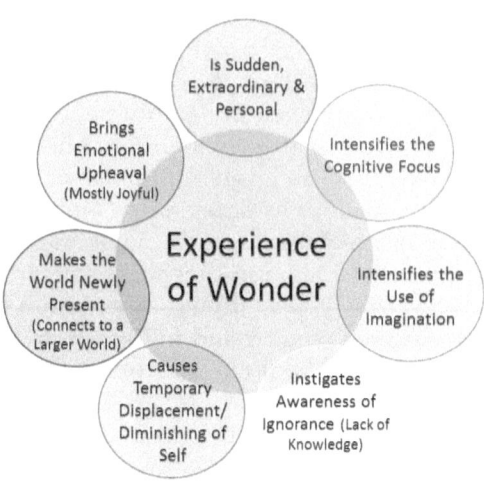

Figure C.1. The 7 Core Constituents of the Experience of Wonder

disturbs the wonderer's order of things. The imagination seeks to correct this disturbance but fails to provide a fitting cognitive schema, making the wonderer aware of her ignorance or lack of knowledge, and so the experience of wonder becomes at least a temporary displacing matter involving a diminishing of self. This permits us to say that wonder makes the world newly present or to put it differently, it connects the wonderer with a hitherto unknown larger world. All this causes joyful emotional upheaval and only rarely the opposite.

Chapter 1 also focused on the etymology of "wonder," which uncovered the root of the word "wonder" and how "wonder" can be seen as a noun (the ghost in Hamlet is a *wonder* to behold), a verb (I *wonder* how the king came back from the dead), an adjective (Horatio is a *wondering man*) and an adverb (Horatio *wonderingly* approached the ghost). Of the four kind of ways to use the word "wonder," the adverbial is the most interesting because when we are doing something wonderingly we indicate that we wonder in a particular way. This hints to us that wonder can be influenced or moderated by the wonderer.

Addressing the history of wonder enriched our preliminary understanding of the subject because it illuminated how conceptions of wonder changed over time and how wonder, with the advancement of science, lost its status and slipped into obscurity.

Because wonder is sometimes seen as interchangeable with other altered states of mind this was followed by a preliminary taxonomy of altered states similar to wonder through which I sought to distinguish wonder from awe, horror, the sublime, curiosity, astonishment, admiration, and amazement.

Finally, to close the chapter, some possible enemies of wonder were considered, and through the categories of natural and elective enemies of wonder I highlighted why wonder is sometimes shunned or simply missing from our lives.

From these initial investigations it became clear that emotion and imagination are somehow involved in the experience of wonder, and by looking at the work on wonder by contemporary philosophers Robert C. Fuller and Philo Hove, this was given additional support. However, in what capacity wonder qualifies as an emotion, and if wonder could be viewed as exclusively so, remained unclear. Likewise, the role of imagination in wonder was shrouded and called out for further exploration. Fuller and Hove, respectively, also brought the notion of deep wonder and the connection between wonder and fulfillment to the table, leaving us with additional questions about the nature of wonder and how wonder may help us become fulfilled or flourish.

Chapter 2, "Wonder and Emotion," dealt with one of the research questions, namely, in what sense wonder can be viewed as an emotion and if it is possible to classify it exclusively so. To illuminate the possibility that wonder is an emotion in the richest possible way I committed to examining wonder through the lens of the cognitive approach to emotion, leaning on the work of philosophers Aaron Ben-Ze'ev and Adam Morton. Through Ben-Ze'ev's work and its application to a selection of examples of wonder, we found that the experience of wonder shares the same characteristics, components, and dependencies as an emotion. For example, all emotions have a cognitive component and are characterized by being intense to some degree or other, the intensity of which depends on the reality of a particular event. This fits wonder well because during wonderment we are trying to figure out what is going on but because we fail our experience becomes intense. Wondering amid an extraordinary meteor shower like the one described by Kuiper in the *New York Times* is thus intense because it was not merely a rare sight but also very real. In addition, upon the examination of the interesting notion of epistemic emotions advocated by Adam Morton, it became clear that wonder can also be viewed as such. However to say that wonder is exclusively an emotion is an overstatement, which becomes evident upon realizing that wonder can also be viewed as a mood, a value, and an attitude. Thus we concluded that wonder is best viewed as multifaceted.

In chapter 3, "Wonder and Imagination," I investigated the role of imagination in wonder. Like the field of emotion, imagination is a vast and complex subject and thus I opted to focus on the work of contemporary philosophers of imagination Mary Warnock, Ronald Hepburn, and Roger Scruton to gain better understanding of the subject and how imagination works in wonderment.

Warnock's contribution to the philosophy of imagination enabled us to comprehend why the wonder-filled experience can come across as animating, intense, and the conveyer of the universal. Wonder animates us because during wonderment we use the imagination to go beyond what is directly in front of us and to seek satisfying cognitive schemata of what we experience. However, in wonder we never obtain a complete understanding of what is going on and thus the wonder-filled experience is intense because a completely satisfying picture of the object of wonder never arrives. Warnock's approach also prompted us to think about wonder as a conveyer of the universal in the sense that the use of imagination in wonder can give rise to the idea that the object of wonder has a general significance beyond itself. In this respect we looked to ideas emerging from wonderment such as that we are mortal creatures and that we live in a world that is grand and beautiful.

The role of imagination in wonder was explored further by paying attention to Hepburn's idea that our imagination works on three levels. This prompted us to explore wonder as a three-layered experience where the first layer enables us to gather data and appreciate something as wonderful; the second layer enables us to see the object of wonder as significant; and the third layer allows for individual interpretations of the object of wonder informing us about how the world is fundamentally structured. The third layer involving metaphysical imagination is of particular interest because it explains why wonder might have a revelatory or noetic quality. Likewise, it highlights why we must be critical about wonderment because a wonder-filled event can, courtesy of the metaphysical imagination, give rise to incompatible views of how the world fundamentally is depending on the wonderer.

Scruton's approach to imagination took our understanding of wonderment to yet another level as it helped us establish a connection between what is absent in imagination, understood as unasserted thought, and what we in wonder experience as newly present. In wonder we see the world anew and we do this because our frame of reference is displaced allowing us for perhaps merely a moment to assert what is normally unasserted and thus experience ourselves as changed. Scruton's approach also allowed us to consider what it takes to wonder appropriately and in this respect a preliminary acceptance criterion for wonderment was proposed stating that for someone to wonder appropriately she has to wonder at what is extraordinary, vivid, and significant, and that her wonderment can be accepted by others. I am sympathetic to the acceptance criterion but what if "others" around the wonderer resembled Alexander Pope and his followers and were completely hostile to wonder? In such a situation the wonderer will always wonder inappropriately because to wonder is foolish from their point of view and should be shunned. It is therefore important to note that if one's wonder has to be accepted by others in order to pass the test it leaves the wonderer as it were to the tyranny of others. Scruton's approach to imagination likewise prompted thoughts about the continuity between intense experiences and subsequent living in relation to wonder, and it was brought forth that if someone is experiencing wonder in a true sense she experiences being in a state of mind that embraces perhaps a kind of subtle reverence, gratitude, or openness that influence her behavior and may continue to do so over time.

Furthermore, we looked to the notion of cultivating a habit of wonder via educating the imagination, and it was ventured that by training our ability to imagine, we can become accustomed to seek for the richest possible account of something and develop a disposition for seeing the ordinary as conveyer of the extraordinary. In connection with Scruton's approach we likewise focused on the joy of wonder and explored if the joy we feel during an episode of wonder can be exclusively linked to the object of wonder. I concluded that this was not necessarily so because although one might find joy in the object of wonder, a part of the joy might also consist of (1) being displaced/experiencing a diminishing of self, (2) the reverence, openness, and gratitude one might experience, and (3) the awareness of ignorance about the object of wonder and the invitation to undertake further inquiries.

Imagination has an important role to play in wonder and its involvement explains why wonder can be revelatory, present us truths, provoke metaphysical speculation, and have us see what, in a strict sense, is not there. Imagination underlies the intensity of wonder and how we, in wonder, see the world as newly present, but we also need to be mindful about the conclusions we draw during wonderment. Wonderment needs to be balanced because as much as one might like to think of wonder as something joyful and positive there are potentially negative effects to wonder. Wonder, as it were, may lead us astray because through wonderment we may become convinced that we have uncovered the truth about the fundamental structure of the world (which is a big and potentially doubtful claim), or that a given object of wonder was literally there while it in fact was nothing but a product of our imagination.

To increase our understanding of how imagination works in wonder and to foreshadow how wonder is important to human flourishing, chapter 4, "Implications of the Role of Imagination in Wonder," examined how the intense use of imagination in wonder may result in a variety of effects, as depicted in figure C.2.

One possible outcome of wonder is the widening of perception and I demonstrated this effect by looking at: (1) the wonder-filled mannerist

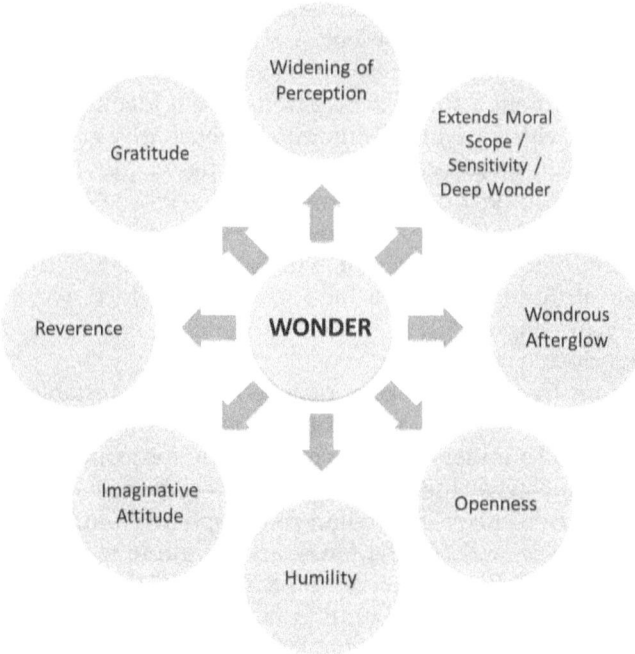

Figure C.2. The Effects of Wonder

painting *Rudolf II as Vertumnus* by Guiseppe Arcimboldo, (2) descriptions of what it is like to see Earth from space by author Frank White, astronaut Edgar Mitchell, and philosopher David Loy, taken from Guy Read's film *Overview*, and finally (3) the microscope and the telescope, both of which I argue qualify as wonder-filled artifacts that when put to use may expand our perception. The widening of perception ultimately helps us increase our understanding of what and who we are and our conception of the world we live in.

The experience of wonder might also extend our "moral scope and sensitivity," which I have sought to demonstrate by engaging with (1) political philosopher Robert Nozick's thought experiment "The Experience Machine," (2) political philosopher John Rawls's thought experiment the "Veil of Ignorance," and (3) the concept of Speciesism advocated by moral philosopher Peter Singer. These examples demonstrated that such "philosophical wonders" are important, not merely because they boost our imagination and encourage us to think about how we live, but also because of their usefulness as educational devices since all of them can induce wonder and may prompt in the wonderer the desire for further inquiry.

The chapter also caught up with the notion of a wondrous afterglow and the experience of deep wonder or deep-leveled wonder promoted by philosophers Philo Hove and Ian Kidd. An important common factor between these effects of wonder is that they are enduring and involve the intense work of the imagination because it is the imagination that gives people such states of mind, the power to venture beyond the given. Having said that the mental states in question are not identical because deep wonder comes with an ethical imperative (hence it is grouped together with an increase in moral scope/sensitivity in figure C.2,) and seems to be an attitude, disposition, or the outcome of philosophical reflection whereas a wondrous afterglow need not involve the ethical and appears to be a mood. Other important effects of wonder are openness, humility, an imaginative attitude, reverence, and gratitude, which were explored superficially in chapter 4 and in greater detail in chapter 5, "Wonder, Human Flourishing, and Virtue."

Building on from the complex picture of wonder established in the previous chapters, chapter 5 brought wonder into the dimension of human flourishing. To understand this new setting for wonder it was essential to understand what the key constitutions of human flourishing are, and via the work of neo-Aristotelian philosophers Douglas Rasmussen, Alasdair MacIntyre, and Martha Nussbaum, a guide to human flourishing was established. Rasmussen revealed a view of the human good that is (1) objective, (2) inclusive, (3) individualized, (4) agent-relative, (5) self-directed, and (6) social. Additionally, Rasmussen brought forth that practical wisdom and human nature are significant to human flourishing. MacIntyre's approach to human flourishing advanced our understanding of human flourishing by highlighting our animality, vulnerability, and dependency on others. Furthermore, he brought to our attention that the process of flourishing demands we become independent practical reasoners and develop virtues that would enable us to make good choices and allow us to find out what is good for us (e.g., questioning if the relationships we are engaged in promotes our flourishing). Nussbaum's approach to human flourishing brought forth the "thick vague conception of the good," and the open-ended list of basic human functional capabilities that may help promote human beings living flourishing lives. The latter has provided us a potential measuring tool against which we can assess whether a given environment (understood not only as our immediate physical surroundings but also the social relations and culture we are situated in) provides the ground for human flourishing.

Based on the concept of human flourishing, I argued that effects of wonder such as gratitude, reverence, openness, humility, and an imaginative attitude might contribute to human flourishing. Openness, for example, contributes to flourishing because not only is it something that everyone, given a choice, would opt to have, it is the antithesis of dogma and helps us discover goods that we perhaps never thought existed. Conversely, it would allow us to critically assess whether the goods we already have or value may or may not contribute to our flourishing. Humility that may spring from a deep felt realization of the vastness and beauty of the universe and the mystery of our existence can likewise contribute to our flourishing, as this could prompt a life of joy, satisfaction, wisdom, and contentment.

Lastly and central to the book, I argued that virtuous wonder or balanced wonder promotes human flourishing in a strong sense. In doing so I demonstrated the problems with the lack of wonder and with wonderment in excess, while wonder works toward our flourishing in a strong sense if practiced in a virtuous or balanced way. Having established this I also acknowledged that obtaining a balanced sense of wonder is not an easy task, partly because there is no concrete tool that could guide one in how to achieve this. However, through in-depth examination of the contribution of both emotion and imagination in the experience of wonder, we did manage to reach a preliminary understanding of how a balanced sense of wonder may be obtained. Much is at play in wonder, including emotional upheaval and the intense use of the imagination, and thus we must do our best not to jump to conclusions about the importance and significance of the object of wonder we perceive, and always seek the richest possible account of what we are experiencing. Importantly, we must also be mindful of the fact that as beings capable of wonder, we may color our experiences and partly be responsible for what we perceive.

In summary, this work has uncovered a fascinating subject of wonder and by in-depth examination of the contribution of both emotion and imagination in the experience of wonder through a neo-Aristotelian lens, it was possible to demonstrate that wonder may contribute to human flourishing via a number of effects (figure C.2), including (but not restricted to) widening of perception, extension of moral scope or sensitivity, and prompting deep wonder, a wondrous afterglow, openness, humility, an imaginative attitude, reverence, and gratitude. A further exploration of wonder revealed that experience of one's wonderment is not an "all-or-none" process and that for wonder to act as a strong contributor to human flourishing one needs to wonder at the right (or appropriate) thing, in the right amount, in the right time, in the right way, and for the right purpose. Cultivating a balanced sense of wonder is thus by no means an easy task, but having a critical attitude toward one's wonderment would aid one to wonder in a virtuous way.

Every piece of academic work suffers limitations and I would like now to address some sources of epistemic worry that one might reasonably entertain with regards to a book of this kind. Firstly, philosophy as "method" of inquiry. Originally titled the *Cynic's Word Book*, Ambrose Bierce's *The Devil's Dictionary* defines philosophy as "a route of many roads leading from nowhere to nothing."[1]

The humorous definition captures well the concerns one might have toward philosophical inquiry in general. Indeed, according to philosopher Bertrand Russell, the value of philosophy is to be sought in its uncertainty.[2] However, philosophy does lead to something. When we philosophize about a given subject we liberate ourselves from the tyranny of certainty and dogmatism. We enlarge and expand our thinking, and although we might lose our feeling of being safely rooted we also gain something as we get to travel "into the region of liberating thought [which] keeps alive our sense of wonder by showing familiar things in an unfamiliar aspect."[3] In this sense the use of philosophy in a study on wonder has prompted us to wonder about wonder, and allowed deeper understanding of the subject matter. In the introduction I presented a preliminary definition of wonder where the subject was defined as "a sudden experience that intensifies the cognitive focus and awareness of ignorance about a given object." Furthermore, I highlighted that it is typically an unsettling yet delightful experience where we become aware that there might be more to the perceived object than meets the eye. Here at the end this still rings true but we are now able to add something to the preliminary definition. We have established that wonder can be an emotion but not exclusively so, and that imagination plays a significant part in wonder. Likewise, by looking at wonder through a neo-Aristotelian lens, we now know that wonder may contribute to human flourishing and if wonder is balanced it qualifies as an activity that contributes strongly to our flourishing. Thus, philosophizing about wonder has complicated matters but as a result we have learned more about the subject matter. Additionally, we have effectively opened up to speculation about wonder, which can lead to further studies and more detailed wonderings about wonder.

The critic may also point out that I am guilty of eclecticism because I have handpicked the theories used to illuminate, in particular, the areas of emotion, imagination, and flourishing. This is a fair critique, but in my defense, each of these areas connected to wonder are worthy of a study in itself because they are all vast and complex. Handpicking theories and examples was thus a necessity to get the study of wonder underway, because it is impossible within the framework of a single book to cover all aspects and approaches to such fields. One might argue that the book would have been different and perhaps more convincing if I had chosen different theories and examples. For example, it would be interesting to see what light could be cast on wonder if viewed through the lens of William James's approach to emotions. A Jamesian approach to the emotion of wonder would entail that after perceiving a wonder, such as a massive meteor shower, a particular bodily state would follow which then would give rise to the emotion of wonder. What this bodily state consists of is interesting for the student of wonder because it connects to human embodiment and human flourishing. Nevertheless, I chose to focus on the cognitive approach to emotions because it helped us build a rich conception of wonder, including the notion that wonder can also be viewed as something other than an emotion.

I would like to end this conclusion by giving one last example of wonder in order to recapitulate the essence of the wonder-filled experience. In 1999, I was working as a nurse in the emergency department at the local hospital in the city of Hjørring, Northern Jutland, Denmark, where I grew up. I was working nights, and around 10 o'clock after an altogether merry evening at my parents' house I prepared to go to work. As I approached the front door I noticed that the trees and bushes outside were engulfed in a strange red and slightly flickering light. As I looked closer I marked that the light extended to the street and the houses on the opposite side of it. I paused, pondering what could be the cause of such illumination and deduced with some alarm that something big, perhaps a house or a car outside my field of vision, must be on fire and that the light was in fact the red light of flames. I quickly opened the door to investigate the matter closer but to my surprise I saw no fire and heard no sound. It was a perfectly calm autumn evening but I became increasing uneasy because I now realized that everything around me, including my own clothing and hands, was engulfed in the red light. Further deductions led me to think that the source of the light had to come from somewhere to my left but there was nothing to see except more illuminated trees and houses. Something then compelled me to look up into the southwestern sky and what I saw, to put it mildly, is still burned into my memory and makes me smile. Instead of the normal night sky with its usual constellations of stars only a black hole the size of the mid-day sun was visible and from its edges gigantic arms of swirling light painted the whole sky before me in translucent red. The sight was utterly surprising and I think I stood somewhat paralyzed for a few seconds before I realized what was going on. Above me was the Aurora Borealis in the form of a corona of fantastic proportion, which I at the time had never seen before and have never seen since. Full of joy I quickly ran back into the house and ushered my parents out into the garden because I wanted them to see the spectacle and to confirm that what I had seen was actually real. My parents acknowledged the reality of the phenomenon and as we all beheld the extraordinary beautiful display of swirling lights I could not contain my excitement any longer. I threw my arms up in the air in celebration and shouted out loud "It is fantastic," whereto my mother with her eyes still fixed upon the spectacle calmly replied "hush son . . . the neighbors." The spectacle disappeared after approximately ten minutes and as I later headed for work, a sense of gratitude came over me because on this particular evening I had seen something rare and quite special.

I like to think of this experience not only as the witnessing of a well-known natural phenomenon but also an experience of wonder. Seeing the black hole and the swirling red lights in the sky was unexpected and quite unlike anything I had ever seen before (extraordinary, sudden, and personal). For a moment I struggled to capture (intensification of cognitive focus) and understand (intensification of imagination, awareness of ignorance) the phenomenon, which had changed the southwestern sky and sense of normality in a dramatic yet beautiful way, but failed (displacement/diminishing of self, world appears newly present, caused emotional upheaval). Additionally, it can be said that the experience of wonder contributed to my flourishing by presenting me something beautiful and by prompting a sense of gratitude, which I to this day do not fully understand but regard as immensely positive.

Can we say that the experience contributed to my flourishing in a strong sense? Well, at the risk of coming across as self-glorifying I would argue yes, because the spectacle was utterly beautiful and I appreciate having seen it even today, but I have not attached a special meaning to the event that is unreasonable. The event was an extraordinary case of the Aurora Borealis, and like the dramatic meteor shower reported in Elder Samuel Rogers's autobiography, it has served me as a reminder of the fact that we live a vulnerable planetary existence in a world of fantastic proportion and that we can wonder at such things as the Aurora is a wonder in itself.

To end this book I can think of no better way than drawing attention to philosopher Alfred North Whitehead, who writes:

> Philosophy begins in wonder. And, at the end, when philosophic thought has done its best, the wonder remains. There have been added, however, some grasp of the immensity of things, some purification of emotion by understanding.[4]

Thank you for your attention.

NOTES

1. See Ambrose Bierce, *The Devil's Dictionary* (Hertfordshire, UK: Wordsworth Editions Ltd, 1996).
2. Bertrand Russell, *The Problems of Philosophy* (Charleston, SC: Bibliobazaar, 2010), 128.
3. Ibid.
4. Alfred Whitehead, *Nature and Life* (Cambridge, UK: Cambridge University Press, 1934).

Bibliography

Alexander, John M. *Capabilities and Social Justice: The Political Philosophy of Amartya Sen and Martha Nussbaum*. Farnham, UK: Ashgate Publishing, 2008.
Alighieri, Dante. *The Devine Comedy*. London, UK: Everyman's Library, 1995.
Anscombe, G. E. M. "Modern Moral Philosophy" in *Philosophy*, 33, 1958.
Arellano, Jeronimo. "From the Space of the Wunderkammer to Macondo's Wonder Rooms: The Collection of Marvels in Cien anos de solodad" in *Hispanic Review*, 78(3), 2010.
Aristotle. *The Art of Rhetoric*. Translated by. J. H. Freese. LCL. Cambridge: Harvard University Press, 1926.
———. *The Metaphysics*. Translated by H. Tredennick. LCL. Cambridge: Harvard University Press, 1989.
———. *Meteorologica*. Translated by H. D. P. Lee. LCL. Cambridge: Harvard University Press, 1951.
———. *Nicomachean Ethics*. Translated by H. Rackham. LCL. Cambridge: Harvard University Press, 2003.
———. *On the Soul. Parva Naturalia. On Breath*. Translated by Walter Stanley Hett. LCL. Cambridge: Harvard University Press, 1957.
———. *Poetics*. Translated by J. Sachs. Bemidji, MN: Focus Publishing, 2006.
———. *Poetics*. Translated by S. Halliwell. LCL. Cambridge: Harvard University Press, 1995.
———. *Politics*. Translated by H. Rackham. LCL. Cambridge: Harvard University Press, 1967.
Attfield, Robin. *Wonder, Value and God*. London: Routledge, 2017.
Augustin. *Om Guds stad*. Aarhus, Denmark: Århus Universitetsforlag, 2002.
Augustine. *Confessions*. Translated by William Watts. LCL. Cambridge: Harvard University Press, 2006.
Bacon, Francis. *The Advancement of Learning*. Project Gutenberg, 1971.
Bæksted, Anders. *Nordiske Guder og Helte*. Copenhagen, Denmark: Politikkens Forlag, 1990.
Beckett, Samuel. "Molloy" in *The Beckett Trilogy*. London: Picador Books, 1979.
Ben-Ze'ev, Aaron. "The Thing Called Emotion" in *The Oxford Handbook of Philosophy of Emotion*. Edited by Peter Goldie. Oxford: Oxford University Press, 2010.
Bentham, Jeremy. *A Fragment on Government*. Cambridge: Cambridge University Press, 1988.
———. *An Introduction to the Principles of Morals and Legislation*. Oxford: Oxford University Press, 1879.
Berlin, Isaiah. *The Roots of Romanticism*. Edited by Henry Hardy. Princeton, NJ: Princeton University Press, 2001.
Bierce, Ambrose. *The Devil's Dictionary*. Hertfordshire, UK: Wordsworth Editions Ltd, 1996.
Blackburn, Simon. "Précis of Ruling Passions" in *Philosophy and Phenomenological Research, LXV*(1), 2002.
———. *Ruling Passions*. Oxford: Oxford University Press, 1998.
Blum, Elisabeth and Paul Richard. "Wonder and Wondering in the Renaissance" in *Philosophy Begins in Wonder: An Introduction to Early Modern Philosophy, Theology and Science*. Edited by Michael Funk Deckard and Peter Losonczi. Cambridge, UK: James Clarke and Co., 2011.

Boler, Megan. "Taming the Labile Other" in *Philosophical of Education Yearbook*. Edited by S. Laird. Philosophy of Education Society, 1997.
Bostrom, Nick. "A History of Transhumanist Thought" in *Journal of Evolution and Technology*, 14(1), 2005.
Boyles, Robert. "Some Observations about Shining Flesh, Both of Veal and Pullet, and That without any Sensible Putrefaction in Those Bodies" [1672], in *The Works of the Honourable Robert Boyle*, [6 vols.]. Edited by Thomas Birch, vol. 3, 1772. Hildesheim, Germany: Georg Olms, 1965–1966, vol. 3.
Brann, Eva T. H. *The World of the Imagination*. Lanham, MD: Rowman and Littlefield Publishers Inc., 1991.
Braud, William. "Experiencing Tears of Wonder-Joy: Seeing with the Heart's Eye" in *The Journal of Transpersonal Psychology*, 33(2), 2001, 99.
Brock, Dan. "Quality of Life in Health Care and Medical Ethics" in *The Quality of Life*. Edited by M. Nussbaum and A. Sen. Oxford: Oxford University Press, 1993.
Burke, Edmund A. *A Philosophical Enquiry into the Origin of Our Ideas of the Sublime and Beautiful*. Edited by A. Philips. Oxford: Oxford University Press, 1990.
Burr, Vivien. *Social Constructionism*. London: Routledge, 2003.
Burrell, David B. "Wonderment Today in the Abrahamic Traditions" in *Practices of Wonder: Cross-Disciplinary Perspectives*. Edited by S. Vasalou. Eugene, OR: Pickwick Publications, 2012.
Byron, Lord. "Don Juan" in *The Works of Lord Byron*. London: John Murray, 1833.
C3 Collaborating for Health. *The Benefits of Physical Activity for Health and Well-Being*, 2012. www.c3health.org.
Caldwell, David F. and Mobjerg, Dennis. "An Exploratory Investigation of the Effect of Ethical Culture in Activating Moral Imagination" in *Journal of Business Ethics*, 73(2), 2007.
Carson, Rachel. *The Sense of Wonder*. New York: HarperCollins, 1984.
Cartledge, Paul. *Spartan Reflection*. London: Duckworth, 2001.
Chen, Jianhong. "On Thomas Hobbes's Concept of Wonder" in *Philosophy begins in Wonder: An Introduction to Early Modern Philosophy, Theology, and Science*. Edited by M. F. Deckard and P. Losonczi. Cambridge, UK: James Clark and Co., 2011.
Chrysakopoulou, Sylvana. "Wonder and the Beginning of Philosophy in Plato" in *Practices of Wonder, Cross-Disciplinary Perspectives*. Edited by S. Vasalou. Eugene, OR: Pickwick Publications, 2012.
Cicero, *De Inventione*. Translated by H. M. Hubbell. LCL. Cambridge: Harvard University Press, 1989.
———. *Tusculan Disputations*. Translated by J. E. King. LCL. Cambridge: Harvard University Press, 2001.
Cleese, John. *Graham Chapman's Memorial Service*. December 1989.
Clemmer, Pam. "Toto We're Not in Kansas Anymore" in *Leonid MAC, NASA*, 1998.
Coen, Ethan and Joel. *A Serious Man*. Focus Features, 2009.
Coleridge, Samuel Taylor. *Biographia Literaria*. Edited by T. Riikonen and D. Widger. Project Gutenberg, 2004.
Compton, William C. and Hoffman, Edward. *Positive Psychology: The Secret of Happiness and Flourishing*. Wadsworth Cengage Learning, 2013.
Connolly, Peter. *Greece and Rome at War*. London: Greenhill Books, 2006.
Crosby, Eric. "An Aesthetic of Wonderment: IMAX and Affect" in *Journal of Moving Image Studies*, 6, 2007.
Cunningham, James Vincent. *Woe or Wonder: The Emotional Effect of Shakespearean Tragedy*. Swallow Paper Books, 1964.
Dante, Alighieri. *The Divine Comedy*. Translated by A. Mandelbaum. London: Everyman's Library, 1995.
Darwin, Charles. *The Expression of Emotions in Man and Animals*. New York: HarperCollins, 1999.
Daston, Lorraine and Park, Katharine. *Wonders and the Order of Nature*. New York: Zone Books, 1998.

Dawkins, Richard. *Unweaving the Rainbow: Science, Delusion and the Appetite for Wonder.* New York: Penguin, 2006.
De Montaigne, Michel. *Essays of Michel de Montaigne.* Translated by C. Cotton. Edited by W. C. Hazlitt. Project Gutenberg, 2012.
De Pasquale, Juan. "A Wonder Full Life," in *Notre Dame Magazine*, 2003. https://magazine.nd.edu/news/a-wonder-full-life/.
Deane-Drummond, Celia. *Wonder and Wisdom.* London: Darton, Longman, and Todd, 2006.
Deigh, John. "Concepts of Emotion in Modern Philosophy and Psychology" in *The Oxford Handbook of Philosophy of Emotion.* Edited by Peter Goldie. Oxford: Oxford University Press, 2010.
Delanty, Gerad. "The Cosmopolitan Imagination" in *Revista CIDOB d'Afers internacionals* (82/83), 2008.
Descartes, Rene. "The Passions of the Soul." Translated by John Cottingham, in *The Philosophical Works of Descartes*, vol. 1. Cambridge, UK: Cambridge University Press, 1985.
Deutch, Barbette. *Poetry Handbook: A Dictionary of Terms.* New York: Grosset and Dunlap, 1957.
Dore, Gustave. *The Dore Illustrations for Dante's Divine Comedy.* Dover Publications, Inc., 1976.
Doron, Claude-Olivier. "The Microscopic Glance: Spiritual Exercises, The Microscope, and the Practice of Wonder in Early Modern Science" in *Practices of Wonder Cross-Disciplinary Perspectives.* Edited by S. Vasalou. Eugene, OR: Pickwick Publications, 2012.
Douglas, Mary. *Implicit Meanings: Essays in Anthropology.* London, Routledge, 1975.
Eckhart von Hockheim (Meister Eckhart). "On Detachment" in *Meister Eckhart: The Essential Sermons, Commentaries, Treatises, and Defence.* Translated by E. Colledge and B. McGinn. New York: Paulist Press, 1981.
Emmons, Robert A. and Shelton, Charles M. "Gratitude and the Science of Positive Psychology" in *Handbook of Positive Psychology.* Edited by C. R. Snyder and S. J. Lopez. Oxford: Oxford University Press, 2002.
Evans, Martyn H. "Medical Humanities and the Place of Wonder" in *The Edinburgh Companion to the Critical Medical Humanities.* Edited by A. Whitehead and A. Woods. Edinburgh: Edinburgh University Press, 2016.
———. "Wonder and the Clinical Encounter" in *Theoretical Medicine and Bioethics, 33*(2), 2012.
Fink, Hans. "The Conception of Ethics in K. E. Løgstrup's *The Ethical Demand*" in *Concern for the Other. Perspectives on the Ethics of K.E. Løgstrup.* Edited by S. Andersen and K. V. K. Nierkerk. Notre Dame, IN: Notre Dame University Press, 2007.
Fishback, Michael. "Humpback Whale Shows Amazing Appreciation after being Freed from Nets." Retrieved November 19, 2018, from https://www.youtube.com/watch?v=tcXU7G6zhjU.
Fisher, Philip. *Wonder, the Rainbow and the Aesthetics of Rare Experiences.* Cambridge: Harvard University Press, 2003.
Fleischman, Paul R. *Wonder.* Amherst, MA: Small Batch Books, 2013.
Frank, Jason. "Publius and Political Imagination" in *Political Theory, 37*(1).
Fuller, Robert. "From Biology to Spirituality: The Emotional Dynamics of Wonder" in *Practices of Wonder: Cross: Disciplinary Perspectives.* Edited by S. Vasalou. Eugene, OR: Pickwick Publications, 2012.
———. "Wonder and the Religious Sensibility" in *Journal of Religion*, 2006.
———. *Wonder: From Emotion to Spirituality.* Chapel Hill, NC: The University of North Carolina Press, 2006.
Gleaves, Robert. "The Perfect Storm" in *Leonid MAC, NASA,* 2002. Available from: https://leonid.arc.nasa.gov/1966-gleaves.txt.
Goldie, Peter. *The Emotions.* Oxford: Oxford University Press, 2000. 87.

Greenblatt, Stephen. "Resonance and Wonder" in *Bulletin of the American Academy of Arts and Sciences*, 43(4), 1990, 29.
Gullo, Christopher. *In all Sincerity . . . Peter Cushing*. Xlibris, 2004.
Hackford, Taylor. *The Devil's Advocate*. Warner Bros. Pictures, 1997.
Hacking, Ian. *The Social Construction of What?* Cambridge: Harvard University Press, 2001.
Hajos, Elizabeth M. "The Concept of an Engravings Collection in the Year 1565: Quicchelberg, Inscriptions vel Tituli Theatri Amplissimi" in *The Art Bullitin*, 40(2), 1958, 156.
Hamilton, William. *Lectures on Metaphysics and Logic*. Vol. 1, *Metaphysics*. Edited by H. L. Mansel and John Veitch. Boston: Could and Lincoln, 1860.
Harre, Rom. "An Outline of the Social Constructionist Viewpoint" in *The Social Construction of Emotions*. Edited by Rom Harre. Oxford: Basil Blackwell Ltd., 1988.
Harris, Ann Sutherland. *Seventeenth-Century Art and Architecture*. London: Laurence King Publishing, 2004.
Harris, Paul L. *The Work of the Imagination*. Hoboken, NJ: Blackwell, 2000.
Harrison, Andrew. "Imagination by Mary Warnock" in *Mind, New Series*, 87(347), 1978.
Haybron, Daniel M. *The Pursuit of Unhappiness*. Oxford: Oxford University Press. 2008.
Hays, J. N. *Epidemics and Pandemics: Their Impacts on Human History*. Santa Barbara, CA: ABC-CLIO, 2005.
Heidegger, Martin. *Basic Questions of Philosophy*. Translated by R. Rojcewicz and A. Schuwer. Bloomington and Indianapolis: Indiana University Press, 1994.
Henderson, Caspar. *A New Map of Wonders: A Journey in Search of Modern Marvels*. London: Granta, 2017.
Henderson, Virginia and Nie, Gladys. *Principles and Practice of Nursing*, 6th edition. New York: MacMillan, 1978.
Hepburn, Ronald W. "The Inaugural Address: Wonder" in *Proceedings of the Aristotelian Society*. Supplementary Volume, 54, 1980.
———. "Landscape and the Metaphysical Imagination" in *Environmental Values*, 5 (3), 1996.
Hesiod, *Theogony: Works and Days; Testimonia*. Edited and translated by Glenn W. Most. LCL. Cambridge: Harvard University Press, 2007.
Hobbes, Thomas. *Leviathan*. Edited by R. Tuck. Cambridge, UK: Cambridge University Press, 1992.
Hodgson, William Hope. *The Casebook of Carnacki: The Ghost Finder*. Hertfordshire, UK: Wordsworth, 2006.
Holmqvist, Kenneth and Pluciennik, Jotoslaw. "A Short Guide to the Theory of the Sublime" in *Style, Resources in Stylistics and Literary Analysis*, 36(4), 2002.
Holy Bible, The. Tophi Books, 1994.
Horace. *Satires, Epistles, Ars Poetica*. Translated by H. R. Fairclough. LCL. Cambridge: Harvard University Press, 1955.
Hove, Philo H. "The Face of Wonder" in *Journal of Curriculum Studies*, 28(4), 1996.
Hughes, Aaron. "Imagining the Divine: Ghazali on Imagination, Dreams, and Dreaming" in *Journal of the American Academy of Religion*, 70(1), 2002.
Human Development and Capability Association, The. https://hd-ca.org/
Hume, David. *A Treatise of Human Nature*. New York: Penguin, 1985.
James, William. *The Varieties of Religious Experience*. New York: Penguin, 1985.
———. "What is an Emotion?" in *Mind*, 9(34), 1884, 190.
Kant, Immanuel. *The Critique of Judgement*. Translated by W. S. Pluhar. Hackett Publishing Company, Inc., 1987.
———. *Critique of Pure Reason*, Translated by W. S. Pluhar. Indianapolis, IN: Hackett Publishing, 1996.
———. *Lectures on Ethics*. Translated by L. Infield. New York: Harper and Row, 1963.
Keats, John. "Lamia" in *The Complete Poems of John Keats*, 3rd edition. Edited by J. Bernard. New York: Penguin Books, 1988.

———. *The Poems of John Keats*. Cambridge: Harvard University Press, 1978.
Keen, Sam. *Apology for Wonder*. New York: Harper and Row, 1969.
———. *In the Absence of God: Dwelling in the Presence of the Sacred*. New York: Harmony Books, 2010.
Kellenberger, James. "Humility" in *American Philosophical Quarterly*, 47(4), 2010. Richards, Norvin. "Is Humility a Virtue" in *American Philosophical Quarterly*, 25(3), 1988, 253–59.
Keltner, Dasher and Haidt, Jonathan. "Approaching Awe, a Moral, Spiritual, and Aesthetic Emotion" in *Cognition and Emotion*, 17 (2), 2003.
Kiernan, V. G. *Horace: Poetics and Politics*. New York: St. Martins's Press, 1999.
King, H. C. *The History of the Telescope*. London: Charles Griffin and Company, 1955.
Kroll, Barry. "Arguing with Adversaries: Aikido, Rhetoric, and the Art of Peace" in *College Composition and Communication*, 59(3), 2008.
Kuper, Adam. *Culture: The Anthropologists' Account*. Cambrdige: Harvard University Press, 2000.
La Caze, Marguerite. *Wonder and Generosity: Their Role in Ethics and Politics*. New York: SUNY Press, 2013, 1.
Lawrence, D. H. *The Later D. H. Lawrence*. New York: Alfred A. Knopf, 1959.
Layard, Richard. *Happiness Lessons from a New Science*, 2nd ed. New York: Penguin, 2011.
Lebech, Mette. *Venskab Dyder og laster*, Vol. 24. Philosophia—Tidskrift for filosofi, 1995.
Leonid Multi-Instrument Aircraft (Leonid MAC). http://leonid.arc.nasa.gov/index.html .
Lloyd, Genevieve. *Reclaiming Wonder after the Sublime*. Edinburgh: Edinburgh University Press, 2018.
London, Scott. "Renewing Our Sense of Wonder: An Interview with Sam Keen" in *Scott London*. Retrieved November 19, 2018. http://www.scottlondon.com/interviews/keen.html
Lopez, Donald. *Buddhist Scriptures*. New York: Penguin, 2004.
Lovecraft, Howard Phillips. "Celephais" in *Eldritch Tales*. Edited by Stephen Jones. London: Gollancz, 2011.
Lutz, Catherine. *Unnatural Emotions*. Chicago: University of Chicago Press, 1998.
Lutz, Christopher Stephen. *Tradition in the Ethics of Alasdair MacIntyre: Relativism, Thomism, and Philosophy*. Lanham, MD: Lexington Books, 2009.
Lytton, Edward Bulwer. *Paul Clifford*. Whitefish, MT: Kessinger Publishing, 2010.
MacIntyre, Alasdair. *Dependent Rational Animals*. London: Duckworth, 1999.
———. *A Short History of Ethics*. London: Routledge, 1998.
Mann, Thomas. *The Magic Mountain*. Translated by H. T. Lowe-Porter. New York: Vintage, 1927.
Matarvers, Derek. "Wonder and Cognition" in *Practices of Wonder Cross-Disciplinary Perspectives*. Edited by S. Vasalou. Eugene, OR: Pickwick Publications, 2012.
McGinn, Colin. *Mindsight*. Cambridge: Harvard University Press, 2006.
McMullen, Ernan. "Enlarging Imagination" in *Tijdschrift voor Filosofie, 58ste Jaarg* (2), 1996.
McReynolds, Philip. "Nussbaum's Capabilities Approach: A Pragmatic Critique" in *The Journal of Speculative Philosophy, New Series*, 16(2), 2002, 148.
Middelcamp, Catherine Hurt. "The Old Woman and the Rug: The Wonder and Pain of Teaching (and Learning) Chemistry" in *Feminist Teacher*, 19(2), 2009.
Mill, John Stuart. *An Examination of William Hamilton's Philosophy and of the Principal Philosophical Questions Discussed in his Writings*. Harlow, UK: Longmans, Green, Longman, Roberts and Green, 1865.
Miller, Jerome. *In The Throes of Wonder: Intimations of the Sacred in a Post-modern World*. New York: SUNY Press, 1992.
Milton, John. *Paradise Lost*, 2 ed. Harlow, UK: Longman, 1998.
Morsbach, H. and Tyler, W. J. "A Japanese Emotion: Amae" in *The Social Constructions of Emotions*. Edited by Rom Harre. Oxford: Basil Blackwell Ltd., 1988.

Morton, Adam. "Epistemic Emotions" in *The Oxford Handbook of Philosophy of Emotion*. Edited by Peter Goldie. Oxford: Oxford University Press, 2010.
Muchembled, Robert. *A History of the Devil*. Translated by J. Birrell. Cambridge, UK: Polity Press, 2003.
Murray, Christopher John. *Encyclopedia of the Romantic Era: 1760–1850*, Vol. 1. Cambridge, UK: Polity Press, 2004.
Nadis, Frank. *Wonder Shows, Performing Science, Magic and Religion in America*. New Brunswick, NJ: Rutgers University Press, 2005.
Neisser, Ulric. *Cognitive Psychology*. London: Psychology Press, 2014.
Nicolas of Cusa. *Complete Philosophical and Theological Treaties of Nicolas of Cusa*, vol. 1. Translated by J. Hopkins. Minneapolis, MN: The Arthur Banning Press, 2001.
Norman, Ron. *Cultivating Imagination in Adult Education*. Proceedings of the 41st Annual Adult Education Research (AERC), 2000.
Norris, Trevor. "The Refusal of Wonder" in *Philosophy of Education Yearbook*, 2001.
Nozick, Robert. *Anarchy, State and Utopia*. New York: Basic Books, 1974).
Nussbaum, Martha. *Creating Capabilities*. Cambridge: Harvard University Press, 2011.
———. "Aristotelian Social Democracy" in *Liberalism and the Good*. Edited by R. B. Douglass, G. M. Mara and H. S. Richardson. London: Routledge 1990.
———. "Non-relative Virtues" in *The Quality of Life*. Edited by Martha Nussbaum and Amartya Sen. Oxford: Oxford University Press, 1993.
———. *Sex and Social Justice*. Oxford: Oxford University Press, 1999.
———. *Upheavals of Thought*, 8th ed. Cambridge, UK: Cambridge University Press, 2008.
———. *Women and Human Development*. Cambridge, UK: Cambridge University Press, 2001.
Onians, John. "'I Wonder . . .': A Short History of Amazement," in *Sight & Insight: Essays on Art and Culture in Honour of E. H. Gombrich at 85*. Edited by J. Onians. London: Phaidon Press, 1994.
Opdal, Paul Martin. "Curiosity, Wonder and Education seen as Perspective Development" in *Studies in Philosophy and Education*, 20, 2001.
Oppenhaimer, Helen. "Christian Flourishing" in *Christian Studies* 5(2), 1969.
Otto, Rudolf. *The Idea of the Holy*. Translated by J. W. Harvey. Eastford, CT: Mertino Publishing, 2010.
Panchbhai, Arati S. "Wilhelm Conrad Röntgen and the Discovery of X-rays: Revisited after Centennial," in *Journal of Indian Academy of Oral Medicine & Radiology*, Vol. 27, Issue 1, 2015.
Pare, Ambrose. *On Monsters and Marvels*. Translated by J. L. Pallister. The Chicago: University of Chicago Press, 1982.
Park, Katharine Park and Daston, Lorraine J. "Unnatural Conceptions: The Study of Monsters in Sixteenth- and Seventeenth-Century France and England" in *Past & Present*, 92, 1981.
Parsons, Howard L. "A Philosophy of Wonder" in *Philosophy and Phenomenological Research* 30(1), 1969.
Partridge, Eric, *Origins: A Short Etymological Dictionary of Modern English*, 4th edition. New York: Macmillan, 1966.
Pascal, Blaise. *The Pensees*. Translated by J. M. Cohen. New York: Penguin Books, 1961.
Pedersen, Jan B. W. "Howard Phillips Lovecraft: Romantic on the Nightside" in *Lovecraft Annual* No. 18. Edited by S. T. Joshi. New York: Hippocampus Press, 2018.
———. "On Lovecraft's Lifelong Relationship with Wonder" in *Lovecraft Annual* No. 11. Edited by S. T. Joshi. New York: Hippocampus Press, 2017.
Pico, Giovanni della Mirandola. *Oration on the Dignity of Man*. Translated by A. R. Caponigri. Washington, DC: Henry Regnery Company, 1956.
Plato. *Cratylus*, Vol. VI. Translated by H. N. Fowler. Edited by E. Capps. LCL. Cambridge: Harvard University Press, 1926.
———. *Theaetetus*. Translated by H. N. Fowler. LCL. Cambridge: Harvard University Press, 1989.

Plutchik, Robert. *Emotions and Life: Perspectives from Psychology, Biology and Evolution.* American Psychological Association, Washington, DC, 2003.
Pope, Alexander. *The Poetic Works of Alexander Pope.* Edited by A. W. Ward. New York: Macmillan and Co., 1885.
Praetorius, Dean. "Hydrothermal Worm Viewed Under an Electron Microscope" in *The Huffington Post*, July 18th 2011: https://www.huffingtonpost.com/2011/07/18/hydrothermal-worm-electron-microscope_n_901833.html?guccounter=1.
Prinz, Jesse "How Wonder Works" in *Aeon Magazine*, 2012.
Quinn, Dennis. *Iris Exiled—A Synoptic History of Wonder.* Lanham, MD: University Press of America, 2002.
Rachel, Carson. *The Sense of Wonder.* New York: HarperCollins, 1984.
Rasmussen, Douglas. "Human Flourishing and the Appeal to Human Nature" in *Social Philosophy & Policy*, 16, 1999.
Ratcliffe, Matthew. "William James on Emotion and Intentionality" in *International Journal of Philosophical Studies*, 13(2), 2005.
Rawls, John. *A Theory of Justice.* Oxford: Oxford University Press, 2000.
Rogers, Samuel. *Autobiography of Elder Samuel Rogers.* Edited by E. J. I. Rogers. Cincinnati: Cincinnati Standard, 1880.
Rubenstein, Mary-Jane. *Strange Wonder, The Closure of Metaphysics and the Opening of Awe.* New York: Columbia University Press, 2008.
Russell, Bertrand. *The Problems of Philosophy.* Charleston, SC: Bibliobazaar. 2010.
Russell, James. "Culture and the Categorization of Emotions." *Psychology Bulletin*, vol. 110, American Psychology Association, 1991, 426.
Schinkel, Anders. "The Educational Importance of Deep Wonder" in *Journal of Philosophy of Education*, 2017.
Scruton, Roger. *Art and Imagination.* New York: Harper and Row Publishing, 1974.
Seligman, Martin. *Flourish.* Boston: Nicholas Brealey Publishing, 2011.
Sen, Amartya. "Equality of what? Tanner Lecture on Human Values," *Tanner Lectures.* Stanford: Stanford University, 1979.
Seneca. *On the Shortness of Life.* Translated by C. D. N. Costa. New York: Penguin, 1997.
——. "Epistle VIII: On the Philosopher's Seclusion" in *Epistles 1–65*. Translated by Richard M. Gummere. LCL. Cambridge: Harvard University Press, 1917.
Shakespeare, William. "Hamlet," in *Tragedies, Vol. 2.* London: Everyman's Library, 1992.
——. "Much Ado About Nothing" in *Comedies, Vol. 2.* London: Everyman's Library, 1996.
Shaw, Philip. *The Sublime.* London: Routledge, 2006.
Shweder, Richard and Haidt, Jonathan. "The Cultural Psychology of the Emotions: Ancient and New" in *Handbook of Emotions*, 2nd edition. Edited by Michael Lewis and Jeanette M. Haviland-Jones. New York: The Guilford Press, 2000.
Sidgwick, Henry. *The Methods of Ethics.* Chicago: University of Chicago Press, 1874.
Silberbauer, George. "Ethics in Small-Scale Societies" in *A Companion to Ethics.* Edited by Peter Singer. Hoboken, NJ: Blackwell, 2001.
Singer, Peter. *Practical Ethics.* Cambridge, UK: Cambridge University Press, 1993.
Smith, Adam. *Essays on Philosophical Subjects.* Edited by W. B. Wightman, J. C. Bryce and L. S. Ross. Oxford: Oxford University Press, 1980.
——. "The History of Astronomy." in *Essays on Philosophical Subjects.* Edited by W. P. D. Wightman, and J. C. Bryce. Oxford: Oxford University Press, 1980.
Smith, Norman R. "Portentous Births and the Monstrous Imagination in Renaissance Culture." in *Marvels, Monsters, and Miracles: Studies in the Medieval and Early Modern Imaginations.* Edited by ed. T. S. Jones and D. A. Sprunger. Kalamazoo, MI: Medieval Institute, 2002.
Solomon, Robert C. "Back to Basics: On the Very Idea of 'Basic Emotions.'" in *Journal for the Theory of Social Behaviour*, 32:2, 2002.
——. *Spirituality for the Sceptic: Thoughtful Love of Life.* Oxford: Oxford University Press, 2002.

———. *True to Our Feelings*. Oxford: Oxford University Press, 2007.
Speak, Daniel. *The Problem of Evil*. Hoboken: John Wiley and Sons, 2014.
Spinoza, Baruch. *Ethics*. Translated by R. Elwes. London: J. M. Dent, 1989.
Stone, Brad Elliot. "Curiosity as the Thief of Wonder, an Essay on Heidegger's Critique of the Ordinary Conception of Time" in *Kronoscope*, 6(2), 2006.
Sumner, L. W. *Welfare Happiness and Ethics*. Oxford: Oxford University Press.
Szeintuch, Yechiel, Tourgeman, Daniella and Zigdon, Maayan. "The Myth of the Salamander in the Work of Ka-Tzetnik" in *Partial Answers: Journal of Literature and the History of Ideas*, 3(1), 2005.
Talbert, Richard J. A. *Plutarch on Sparta*. New York: Penguin Books, 2005.
Tallis, Raymond. *In Defence of Wonder and Other Philosophical Reflections*. London: Acumen, 2012, 6.
Tanner, Tony. *The Reign of Wonder: Naivety and Reality in the American Literature*. Cambridge: Cambridge University Press, 1965.
Theobald, Robert M. *Shakespeare Studies in Baconian Light*. Whitefish, MT: Gay and Bird/Kessinger Legacy Reprints, 1901.
Thomas Aquinas. *Summa Contra Gentiles*. Translated by Anton. C. Pegis. Notre Dame, IN: University of Notre Dame Press, 1976.
———. *Summa Theologica*. Translated by Fathers of the English Dominican Province. Cincinnati: Benziger Brothers, 2006.
Turpin, Adriana. "The New World Collections of Duke Coismo I de'Medici and Their Role in the Creation of a Kunst- and Wunderkammer in the Palazzo Vecchio" in *Curiosity and Wonder from the Renaissance to the Enlightenment*. Edited by R. J. W. Evans and A. Marr. Farnham, UK: Ashgate, 2006.
Ueshiba, Morihei. *The Heart of Aikido: The Philosophy of Takemusu Aiki*. Translated by J. Stevens. Edited by H. Takahashi. Kodansha International, 2010.
Ullman, Harlan K. and Wade Jr., James P. "Shock and Awe: Achieving Rapid Dominance." Defense Group Inc. for The National Defense University, 1996.
United Nations Educational, Scientific and Cultural Organization (UNESCO) entry on Literacy at https://en.unesco.org/themes/literacy-all.
United Nations General Assembly, 1989, article 29, retrieved November 14, 2018 from http://www.ohchr.org/en/professionalinterest/pages/crc.aspx.
Vasalou, Sophia. "Introduction" in *Practices of Wonder: Cross-Disciplinary Perspectives*. Eugene, OR: Pickwick Publications, 2012.
———. *Wonder: A Grammar*. New York: SUNY Press, 2015.
Verhoeven, Conelis. *The Philosophy of Wonder*. New York: Macmillan Company, 1972.
Vernon, Mark. *The Philosophy of Friendship*. New York: Palgrave Macmillan, 2005.
Warnock, Mary. *Imagination*. London: Faber and Faber Limited, 1976.
———. *Imagination and Time*. Hoboken, NJ: Blackwell, 1994.
———. *The Uses of Philosophy*. Hoboken, NJ: Blackwell Publishers, 1992.
White, Frank. *The Overview Effect, Space Exploration and Human Evolution*. New York: Houghton Mifflin Company, 1987.
Whitehead, Alfred. *Nature and Life*. Cambridge: Cambridge University Press, 1934.
Wittgenstein, Ludwig. *Philosophical Investigations*. Translated by G. E. M. Anscombe in *Philosophical Investigations*. Edited by G. E. M. Anscombe and G. H. von Wright. Oxford: Blackwell, 1983.
Woods, Angela. *The Sublime Object of Psychiatry: Schizophrenia in Clinical and Cultural Theory*. Oxford: Oxford University Press, 2011.
Wordsworth, William. *Poems in Two Volumes*. Vol. 2, 1850. Retrieved from https://itun.es/gb/wDVkE.1.
———. *Wordsworth's Poetical Works*, Vol. 2. Edited by Ed. W. Knight. Project Gutenberg, 1896.
WorkStress, The UK National Work-Stress Network, 2018, http://www.workstress.net/what-stress.
Wotton, Sir Henry. *The Life and Letters of Sir Henry Wotton*, Vol. 1. Edited by L. P. Smith. Oxford: Clarendon Press, 1907.

Young, Matthew. "'Dolphins Saved Me from Shark Attack' Says Champion Swimmer" in *The Daily Star*, 2016. https://www.dailystar.co.uk/news/latest-news/486073/Dolphins-saved-shark-attack-champion-swimmer.

Young, Richard Fox."'Gokyō-dōgen' to 'Bankyō-dōkon': A Study in the Self-Universalization of Ōmoto" in *Japanese Journal of Religious Studies*, 15(4), 1988.

Index

A Serious Man (Film), 120

admiration: altered states and, 38, 49–51; Aristotle and, 1; Augustine and, 25; etymology of, 20, 21; Jakobi, Friedrich Heinrich and, 35; Kant, Immanuel and, 31; Pope, Alexander and, 32; reverence and, 184; Smith, Adam and, 31, 37
affiliation with other human beings, 170
the age of discovery, 28
the age of enlightenment, 30
the age of reason, 30
aikido, 180
amazement: altered states and, 6, 38, 41, 57, 204; Deane-Drummond, Celia and, 72; Heidegger, Martin Freiburg and, 49, 51; Longinus and, 44; Onians, John and, 22
anger, 74, 75, 81, 82, 101, 173, 179, 180, 181, 190
animality, 159, 176, 194, 208
Anscombe, Elizabeth, 3
Aquinas, Thomas, 26–27, 37, 141
Arcimboldo, Guiseppe, 131–133, 134, 147, 185, 207
Aristotle, 1, 2–3, 4, 6, 12, 26, 27, 34, 37, 49, 74, 81, 141, 151, 159, 164, 166, 167, 169, 170, 175, 177, 187–188, 190
astonishment, 6, 25, 31, 32, 38, 40–41, 44, 49, 50–51, 57, 75, 96, 204
astrology, 136–137
Augustine, St., 25–26, 37, 95, 97
aurora borealis, 4, 19, 29, 211, 212
Austen, Jane, 113
awe, 1, 5, 6, 38–39, 40, 48, 50, 51, 57, 70, 82, 183, 204

Bacon, Francis, 28, 37

basic human functional capabilities, 172–173, 194, 208
Beckett, Samuel, 192
Ben-Ze'ev, Aaron, 7, 79–81, 82, 84, 85, 87, 144, 204
Bentham, Jeremy, 34, 145, 146
Berlin, Isaiah, 32
Bierce, Ambrose, 210
Blackburn, Simon, 78
Blum, Elisabeth and Paul Richard, 28
Boyle, Robert, 16, 18, 46, 67, 71, 104, 123
Brann, Eva T., 97, 112
Burke, Edmund, 45, 47, 51
Burr, Vivian, 74, 75
Burrell, David B., 4
Byron, Lord, 33, 37

Came, Charles C., 36
capability approach, 166–175
capacity for pleasure and pain, 169
Carson, Rachel, 183
Caze, Marguerite La, 71
Chauvet cave, 70
Chrysakopoulou, Sylvana, 22
Cicero, 1, 23, 31, 32, 75
civility, 181
Clemmer, Pam, 69, 84–86, 88, 106, 182, 183
cognitive schema, 96, 104, 124, 133, 134, 203, 205
Coleridge, Samuel Taylor, 100–102, 105, 112, 115
conception of the good, 8, 139, 166–167, 168, 170, 173, 176, 192, 194, 208
corruption, 162
Crassous, Philippe, 135
Cunningham, James Vincent, 70
curiosity, 6, 30, 38, 48–49, 51, 54, 56, 57, 82, 83–84, 86, 204
Cushing, Peter, 79

225

226 *Index*

Dante, Alighieri, 97, 98
Darwin, Charles, 24, 34, 35, 75
Daston, Lorraine and Katharine Park, 16, 20, 22, 26, 51
Dawkins, Richard, 4–5
de Pasquale, Juan, 12, 16, 17, 18, 48, 87, 95, 105, 110, 117, 118, 119, 122, 157, 185, 192
Deane-Drummond, Celia, 72
death, 12, 16, 27, 41, 70, 79, 117, 160, 168, 169, 171, 178, 179
the devil, 98, 210
dependence, 74, 159, 162, 184
Descartes, Rene, 29–30, 37, 70, 75
Deutch, Barbette, 112
diminishing of self, 57, 123, 125, 140, 203, 206, 212
the duck-rabbit, 17, 18, 116
Doi, Takeo, 74
Dore, Gustave, 97
Dunsany, Lord, 42

early infant development, 169
Edison, Thomas, 36
education, ix, 32, 54, 97, 99, 102, 105, 124, 157, 172, 174, 177, 208, 231
Elgin Marbles, 4
Emerson, Ralph Waldo, 35
emotion, 6–7, 16, 17, 18, 34, 37, 57, 67–89; basic, 73, 75, 77, 82; cognitive approach to, 7, 77, 78, 82, 204, 211; cultural approach to, 73, 75–77; epistemic, 7, 82, 83, 84, 86, 87, 89, 204

natural approach to, 75, 77

Epicureanism, 23, 32
ergon, 156
ethics, 23, 55, 71, 73, 138, 145, 146, 151, 159, 166, 177, 190
Etna, Mt., 26
eudaimonia, 3, 151
Evans, Martyn, ix, 87, 88
Extraordinary experiences. *See* taxonomy of altered states

fancy, 111, 112–113, 116
fire salamander, 26

Fisher, Philip, 1, 20, 46, 96
Fleischman, Paul R., 72
friendship, 8, 152, 156, 162, 172, 177
Fuji, Mt., 53, 186
fulfillment, 57, 111, 138, 154, 192, 204
Fuller, Robert C., 4, 56, 57, 69–70, 71, 95, 111, 112, 113, 124, 138, 141, 186, 192, 204

Galilei, Galileo, 135, 136–137
ghost, 14, 21, 67, 117, 123, 204
Gleaves, Robert, 69, 84–85, 86, 88, 182–183
God: communication by, 111; existence of, 121; fear of, 24, 40, 47; first cause and, 27; gratitude and, 181; imagination and, 108, 109, 193, 194; knowledge about, 24, 27, 28, 37, 131; light of, 24; love of, 24; infinite and, 28, 135; mysteries of, 28; omnipotence of, 26; power of, 40, 135; presence of, 109; theodicy and, 47; will of, 120
Goldie, Peter, 75
gratitude: emotion and, 73–74, 82, 144, 173, 181, 182; God and, 181; religion and, 181; sense of, 17, 18, 67, 117, 118, 119, 122, 123, 125, 143–144, 147, 182, 184, 206, 211; source of flourishing and, 8, 180–181, 182, 183, 186, 195, 206, 209
grief, 72, 73–74, 75, 82, 181

Hacking, Ian, 73
Hamilton, William, 34, 35
happiness: flourishing and, 3, 133, 151; greatest happiness principle, 34; nil admirari and, 31, 33, 34
Harris, Paul L., 97
hedonism: classical, 151; Epicurianism and, 23; Nozick, Robert and, 137
Heidegger, Martin Freiburg: admiration and, 50, 51; amazement and, 49, 51; astonishment and, 50–51; being and, 54; curiosity and, 51, 54; motivator for inquiry and, 51
Henderson, Virginia, 178
Hepburn, Ronald, 7, 38, 106–124, 205
Hesiod, 22–23, 37

Hippocates, 178
Hobbes, Thomas, 48, 49, 75
Honnold, Alex, 153
horror, 38, 41–42, 51, 57, 75, 204
Houdini, Harry, 36
human body, 168
human condition, 50, 131, 144, 160, 162, 170
human flourishing, 3–4, 6, 8, 57, 138, 148, 151–195, 207, 208–209, 210–211
human functional capabilities, 8, 166, 172, 173, 174, 176, 194, 208
human good, 23, 151–152, 155, 156, 164, 166, 180, 208
human nature, 8, 28, 151, 152, 156, 157, 158–160, 165, 176, 194, 208
human rights, 174
Hume, David, 97
humility, 8, 82, 180, 182, 187–189, 195, 208, 209
humor, 8, 157, 177, 178, 179, 192, 210

imagination: animator and, 104; art and, 97, 114; collective, 98; commensurability and, 111; conveyer of truth and, 110–111; education and, 102–103, 105, 123; etymology of, 97; history of, 97; layered, 106–113, 124; metaphysical, 106, 107–108, 111; perception and, 99, 100, 102, 103; philosophy and, 97, 98, 99; poetry and, 34, 102; psychology and, 97; religion and, 98; Romantic, 99–106, 124; seeing as and, 114–116, 119, 125, 145, 146; unasserted thought and, 114, 116–117, 118, 125, 206; universality of, 105; wonder and, 1, 6, 7, 17, 18, 32, 35, 57, 89, 95–96, 99, 104, 126; world-creating and, 100
independent practical reasoner, 8, 159, 161, 162–163, 176, 191, 192, 194, 208
Iris, 22–23, 29, 37, 57

Jakobi, Friedrich Heinrich, 34
James, William, 77, 108, 211
Jansen, Zacharias, 135
Joblot, Louis, 135

Kant, Immanuel, 31, 35, 37, 45, 46, 47–48, 51, 100, 104, 118, 141, 166
Katterfelto, Gustave, 67
Keats, John, 4, 32, 33
Keen, Sam, 17, 18, 47, 67, 117, 118, 119, 122, 143–144, 147, 181, 182, 184, 185, 190–191, 192
Kidd, Ian, ix, 5, 144–145, 208
Kuiper, Gerald, 68, 69, 188, 204
Kuper, Adam, 158

Lawrence, D. H., 192
Li Chi, 75
libertarianism, 175
Lippershey, Hans, 136
Lisbon earthquake (1755), 45, 47
literacy, 8, 172, 177
longing, 46, 173, 181
Longinus, 43, 44–45, 51
Lovecraft, Howard Phillips, x, 42
Loy, David, 133–134, 207
Lucretius, 45
Lutz, Catherine, 74

MacIntyre, Alasdair, 1, 8, 158–160, 160–162, 162–165, 166, 176, 177, 179, 189, 191, 194, 208
Mann, Thomas, 15, 16, 18, 36, 47, 110
Matravers, Derek, 1
Mee, Arthur, 36
memento mori, 15–16
meteor shower: Leonid meteor shower (1833), 11–12, 18, 68, 106, 109, 193–194, 204, 212; Leonid meteor shower (1966), 68–69, 84–85, 86, 88, 106, 182–183, 188
microscopy, 135, 136, 137, 147, 185, 207
Mill, John Stuart, 35, 153
Miller, Jerome, 41, 42, 96
Milton, John, 98, 112
Mirandola, Giovanni Pico della, 28, 37, 132–133
Mitchell, Edgar, 133, 134, 207
Montaigne, Michel de, 113
Monty Python, 178
moral scope, development of, 7, 95, 137, 138, 140, 141–143, 147, 185, 208, 209

mortality, 4, 12, 18, 48, 95, 105, 110, 117, 118, 119, 122, 145, 146, 168, 179, 185
Morton, Adam, 7, 82–84, 86, 204
Muchembled, Robert, 98

Nadis, Frank, 22, 36
naturalistic fallacy, 156
Natyashastra, 75
neo-Aristotelian, 1, 6, 8, 148, 151–152, 153, 155–156, 177–178, 189, 194, 208, 209, 210
Nicholas of Cusa, 28, 37
noetic, 108–109, 110, 111, 124, 205
nonhuman animals, 49, 70, 132, 141, 146, 159, 168, 170, 173, 174, 192
Norman, Ron, 97
Norris, Trevor, 54, 55, 56
Nozick, Robert, 137–139, 142, 147, 185, 208
Nussbaum, Martha, 1, 8, 40, 71–72, 73, 78, 165–176, 177, 181, 189, 191, 192, 193, 194, 208

Onians, John, 22
ontological 'imagineering,' 113
Opdal, Paul Martin, 2, 105, 122
openness, 3, 8, 53, 122, 123, 125, 140, 180, 182, 186–187, 195, 206, 208, 209
Otto, Rudolf, 38
Overview (film), 133, 134, 207
overview effect, 133, 134

Parsons, Howard L., 4, 87, 88
Partridge, Eric, 20
Pascal, Blaise, 182
Paul, St., 39–40
physical exercise, 8, 23, 177, 179, 180
Plato, 4, 19, 22, 23, 37, 55, 70, 76
Pliny the Elder, 26
Plotinus, 28
Plutchik, Robert, 75
Pope, Alexander, 31, 32, 33, 76, 206
practical reason, 8, 46, 103–163, 156, 159, 161–162, 170, 173, 175, 176, 189, 191, 194, 208
Prinz, Jesse, 70
psychedelic experience, 190–191

quality of life, 151, 166

Quinn, Dennis, 1, 5, 20, 22, 23, 28, 31, 36, 37, 50, 70, 73

Rasmussen, Douglas, 1, 8, 151–158, 165, 166, 176, 177, 189, 192, 193, 194, 208
Rawls, John, 139, 140, 147, 167, 185, 208
reformation, 28
renaissance, 28, 32, 48, 70, 131, 133, 135
reverence, 8, 48, 57, 69, 82, 122, 123, 125, 180, 184, 186, 195, 206, 208, 209
Rogers, Elder Samuel, 11–12, 17, 18, 68, 106, 109, 193, 193–194, 212
Romanticism, 32–35
Röntgen, William, Conrad, 36
Russell, Bertrand, 210
Ryder, Richard D., 141, 142

savikalpa samadhi, 134
Schelling, Friedrich, 100, 102
Scruton, Roger, x, 7, 114–126, 145, 186, 205, 206
Seneca, 11, 23, 57
separateness, 171–172
Shakespeare, William, 14, 16, 18, 20, 21, 38, 46–47, 67, 123, 204
Shaw, Philip, 43, 45, 46
Shelley, Percy, 33
Sidgwick, Henry, 153, 187
Silberbauer, George, 164
Singer, Peter, 141, 142, 147, 208
Smith, Adam, 31, 37, 54, 70
social constructionism, 74, 75
Socrates, 6, 23, 24, 25, 55
Solomon, Robert C., 73, 74, 184
sorrow, 12, 70, 74, 75, 79
Sparta, 158
speciesism, 141, 142, 147, 185, 208
stargazers, 69, 84, 85, 86, 88, 193
stoicism, 11, 23, 32
stress, 161, 179
the sublime: definition of, 38, 43–44; Burke, Edmund and, 45, 47, 51; Kant, Immanuel and, 45–46, 47–48, 51; Longinus and, 44, 45, 51

Tallis, Raymond, 52–53, 56, 57, 190
Tanner, Tony, 35
taxonomy of altered states, 38–56

telescope, 16, 135, 136, 137, 147, 185, 207
telos, 156
Theobald, Robert M., 20
the "thick vague conception of the good," 166, 194, 208
Thoreau, Henry David, 35

utopia, 33

Vasalou, Sophia, 71, 96
venus of Willendorf, 70
Verhoeven, Conelis, 1–2, 41, 122
vervunderung, 31
virtue, 1, 2, 6, 8, 41, 82–83, 84, 96, 105, 146, 152–153, 154, 155, 156, 158, 159, 161–162, 162–164, 175, 176, 177, 187, 189, 190, 192, 194, 208
vulnerability, 57, 95, 145, 146, 159, 160, 161, 162, 176, 184, 194, 208

Warnock, Mary, 7, 97, 99–103, 108, 124, 205
well-being, 3, 80, 133, 151, 166, 178, 179
White, Frank, 133, 134, 207
Whitehead, Alfred North, 212–213
Whitman, Walt, 35
wisdom: general, ix, 31, 72, 144, 145, 152, 156, 188, 209; inner, 108; practical, 152, 156, 176, 189, 194, 208
Wittgenstein, Ludwig, 17
wonder: acceptance criterion of, 119, 125, 206; as adjective, 6, 21–44, 205; as adverb, 6, 21, 57, 204; as attitude, 7, 88–89, 96, 133, 140, 146, 147, 204, 208; awareness of ignorance, 1, 16, 18, 47, 57, 96, 123, 125, 140, 147, 192, 206, 210, 212; awed, 5; balanced, 1–2, 3, 8, 56, 57, 148, 176, 180, 189–190, 193, 194, 195, 203, 207, 209, 210; cognitive focus and, 1, 16, 17, 18, 57, 96, 140, 192, 203, 210, 212; conveyer of the universal and, 105, 106, 124, 205; cultivating a habit of, 122, 125, 206; deep, 5, 7, 57, 143, 145, 146–169, 204, 208, 209; deficient, 3, 192; definition of, 1, 96, 210; density of, 121; effects of, 57, 143, 180, 207, 208, 209; emotion and, 57, 67–89; emotional upheaval and, 16, 18, 57, 123, 138, 140, 194, 203, 209, 212; enemies of, 6, 51–56, 57, 204; etymology of, 19–21, 105; examples of, 6, 11–18, 67, 68, 69, 204; excess and, 2, 190–191, 209; extension of moral scope and sensitivity, and, 7, 95, 137, 138, 140, 141, 142, 143, 185, 208, 209; first of all the passions and, 29, 37; history of, 6, 22–37, 57, 70, 95, 204; intense use of the imagination and, 7, 142, 145, 147, 207, 208, 209; joy of, 1, 20, 21, 40, 46, 51, 53, 57, 67, 118, 123, 125, 183, 186, 191, 206–207, 211; as mood, 7, 87, 89, 144, 146, 147, 179, 185, 204, 208; multifaceted, 87, 88, 89, 204; as noun, 2, 21, 57, 121, 204; as pain, 20, 55–56; perception and, 7, 12, 17, 18, 56, 95, 131, 133, 134, 135, 137, 138, 147, 207, 209; refusal to, 54, 55, 141, 143; seven constituents of, 12, 18, 33, 203; shallow, 5, 144, 145; shared, 12, 53, 109, 186; shows, 22, 23, 36; source of flourishing and, 8, 180–195; suddenness and, 1, 2, 12, 16, 17, 18, 40, 55, 57, 88, 96, 118, 203, 210, 212; temporary displacement/diminishing of the self and, 48, 53, 57, 119, 123, 147, 211, 212; as value, 7, 34, 71, 87, 88, 89, 143, 168, 204; as verb, 6, 20, 21, 57, 204; vulgarization of, 2, 32, 48, 189; world as newly present and, 117, 118, 140, 203; as wound, 20, 21, 46, 88
wonder-joy-tears, 183
Wordsworth, William, 22, 33, 69
Wotton, Sir Henry, 136

x-ray, 15, 16, 36, 135

About the Author

Jan B. W. Pedersen, PhD (Dunelm), is lecturer at University College Diakonissestiftelsen, Frederiksberg, Denmark, where he teaches in the areas of ethics, philosophy of science, and philosophy of education.

www.ingramcontent.com/pod-product-compliance
Lightning Source LLC
Chambersburg PA
CBHW021547020526
44115CB00038B/848